WITHDRAWN

*Teaching Creative Music
in Secondary Schools*

Student-composers of the Newton (Mass.) Creative Arts Summer Program rehearsing an original composition created and orchestrated by a member of their group. Guiding them is the author, while other composers listen attentively.

Teaching Creative Music in Secondary Schools

HENRY LASKER

Instructor of Music
Newton High School
Newtonville, Mass.

ALLYN AND BACON, Inc.
Boston

Library of Congress Catalogue Card Number: 79–124939

DEDICATION

To my wife, Gertrude, whose support, understanding, and patience have always been an inspiration to all my creative projects.

ACKNOWLEDGMENTS

To the young composers whose creative seeds have been the inspiration for this book; to *The Christian Science Monitor, The Boston Globe, The Boston Herald Traveler,* and *The Boston Record American* for their permission to publish excerpts written by their music critics of the public performances of many of these pieces; to Malcolm E. Bessom for his wise counsel and guidance in its organization.

Table of Contents

Foreword   ix

Introduction   x

1. *Creativity—Why and How?*   1

2. *Teaching Approaches in Creativity*   8
   Singing Approach   8
   Jingle Approach   10
   Tone Row Approach   19
   Rhythm Approach   21
   Melodic Approach   25
   Harmonic Approach   26

3. *Teaching the Essentials*   31
   Structural Elements   31
   Forms   32
   Melodic Treatment   35
   Rhythmic Treatment   36
   Instrumental and Vocal Treatment   37
   Procedure for Rhythmic Notation   39
   Compositional Techniques   39
   Twentieth Century Idioms   45
   Development of Stylistic Individuality   48

4. *Establishing a Creative Climate*   49

5. *Middle and Junior High Schools*   58
   VOCAL PIECES:
   The Animals' Discussion, LINDA TUFTS   60

vii

Books, MARJORIE KAPLAN   66
The Swing, BETSY BANKS   73
Travel, GUILA DULFANO   78
Summertime, STUART GLAZER   85
You Can Always Tell the English,
    JUDY ALEXANDER   88
Thoughts of Spring, JONNA AMICANGIOLI   94
Trial and Error No. $\frac{3}{4}$, AUDREY SHAFRAN   101
INSTRUMENTAL PIECES:
Piece for Flute, JOANNE SAPERS   112
String Quartet, BEVERLY GERSON   117
The Playful Pup, MICHÈLE COOKE   121
Piece for Instrumental Ensemble,
    DONNA MEYERS   126
Study in Jazz, BARBARA SANDLER   134
Quintet for Strings and Flute, DANIEL STARR   139
Frolic for Clarinet and Piano, ROSALIE PHILLIPS   146
Concerto for Piano More or Less, JOEY SINGER   151
Neophyte Rondo, RONNIE SMOLLER   163

6. *Senior High School*   171
VOCAL PIECES:
Ne'er to Part, LINDA FISHER   174
The Land of Counterpane, DOTTIE CASE   186
Shout Unto the Lord—Psalm 98,
    DEBBY ROTHSTEIN   193
INSTRUMENTAL PIECES:
Chorale with Theme and Variations,
    DAVID JODREY   201
Duet for Flutes, CHRISTINE OLTON   217
Zwei Tänze, DONNA LAWSON   226
Episode No. 1, MICHAEL BIELSKI   237
Fantasy Gavotte, JOHN HARUTUNIAN   248
Capriccio, ROSS CAPON   267
Shades of Thought, DALE SHUMAN   286
Conflict in Solitude, TINA CURRENS   295
Les Emotions Changeantes, LIZ LITTLE   307
Huapangos, GEOFFREY HALE   324
Study for Orchestra, WALTER WAGENKNECHT   338
Toccata, CLAIRE RUBIN   355
Conclusion to Chapters 5 and 6   367

Conclusion   369

Appendix   372

Index   375

Foreword

It would have been inconceivable fifty years ago for high school students in the United States to be writing serious music, and for the music to be played by professional musicians of the Boston Symphony Orchestra. Yet this is what is happening in Boston today.

The Boston Symphony Youth Concerts have presented over the past several years a number of original compositions, all composed and orchestrated by students of Newton High School. For me it has been a real pleasure to have been part of these exciting programs.

Their teacher, Henry Lasker, himself a fine composer and performer, has proven, through his own insight, imagination, and great belief in young people, that creative music can become an integral part not only of a High School curriculum but also of a Junior High and Elementary program, as brought out in his book.

No one claims, least of all Mr. Lasker, that all of these young composers will become second Beethovens, Bartóks, or Bernsteins. But whether or not they go on to become professional composers, their lives will have been enriched by this wonderful opportunity of expression through the creation of music.

At the very least they will have become acquainted with the discipline, the logic, the mystery and the joy of one of Man's greatest achievements—the Art of Music Creativity.

HARRY ELLIS DICKSON
Music Director, Boston Symphony
Orchestra Youth Concerts

Introduction

To live is not merely to exist. So that living may have significance, a person must establish for himself, as a guiding light, criteria based upon values and ideals acquired through enlightenment, knowledge, and understanding. These standards are made more meaningful through creativity in any field of endeavor, be it science or the arts.

I have always believed that everyone is instinctively creative, but if this creativity is not naturally self-expressed, a stimulus is needed as a spark to lighten the way. In most people, their innate talent lies latent. In many cases, it is lost either because of fear, apathy, or lack of proper guidance. This is especially evident in the area of musical creativity, which, through the years, has been a rather barren field for many reasons.

The opinion of lay people has been that musical creativity is a formidable task relegated to the extremely talented student and professional. Consequently lay people develop a defeatist attitude, believing that if they attempt to compose, their efforts will be doomed to utter failure. This attitude can be easily dispelled by convincing them that their talent to create is a vital part of their birthright and heritage. Aware of this reality and with their self-confidence assured, here is no predicting what they can produce.

Quality is not the issue at this stage. This can always develop and improve through study, perseverance, and exposure to good musical literature. The initial step is most important—to break the ice and to remove the barrier which keeps people from realizing their productivity.

Consequently, I have felt the need of a book which can serve as a practical guide primarily for the college and graduate students who will be future music educators and for in-service teachers, to instruct them how to teach creative music. These teachers need not necessarily be specialists in composition. All that is expected of them is:

1. A love for music
2. An academic background involving the knowledge of the simple elements of music
3. An elementary exposure to applied music in any form
4. An empathy toward and an understanding of youngsters. (Possibly this should have priority)

This book is unique and beneficial because it uses step-by-step, positive approaches and procedures in the teaching of creativity. It is based upon actual experiences that have proven successful here and in Europe. Teachers, with or without experience, will benefit greatly from it because of the stimulus it will provide them and, eventually, their students whose creativity will be inevitable. Reading this will open up new vistas, which will be most exciting and gratifying for both student and teacher.

Among the special features of the book are:

1. A variety of approaches for stimulating and launching students in their creative opuses
2. Techniques for teaching music essentials that are basically applied in the students' work
3. Guidelines for developing student composition in a variety of styles historically, including contemporary idioms
4. Methods of establishing a creative climate for music classes in the secondary school
5. Procedures for the organization of creative classes in music theory at the high school level, and the involvement of vocal and instrumental performance groups in programming original compositions for concerts
6. Analysis of compositions arranged and orchestrated by middle, junior, and senior high school students

The success of procedures presented in this book is illustrated in Chapters 5 and 6 by the works produced by students involved in the creative experience. Compositions by some of these students, none of whom had composed previously, have been performed for several years by the Boston Symphony Orchestra in their Youth Concert series, Harry

Ellis Dickson, conductor, by the Boston Pops Orchestra, directed by Arthur Fiedler, and by the Newton Civic Symphony Orchestra, Michel Sasson, conductor. Reaction by professional music critics to the merits of these pieces has been most commendable.

Music, and especially musical creativity, is a vital force in our society. Our young people must be encouraged to create in order to ensure for them an artistically and culturally healthful and wholesome atmosphere.

HENRY LASKER

*Teaching Creative Music
in Secondary Schools*

I

Creativity—Why and How?

Self-expression, creativity, invention, and imagination are gifts to be treasured. They are innate in every human being, and, if developed, open up new horizons, which may heighten every aspect of living. Full fruition of these gifts can be achieved only with proper guidance, encouragement, and motivation.

My objective here is not to set down guidelines for producing professional composers; my hope is to help produce healthy human beings, individuals who are culturally stimulated, intellectually appreciative, emotionally stable, and psychologically tolerant. Creativity can be channeled in many directions by inspired teaching; it can become the foundation for enterprise not only in music and the arts, but also in such fields as medicine, engineering, science, education, and law.

Many educators have conceived wrongly that music can be composed only by the advanced college student or the professional composer. In this book, I shall attempt to show otherwise. I am convinced that exposure to a creative musical experience should begin early in life, particularly in the earliest stages of a child's general education. In the primary grades a child draws and finger paints. Why can he not compose?

Anyone with a little imagination and craft, acquiring skills and technical knowledge as he grows, can compose. If, under competent musical guidance, a child applies himself consistently throughout his

1

early education, the simplicity of his early compositions will gradually come to embrace harmonic, rhythmic, and contrapuntal principles. Pieces of all types will evolve naturally. Arrangements for various choral and chamber groups and full orchestra become possible, stimulating concepts of color, contrast, and dynamics. The developmental process naturally depends upon each individual child or adolescent, upon the age at which he is exposed to and inspired by music, and upon his temperament, ingenuity, willingness to work, and inherent musical ability. The term "talent" is conspicuously absent from these qualifications. Talent is relative; musical dedication and tenacity are qualities that take precedence over a talent that will manifest itself only if the child desires to work. Every boy and girl, regardless of I.Q., apparent lack of musical fertility, degree of ability or past experience, or social, economic, and racial background, is capable of creative musical activity.

Current concepts of progressive education, especially those with a functional and flexible approach, must be used if the young musician is to realize his fullest potential. Traditionally, education has concentrated on the acquisition of facts and skills given out by a teacher. Called the mechanistic or atomistic philosophy, this method is neither functional nor flexible; the pupil merely stores up knowledge without first having had experience. In the more recent so-called "organismic" theory, a creative approach to expanding experiences is more important than technique in the development of the creative process. Accordingly, the child benefits from experience *before* he has knowledge; he learns by doing. Within the organismic approach, the child should not be pressured externally; ideas should come from within and be spontaneously and emotionally motivated. For the young composer, this means the freedom to select, plan, execute, and evaluate, regardless of his previous experience, or lack of it. He should be prompted by native intelligence and instinct. Obviously, this theory is more constructive than the older method of facts first followed by practice.

A young child, completely uninhibited and unrestrained, reacts only in a natural way. If society does not place any restrictions on the spontaneity of his creative thought, this freedom has been known to last until age nine (fourth grade), when society begins to clamp down, parents exercise more control, and teachers impose more rigid disciplines upon their pupils. However, in recent years television and the social upheaval racially, politically, and morally have had their effect on children, so that the free childhood spirit does not extend as long as it did ten or fifteen years ago. Evidences of change may begin to show as early as the third grade. In addition to these outward restrictions, the natural development of shyness and diffidence inhibits the eight-

and nine-year-old. Sudden awareness of approaching preadolescence makes him self-conscious. Though creativity is usually strong at this time, its development takes longer than with younger children. With the preadolescent, it is the increasingly important role of school, administration, and teacher to break through inhibiting barriers and to establish a climate that will best encourage him to express his creative ideas. With the middle, junior, and senior high school student, these inhibitions are more evident, so the responsibility of the school and teacher is even greater. Still, when the ice is broken and a dynamic musical experience is achieved, the pleasure, excitement, and enthusiasm for further creativity definitely can be inspired at any age.

Many boys and girls have become manufactured musical automatons, both instrumentally and vocally, during their early years of private study. Instruction in the basics of real musicianship in the areas of solfeggio, theory, harmony, and form are usually neglected. Students need to acquire, for example, the vital ability to relate the symbol of a written note to the production of its sound, an ability that in turn becomes a mental concept through the development of relative pitch.

In addition to obvious psychological barriers, some children show pitch discrepancies. These disappear gradually by encouraging them to try to concentrate. Patience, guidance, and especially kindness on the part of the teacher are essential. These children should never be embarrassed in front of their colleagues; doing so only makes them withdraw deeper into their shells, with resulting feelings of defeat, dejection, resentment, antipathy, hostility, and anxiety. To prevent this, the teacher should take these youngsters aside and work with them individually. The teacher must bear the responsibility for administering the proper therapy.

The ultimate aim for every student should be the ability to "hear" music with his eyes. The importance of hearing mentally, without the aid of piano or other mechanical devices, cannot be emphasized enough. Only by developing this independence can there be assurance of real musicianship, something which is sadly lacking in the great majority of music students. Mental hearing is often neglected by those who profess that perfect pitch is a prerequisite. Perfect pitch, to be sure, is a quality that arouses the admiration and amazement of those who do not have it. Actually, this endowment is no different from being born with blue eyes; it has advantages and disadvantages, but little relevance to musical ability. Far more important is the development of relative pitch, something requiring work, patience, intelligence, and sincerity. He who has added this faculty to his musical equipment has a great advantage over one, who by nature or accident, has perfect pitch.

For too many years, vocal music has been taught principally by rote, an approach that does have some advantages in the early stages of musical development. The justification for this method is to win the confidence of the child in the elementary grades, to maintain his interest in music learning, to make it fun for him to sing, and, by this learning process, to keep his enthusiasm for further musical activity. This is all right up to a point; but the time comes when the child will begin to request instruction in music reading, since fundamentally he wishes to progress, and his inner sense of values will make him realize that rote learning leads to a dead end. At a given point in his experience, perhaps the third or fourth grade, he ought to begin to read and understand music intelligently, as he would any language. With this understanding, he will feel excited, confident, and eager for further learning.

After experimenting with creativity by instinct, a young child naturally accepts the acquisition of technical abilities and knowledge to enhance his intellectual and creative satisfaction. He is an apt pupil in the language of music, which puts at his disposal tools and techniques that help him to further his creative experience. In my experiences with teaching children in grades 1 through 4, ranging in age from 5 through 10, as well as students in the middle, junior, and senior high school, I can state categorically that all children can create if given the opportunity.

For several summers, I have been associated with the Creative Arts Program in Newton, Massachusetts—a program designed to give children from the sixth to the eleventh grades an opportunity to explore creativity in the areas of art, dance, music, theatre, film-making, and crafts. The great majority are in junior high school. The group meets for five weeks, five mornings a week; an intense and concentrated approach is necessary in order to accomplish as much as possible. By selecting a heterogeneous group in terms of musical background, general intelligence, and ability, every child can be guided both individually and collectively. Performance of an original piece becomes an object of interest to all. Each child benefits not only from his own accomplishments, but also from those of his colleagues.

Although most children in this program had some ability to read and notate, none had ever composed. Generally, their knowledge of theory and harmony was nonexistent or, as with some students, superficial and fragmentary. The theory they knew had been learned mechanically, in relation to an instrument. Most of the vocalists had no theoretical knowledge. Therefore, it was necessary to start from scratch.

These children were at first inducted into the so-called "mysteries" of composing by taking a jingle, scanning it rhythmically and then supplying a melody based upon a motif created in a natural way. The motifs were then developed into musical phrases and sentences. Using a simple major scale construction and the primary triads, each child went on to create a *complete* piece around his or her instinctive and original motif. Gradually, students learned to incorporate melodic, harmonic, contrapuntal, and rhythmic techniques, which made their compositions more exciting. Each composition was discussed by the group for the use of: constructive principles of unity, variety, and coherence; cadences, harmonies, dissonance, and consonance; and foreign tones and motion. In this way, the creative concept became meaningful.

For many years I have taught Music Appreciation, General Humanities, and Music Theory I and II at the high school level. At this level, the teacher finds a heterogeneous group with whom he works for an entire academic year. Unlike the earlier grades, he presumably meets with these students in a theory class several times a week, during which time he teaches the disciplines, restrictions, regulations, and procedures of any thorough theory or harmony course. The objective of this course is to develop the power of discrimination between good and bad, according to standards generally determined by musical authorities, and the taste for simplicity and clarity. Thus, when allowed to create spontaneously, the students are able to break rules justifiably.

Even in the advanced theory class, the student uses constructions in his compositions, which have not been taught. With his greater flexibility, understanding, and experience, he usually engages in challenges much more readily than the younger musician. In these compositions, individual differences of temperament, talent, and musical background become significantly more marked. There may be students in elementary theory who are more daring than those in advanced theory. Conversely, there may be slow bloomers in elementary theory who suddenly become mature composers in the advanced class, even using twentieth century techniques with taste and discrimination.

At both academic levels, the fundamental principles of composition—unity, variety, coherence—remain essential objectives. The student's common sense and intelligence help him understand the meaning of such basic concepts as motif, theme, fore-phrase, after-phrase, musical sentence. In early experiments in either junior or senior high school, a student cannot be expected to compose a sonata, a symphony, or a fugue. Working in two-part, three-part, and rondo forms will encourage more complicated compositions. It is the teacher's responsibility to guide him correctly and scientifically in these areas. Through proper guidance, the student learns to evaluate and criticize his own material as well as the material of his colleagues. He learns not only to create musical ideas, but also to express them with color, shading, and dynamics.

Orchestrating a piece will almost certainly be a new experience for every student. He learns how to relate different classes of instruments to their appropriate melodic, harmonic, and contrapuntal lines; learns their ranges, registers, and the method of writing them; learns the various clefs and other aspects of orchestration, such as dynamics, phrasing, tempo indications, and the many different directions associated with instruments of different choirs.

The student should become acquainted with instruments of the symphony orchestra. The teacher should encourage him to listen to live or television concerts, symphonic records, and records and films illustrating the different instruments. He should also have access to the different instruments, hear and see them in live performance, acquire a superficial understanding of how each is played, and study the highlights of each instrument in a textbook. All of these can be approached by the student in a spirit of exploration and fun.

In most cases, the high school student will be in a more exciting situation in terms of orchestral composition than the junior high school student, because of his probable access to a school orchestra of greater size and variety. This depends on each community and the availability of student musicians. Under ordinary circumstances, superior orchestral opportunities encourage the high school student to score correspondingly and thereby make his task of understanding the orchestra more demanding and more satisfying.

The pieces presented in Chapters 5 and 6, composed by students at the middle, junior, and senior high school levels, have been selected for analysis because of their value as examples of musical creativity. The pieces range from simple jingles to fully orchestrated compositions. The composers had some or at least adequate technical and mechanical training as instrumentalists and vocalists, but had little or no understanding of the construction, compositional techniques, and procedures for the development of the material with which they dealt. They learned by doing, gradually channeling their spontaneous individual impulses, their creative seeds, into a solid musical framework. The processes discussed in the evolution of these pieces are general ones. Significant harmonies and foreign tones have been indicated on the piano scores. In the case of pieces written for chamber music ensembles and symphony orchestra, instrumentation has been inscribed where necessary on the piano reductions.

Teachers, to inspire students toward the creation of musical pieces, should use techniques of their own for a particular child, but it is my hope that the fundamental principles brought out in this book may serve as solid guidelines.

What, then, is the essence of the creative teaching of music? First, it is recognizing that good teaching is not a one-way street; the teacher must appreciate individual differences and treat each student accordingly. Second, creative teaching demands that children experience the creative process *before* they learn the rules and techniques involved. There is nothing objectionable in following a model. Walter Piston often suggests composing a piece based on the form and musical construction of an earlier master. This technique is suitable for the experienced composer-musician with a great deal of theoretical background. For the neophyte, however, it is wise to encourage him to function naturally, to enjoy his spontaneous accomplishments, and to feel that the piece is entirely his own. Eventually, he will want to examine the scores of the great composers for the many lessons they can teach. Meanwhile, with the sensitive guidance of a good teacher and constructive criticisms from both teacher and colleagues, the child can learn where improvements may be made through his own experiences. The teacher, too, must warmly encourage, inspire, and understand the child.

If teacher and student are reciprocally motivated toward these creative objectives, there is no way of gauging how rich the rewards will be for both. With properly guided musical exposure throughout early life and adolescence, the creative output of the child can be unlimited by the time he reaches maturity. Who knows how many of these youngsters will become America's future composers?

2

Teaching Approaches in Creativity

Musical creativity in the classroom is a beautiful experience and a delightful joy for both students and teacher. Very often the classic question is asked, "How does this activity begin?" The answer is quite simple. The teacher impresses upon the students that they *are* potential composers because they are human beings, that composing is a natural phenomenon, and that their creative efforts will give great gratification and satisfaction. Immediately, the students feel important. Their confidence is won, and the door to their creative efforts is opened. With this positive atmosphere established, various approaches and techniques can be used to the advantage of both teacher and students.

SINGING APPROACH

Singing is the first natural step in composing, especially for a neophyte who has not been exposed to any activity in music. The students must adopt a positive attitude toward song. They should realize that singing is an important part of their lives, that it is a wholesome, happy, and relaxing activity, and that it helps them let off steam during moments of anguish, apprehension, and anxiety. Some students may be indifferent, recalcitrant, insecure, or shy because of previous traumatic experiences, but with understanding and encouragement by the teacher, they can be easily convinced that participation in this activity will be rewarding. Let them realize that anyone who speaks can sing.

Singing should be used not only to introduce the neophyte to music, but also to help him develop a sensitivity to pitch. Many methods exist that can be used to develop relative pitch. To begin, the child must be relaxed physically. Once he is, the teacher may start with one note, then two notes, then three notes, asking the child to match each one as it is sung or played, making sure that there is no tension in the student's throat as he sings. The teacher should skip arbitrarily tones that are to be matched by the child who must be alert in his response. Another experiment in developing the ear is to let the child sing a note, which he must try to match on the piano or any other instrument. The piano is preferable since it is a tempered instrument and involves simply a finding and striking technique. Other instruments may be inconvenient and difficult for him unless he is acquainted with the technique of playing them, even superficially. Another method is for the music student to assign himself a "Do" or "I" or "Ah" associated with the first note of a scale. With this as a basis, he learns to relate the notes in the series without difficulty. The majority of students need this discipline and conditioning. Combining both the pitch identifications with their respective rhythmic values forms the beginning of the student's understanding of melody and development of his musicianship.

The approach to creativity ought to be gradual. Begin by having the students sing a song or two that they know. This warming-up period relaxes them and establishes a suitable climate for creativity. Then let them engage in an improvised musical conversation in a recitative manner, a sort of spontaneous "opera." This further secures the establishment of a creative mood. Done properly, by avoiding boisterous singing and maintaining decorum, while acknowledging in an orderly manner each student as he contributes his musical idea, a narrative type song results, which creates alertness, stimulates the imagination, and fosters a feeling of democratic musical dialogue.

By this time the students are receptive to more objective creativity. Two experiments may be used:

1. Individual members of the class are invited to write a brief story. Each is read aloud by the teacher. A majority vote by the students selects the most desirable one. With voluntary contributions from all members of the class, a cooperative effort

converts the highlights of the story into a rhymed couplet or quatrain.

2. If time is short, the teacher may present a jingle or poem, either standard or original.

In either approach, the final objective is the creation of original music. My personal preference is the first approach, since it has the advantages of stimulating creativity, initially, in the use of language and of encouraging young people to relate and convert prose to rhymed verse. With the couplet or quatrain consummated, the musical stage is set. However, before the creative musical experience begins, the class must understand clearly the rhythmical construction of the verse, since music, like verse, is conditioned by meter, the basis of rhythm, which is the most fundamental natural element of music. Rhythm is inherent in every human being. Everything in life is rhythm —the human heart beat, respiration, the ticking of a clock, the wheels of a locomotive. Nature's expression of rhythm is simplicity itself.

The next step is to teach the students to feel rhythm instinctively. The measurement of music, meter with its accented and unaccented beats, is basically either duple, triple, or quadruple. The students can experience meter in a physical activity, such as setting-up exercises or calisthenics, by coordinating the activity with the counting aloud process of 1, 2 or 1, 2, 3 or 1, 2, 3, 4, emphasizing the first accented beat. They may clap their hands, walk, and dance to music written in these basic meters. In this way, the students begin to understand meter by actually coordinating it with their own physical experience.

The neophytes will eventually want to see the notation of the rhythm and to intellectualize upon it. Only then should the teacher introduce an academic approach to meter—the function of the upper and lower numbers. The students who have already been introduced to these technical aspects outside of school will have an advantage over their neophyte colleagues.

JINGLE APPROACH

With an understanding of the relationship between words and music in terms of rhythm and meter, the next step is to explore the way music can be created successfully to a jingle in the form of a couplet.

For the first meeting of a recent summer Creative Arts session, the following jingle was used, inspired both by the beautiful morning and by the anticipated enthusiasm of a new creative experience:

STEP 1

    Good morning, good morning, good morning to you.

    The sky up above is so limpid and blue.

    Since the results were gratifying, it would be well to present this jingle, or one similar, to the class. The jingle should be written on either the chalkboard or on a transparency if an overhead projector is available.

    To determine the accented syllables, the class scans the lines aloud, exaggerating the pronunciation of syllables they instinctively and intellectually sense are strong. In this way, they feel the rhythm more decisively. Adding the graphic sign "/" over each accented syllable and an "‿" over each unaccented syllable, the couplet appears this way:

STEP 2

    ‿ / ‿ ‿ / ‿ ‿ / ‿ ‿ /
    Good morning, good morning, good morning to you.

    ‿ / ‿ ‿/ ‿ ‿ / ‿ ‿ /
    The sky up above is so limpid and blue.

Bar lines are then placed before the accented syllables to impress upon the students the significance of bar lines and measures in relation to melodic concept. All students, the experienced and inexperienced, learn to associate a strong beat with the bar line:

STEP 3

    ‿ | / ‿ ‿ | / ‿ ‿ | / ‿ ‿ | /
    Good | morning, good | morning, good | morning to | you.

    ‿ | / ‿ ‿| / ‿ ‿ | / ‿ ‿ | /
    The | sky up a|bove is so | limpid and | blue.

Immediately a question arises, "What about the first 'good'?" Here is an excellent example of the so-called pick-up or anacrusis, the fractional part of the measure, which in this case is felt to be the same length as each syllable of the subsequent words "morning," "good," and "to." The word "The" also has the same length in time value. Instinctively, the students will hold the words "you" and "blue" twice as long as any of the other syllables preceding it. In the final analysis, the couplet appears as follows, with horizontal lines indicating an additional beat for "you" and "blue":

STEP 4

⌣ | / ⌣ ⌣ | / ⌣ ⌣ | / ⌣ ⌣ | /—
Good | morning, good | morning, good | morning to | you.

⌣ | / ⌣ ⌣ | / ⌣ ⌣ | / ⌣ ⌣ | /— ‖
The | sky up a|bove is so | limpid and | blue.

Taking the area between two consecutive bar lines as a measured unit, the class determines whether the couplet is duple or triple meter by counting the number of syllables in a measure. They realize that a majority of units have three syllables, all equal in time; this establishes the meter as triple, or a ¾ rhythm. Since the word "you" is held for two beats, the unaccented word "The" at the beginning of the second line can suitably be added to that unit as its third count. In this way, the accented word "sky" becomes the beginning of the second line musically. It should be explained that the anacrusis "good" and the word "blue" together represent a broken measure, both words being equivalent to the three required counts in a measure unit.

At this point, the teacher will review the theory of ¾ meter for the experienced students and will teach it to the inexperienced ones. In so doing, enlist the patience of the former to help the latter feel secure and comfortable in this area new to them. The inexperienced will be introduced to quarter and half notes, and their simple relationship to meter, note value, and rhythm.

Intelligibly, the students will understand the next procedure. In place of the accented and unaccented graphic signs, note symbols and counts will now be placed above the words of the couplet:

STEP 5

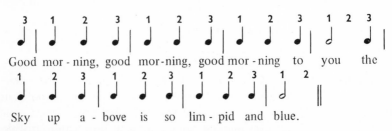

The prevalence of quarter notes indicates the equal value of the majority of the syllables. Only the words "you" and "blue" are half notes, each held twice as long as the others. Now the class claps the rhythm, while counting aloud "1, 2, 3" continuously, steadily, and staccato-like, exaggerating each accented beat. The number of claps should equal the number of syllables—22 in all—one clap for each quarter note and one for each half note, with hands clasped for the second count of the half notes. With this rhythmic feeling established, the class begins to substitute words for the previous number count, while their hands take over the function of clapping on *every* beat. Obviously, they cannot recite the words and count simultaneously. Half the class should recite, while the other half counts, and vice versa so each child gets the total rhythmic experience of relating word syllables to the actual counting. The words "you" and "blue" should be articulated as follows: "you-oo" and "blue-oo," to indicate two counts while the hands keep the beat moving steadily.

With this basic rhythm established, print the words of the jingle in the space below the staffs, indicating measure divisions on the staff at the proper places. Rhythmic values of the notes of each syllable will be placed above the staffs, the counts being unnecessary at this point. Draw the treble clef and add the $\frac{3}{4}$ rhythm signature:

STEP 6

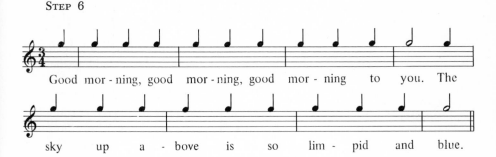

Good mor - ning, good mor - ning, good mor - ning to you. The

sky up a - bove is so lim - pid and blue.

Notice that the note values above the staff serve as guides for the rhythmic values of the melody-to-be, which will consist of a musical sentence of eight measures.

Having formulated these preliminaries, each student should be urged to improvise vocally a spontaneous melody appropriate to the words. To help launch the students on this new experiment, a C-major triad, followed by a C-major scale, should be played on the piano. Beginning with this simple key often relieves any fears youngsters may have developed toward those with more involved signatures.

After the initial use of the C-major scale, it is wise to urge the older child in junior high school, and especially in senior high school, to explore in other keys to make him realize that one key is no more difficult than any other. When knowledge of theory and harmony increases, this exploration may be expected of him; with good teaching, he can feel that no key poses insurmountable difficulties, that all keys are relative, and that any signature need not be frightening, no matter how formidable its appearance. The greater his confidence in understanding scale construction, the more comfortable he will be in any key. In this way, he may realize that each key has its own characteristic, color, and descriptive quality, and that a composer eventually may work in any one, which will best help him to fulfill his creative objectives.

After hearing the C-major scale played up and down, the students should sing it first with the piano and then without, using syllables, numbers, or a neutral syllable "Ah." This helps them relate to a tonality. Then on a chalkboard, or transparency, write the scale. They now can visualize as they sing. Following this procedure, they should sing any note that the teacher arbitrarily points to, progressing by step and skip. This helps them to establish in their minds the sound of each note and its relationship to other notes. Thus, they begin to acquire the concept of a melodic line.

There may be some students who would prefer to experiment with scales by using a musical instrument such as the piano or xylophone. However, the singing experience ought to be encouraged at first, since it is basic to every individual.

Now the students are ready to improvise their own melody to the jingle. Each youngster may start on any note of the scale he wishes and follow it by notes he considers suitable for a song. This step very often brings a period of silence and bewilderment. To break the impasse, the teacher may again encourage the class to engage in spontaneous musical conversation—a sort of miniature opera. This stimulates imagination, eases tension, and brings out a spirit of fun. After repeated playing and singing of the C-major triad and scale, the students are usually ready to function creatively on their own. The following is a melody improvised by a student, which I wrote on the chalkboard as it was being sung:

EXAMPLE II-1

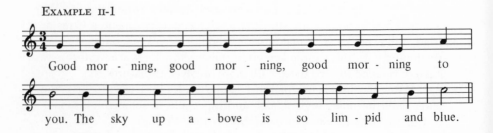

Good mor - ning, good mor - ning, good mor - ning to
you. The sky up a - bove is so lim - pid and blue.

After hearing the tonic note of the scale on the piano, the class sang the melody, at first without the piano to see if they could sense melodic direction and the proper relationship of pitches, and then with the piano and harmonic support. Fortunately, there was little difficulty because of the natural and simple line of the melody. It is important to condition students to a *mental* response to notes—hearing specific tones in their minds after the tonic has been sounded. Having them think of the sound of each component of the melody before actually singing it aloud is helpful and the results often gratifying.

Representation of the improvisation may be done in one of two ways. If the teacher has perfect or relative pitch, he may record the melody on the chalkboard or transparency. If this is not feasible, a tape recorder can be used, which will help in the teaching of the song by rote. Eventually, the melody could be recorded for the eyes to see.

If time is available and if the occasion is expedient, more improvisations by as many of the students as possible should be encouraged. Let each one contribute in a serious but cheerful manner. Keep the experiment at a high level. It may be well to have the class copy Step 6, take it home, and practice improvising tunes to it. There will be some who will actually write the tunes down. Let them create their own jingles to which they will adapt melodies.

To return to the "Good Morning" experiment, the form, structure, and melodic line should be analyzed. The class will see that the melody has eight measures, already defined in Step 6 as a musical sentence. The class learns the construction of a musical sentence consisting of eight measures, divided equally into two 4-measure phrases (the first phrase called the fore-phrase or antecedent, the second called the after-phrase or consequent). They also discover the question-and-answer principle, by which the first four measures ask a question, which is answered by the next four measures. They develop a melodic sense for phrase and balance. They realize the relationship between the question with the half- or rising cadence at the end of the fore-phrase in measure 4, and the relationship between the answer with the authentic cadence at the end of the after-phrase in measures 7 and 8.

A cadence is an objective point produced by a progression of chords. The half-cadence utilizes the dominant harmony, giving the psychological impression of a pause, with a desire to continue after it. The authentic cadence with the super-tonic and dominant harmonies in measure 7, followed by the tonic harmony in measure 8, creates the feeling of completion of a melodic thought. To help the class better understand the construction of the musical sentence, the half-cadence may be likened to a comma, creating a feeling of pause and also continuity between the fore-phrase and after-phrase. The authentic cadence may be likened to a period, creating a feeling of finality, for it ends the 8-measure sentence. Cadences may be feminine or masculine. In the former, the tonic chord occurs on the weak or second beat, while in the latter it occurs on the strong or first beat. When the root of the tonic is in the soprano and bass, the cadence is perfect; otherwise, it is imperfect.

As the teacher introduces new concepts or techniques to the class, it might be helpful to play recorded musical examples of these from the classical repertoire so the students may hear them mentally as well as understand them intellectually. Musical techniques and concepts with reference to classic musical examples are discussed in Chapter 3.

The importance of the motif, the germ of any melody, should be emphasized next in analyzing the melodic construction of the couplet. Motifs are parallel to a topic sentence in a paragraph, a design in a painting, a movement in a dance, a character in a play. The motif is the introductory group of notes, made up of a distinct rhythmic pattern, which is coordinated with a succession of pitches in such a way as to sound intelligible. Motifs are developed throughout a piece by many devices, such as repetition, imitation, inversion, transposition, sequence, modulation, variation, augmentation, and diminution.

In the "Good Morning" experiment, the motif consists of:

EXAMPLE II-2

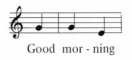

Good mor - ning

The words "Good morning" and their corresponding musical notation is the essence of the fore-phrase. Here the words and notes together give a feeling of exuberance, excitement, and optimism. Subsequently, the motif is repeated literally twice to achieve unity, the basic principle of any creative work.

On the third beats of both the first full measure and measure 2, the note "G" occurs. On the third beat of measure 3, after the three appearances of the motif, the "G" has been transposed to "A," one whole step higher, to avoid monotony. Musically, a 4-measure phrase is divided into two 2-measure sections. To have the "A" occur in the third measure, or first measure of the second section, seems logical tonally.

It not only produces variety, but also provides emphasis, because it is a high point in the melodic line and logically moves further upward by step to "B" on the half-cadence. Coherence is achieved, since the musical material is coordinated through unity and variety.

How elementary this appears to be, but how important! Each component of the material is dependent on the other and forms a mutual relationship with the whole. So, the motif, by repetition and variety, however slight, graduates into a phrase, as indicated by the first four measures in the couplet.

Now let us analyze the after-phrase in which the rhythm of the motif is continued, but with melodic variety. In the first two measures, the text seems to direct the melody upward to "E," the climax, only to return to "C," the original level. This is followed by a rise by step to "D," a secondary high point at the beginning of the next two measures. The word "limpid," when spoken, has a downward motion. If the syllable "lim" is accented, it seems natural for the voice to phrase the syllable "pid" downward. Observe the notes used with this word:

EXAMPLE II-3

lim - pid

Here again we have a natural relationship between word and music.

Finally, two notes associated with the dominant and tonic chords ("B" to "C") on the words "and blue" conclude the after-phrase. The last note, the tonic, makes a perfect ending.

The range of the tune, an exact octave from first line "E" to fourth space "E," is convenient for any voice. For the average layman, a range should never exceed ten notes.

With the melody completed, draw a line connecting one note to the next. The class should then evaluate the direction of the line:

EXAMPLE II-4

and observe the melody's wave-like structure, rising and falling, with a gradual ascent to the climactic point at the high "E" and a gradual descent and last rise to the final note. They will realize that a pattern of this type contributes to a song whose text and melodic simplicity has merit, whose range is comfortable, and whose construction displays over-all coherence, unity, and variety.

Without any previous technical indoctrination, students will have been exposed to an experiment in which the following procedures were used:

1. Delineating accented and unaccented syllables through word scanning
2. Indicating bar lines to emphasize the association of words with a measure or bar musically
3. Defining the pick-up beat or anacrusis
4. Defining the meter as ¾ and realizing that the majority of the syllables use a quarter note unit (with the exception of two half notes)
5. Creating a melodic line, coordinated with the words in terms of motif, phrase, sentence, cadence, form, structure, logic, character, range, unity, variety, and coherence
6. Drawing a geometric diagram—with waves, climax, and finality—to show what constitutes good melodic writing.

In this way, the door to a creative musical experience will be opened. Whether it leads to satisfying the students' curiosity, fulfilling a musical challenge, or simply encouraging them to create does not really matter at this point. A task will be accomplished, which is not only musically significant, but also psychologically valuable in that the students will mature creatively in only a matter of minutes. This will make them aware, at an early stage, that composing is not relegated to the exceptionally talented.

With this basic experience as a launching pad, the couplet could be extended with the addition of more words and music, both bearing a relationship to the original. For example, the next eight measures could be a musical repetition or slight variation, to avoid monotony, with different words followed by new music and new text for the succeeding eight measures. Finally, the original eight measures could return either with the original text or a variation of it. Stated diagrammatically, it would appear as follows:

Text	Music
a	A
b	A or A'
c	B
a or a'	A or A'

The "prime" of course indicates variation. Musically, it is a 32-measure piece in three-part song form. The rhyming scheme throughout could follow that of the first couplet.

The students should now select a poem from the standard literary repertoire to which original music may be set. As an alternative, they could create one of their own, preferably containing not more than four stanzas, all with the same meter and each one having four lines. Each stanza also should follow one of these rhyming schemes: A, A, B, B, in which lines 1 and 2 (AA) and lines 3 and 4 (BB) rhyme; A, B, A, B, in which lines 1 and 3 and lines 2 and 4 rhyme; or A, B, C, A, in which only lines 1 and 4 rhyme. It should be explained here that in the process of writing an original poem, changes in words for the sake of euphony, rhythm, or rhyme become necessary. Synonyms are helpful. Poetic license allows altering the position of words in order to achieve the proper feeling of rhythm and rhyme. To these lines an original melody is written, which consists initially of at least eight measures, which can be developed further with more stanzas. (If a familiar tune is used for which original words are supplied, the rhythmic limitations are naturally more apparent; one would hesitate to change a note of a familiar melody to conform to original words.) To motivate some students who, at first, may appear hesitant, the tone row approach may be tried, and with very encouraging results.

TONE ROW APPROACH

Begin with the scale of C-major. Arrange the notes in a tone row series arbitrarily, avoiding too many consecutive skips. Taste, judgment, and common sense, as well as experience, will all help to provide an intelligible row which can be sung easily. A reasonable number of conjunct and disjunct intervals should be used. Conjunct intervals proceed by step, while disjunct intervals proceed by skip. For example:

EXAMPLE II-5

Notice that each of the above notes is numbered according to its numerical position in the scale. In all, there are three conjunct intervals marked with C and three disjunct intervals marked with D. In only

two places are disjunct intervals used consecutively; the second one in
an upward direction, followed immediately by a conjunct interval in
a downward direction. Customarily, if there is an interval skip of a
fourth or more, it is advisable to follow it by step-wise motion in the
opposite direction.

Next, let the class arrange the notes of the C-major scale in a
4-measure phrase to be written in $\frac{4}{4}$ rhythm, since $\frac{2}{4}$ is not too much of
a challenge, and since the "Good Morning" jingle already has used
a $\frac{3}{4}$ rhythm. This time let them include quarter, half, dotted half, and
whole notes, the values of which they should understand mathemati-
cally. They then should list all the possible formulas that might use
these notes in different orders, all in $\frac{4}{4}$ rhythm. Their response should
be as follows:

EXAMPLE II-6

Any of these formulas may be chosen and even repeated to help
establish a 4-measure phrase. Four such series are:

EXAMPLE II-7

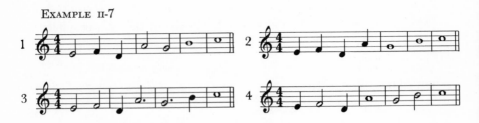

By creating many varieties of interesting tone rows based upon
the principle of good melodic construction, the students will increase
their musical vocabulary and become more confident to proceed indi-

vidually. Before allowing them to continue on their own, however, they should be encouraged to sing the original tone series, followed by its various rhythmic patterns. In this way, they will be introduced to pitch discrimination and ear training. The first note of the scale, "Do," should be sounded (playing a C-major triad can also be very helpful). This is necessary for a starting point, as well as to build confidence.

Each of these 4-measure fore-phrases may be literally repeated to establish the 4-measure after-phrase to consummate an 8-measure sentence. The expected monotony can be avoided by slight alterations wherever possible. Let the students experiment to discover how effectively these alterations will relate to the music preceding and following. With the proper guidance, let their decisions to reject or accept be based upon their own taste, judgment, and experience. Since each of the phrases concludes on the authentic cadence, it may be well to suggest that each could end on any note belonging to the V harmony (see p. 26 for a discussion of the harmonic approach) to give the feeling of desired pause, which a half-cadence affords. This can be accomplished, without disturbing the musical quality, by reversing the last two notes of each phrase. With this arrangement, these four measures now represent the fore-phrase, while the original four measures function as the after-phrase. Henceforth, this can be extended in the same way as the jingle. The various techniques used in the twelve-tone system, such as inversion, retrograde, inversion of the retrograde, and retrograde of the inversion, may be applied with exciting results.

Canonic imitation for two or three voices, applying the techniques mentioned, would be a challenge to the enterprising student. Tone rows may be either vocal or instrumental. In the former, a neutral syllable "Ah" may be used or original words may be created.

Having experimented with a tone row from the C-major scale in various simple rhythmic patterns, the students are now ready to include eighth notes and dotted eighth notes if necessary, as well as syncopation and rests wherever feasible. It is assumed that these principles would have been taught already, giving the students carte blanche to create whatever seems appropriate and logical. Let them explore in keys other than C-major.

RHYTHM APPROACH

Starting with a rhythmic idea is another way to stimulate and induce creativity. Again the theory of learning by doing should be applied.

In terms of rhythm, students can develop a feeling for the measure, phrase, and form through physical responses. These exercises in turn eventually lead to rhythmic improvisation. The practice of antiphonal rhythms between teacher and students is a favorite device, the former supplying a rhythmic motif, the latter answering by instinct, by ear, by imitation. Subsequently, an improvisation begins to take form, which constitutes a development of the motif.

After experimenting in this improvisational area, students will want to intellectualize, to wish to understand what they are doing, since a musical idea is intelligible only if its rhythm is intelligible. Music without rhythm cannot exist.

An intellectual understanding of the notation and performance of rhythm requires discipline on the part of students. Above all, a thorough understanding of rhythmic concepts demands patience and desire on the part of students to learn and teachers to teach. Analysis and comprehension of rhythmic formulas, from the most elementary to the most complex, will develop for the students not only performing facility, but also definite creative potential. With a good rhythmic background, the students will not only derive emotional satisfaction from their work but will also gain confidence. Basic to such growth is the ever-present teacher's respect for the students as people, an enduring faith in their ability to achieve, and a dedication to secure within them a solid foundation that will enable them to work out rhythmic problems independently. Success in this area produces more success.

Rhythmic understanding will help the students produce a pattern that can develop into an adequately proportioned piece. For example, this rhythmic motif was suggested by a student at the Creative Arts center:

EXAMPLE II-8

Because of the triple meter, a minuet-type piece was suggested. Examples from the standard classical and romantic repertoire were then played. (Under similar circumstances, illustrations may be presented either on recordings or on the piano if the teacher or any student is a capable pianist.) It was then agreed that the rhythmic motif be utilized and developed into a 32-measure, three-part song form construction, A, A, B, A.

The following was one of the several experiments. It warrants analysis:

EXAMPLE II-9

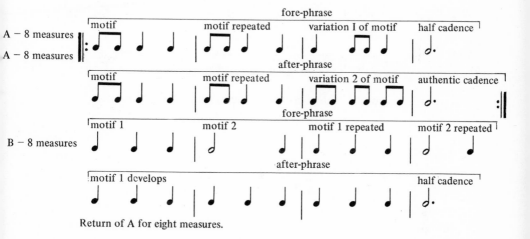

Return of A for eight measures.

Notice particularly that the two motifs of the B theme are less active rhythmically than the material of A. Unity by repetition, variety by contrast of rhythms, and coherence by consolidation of the material are achieved.

After completing this project, a melody was created with the following result:

EXAMPLE II-10

In measure 1, the motif is stated. The melodic direction is upward:

EXAMPLE II-11

In measure 2, the motif is repeated. A variation of it occurs in measure 3 in a downward direction as contrast to measures 1 and 2:

EXAMPLE II-12

leading to the half-cadence in measure 4.

In the after-phrase, the first two measures, 5 and 6, are a transposition upward by step of the first two measures of the fore-phrase. This is followed in the next measure, 7, by the second variation of the motif consisting of eighth notes starting at a higher point and leading down diatonically:

EXAMPLE II-13

The authentic cadence is in measure 8. The entire 8-measure sentence is repeated forming the second appearance of A.

In measure 17, a new theme, B, enters with the presentation of two motifs consecutively:

EXAMPLE II-14

EXAMPLE II-15

Each is transposed down by step in measures 19 and 20 respectively. Motif 1 appears again transposed down another step in measure 21, and is then transposed upward twice by an interval of a third, forming a sequence which helps to develop the motif.

In measure 24, the half-cadence appears. For the next eight measures, the material of A returns, this time as A′ because of the change in the authentic cadence beginning in measure 31. Here the original downward diatonic scale is interrupted by an ascending passage leading to the upper tonic in measure 32. In this way, a wave-like formation is achieved, and the cadential interest is increased because of the contrast to the original one at A.

From the above analysis, it is obvious that the constructive principles of music have been easily achieved because of the repetition, contrast, and cohesion of the music. It must be remembered that the constructive principles already were present in the original rhythmic construction.

MELODIC APPROACH

The melodic motif approach can be related to the tone row series, in which the tone row may be applied to and converted into a rhythmic pattern to make an intelligible melody. In other words, reverse the procedure. Start with the pitches:

EXAMPLE II-16

and incorporate this tone row into the rhythmic motif:

EXAMPLE II-17

Immediately, a melodic motif is born for vocal or instrumental purposes.

The tone row, rhythmic, and melodic motif approaches are all related to the jingle approach, in which the rhythm and character of the words suggest both the rhythm and character of the melody.

It may be well, even before using the previous approaches, to question the composers as to what they would do with a motif after it is once conceived. Explore with them the possibilities based on their common sense and experience. The next step is to expose the students to harmonic progressions from which they may derive melodic ideas.

HARMONIC APPROACH

At this point, because of the students' previous musical experiences in school as well as extracurricularly, it is assumed that they have been exposed to the sound of a scale and have learned that it is made up of eight notes constructed on consecutive degrees. Let them sing a major scale in unison. Then encourage them to sing again in unison, on each of the seven different notes, a series of three notes alternately arranged in the form of arpeggios, that is, 1, 3, 5; 2, 4, 6; 3, 5, 7; etc. By dividing the class into three equal parts, or by working with three individual students, the simultaneous singing of the notes of each of the seven arpeggios will establish the principle of triad formation. Apply these procedures also to the minor scales and the modes.

Each group must listen not only to the note it is singing, but also to the notes sung by the other groups, so that each group can benefit from the fusion of all three notes. This same procedure can be used by three individual students. Each of the seven formations ought to be performed by each student on the piano both as arpeggios and triads.

From all these experiences, the students will be fascinated by the sounds emanating from these combinations, which introduce them to the important part harmony plays in musical creativity. (The above procedures may be applied in the formation of arpeggios and chords of the seventh such as 1, 3, 5, 7; 2, 4, 6, 8; 3, 5, 7, 9; etc., each sung and performed on the piano in four parts.)

At this point the teacher should emphasize the significance intervals play in the construction of chords. In a television youth concert program entitled "Musical Atoms, A Study of Intervals," presented by Leonard Bernstein and the New York Philharmonic Orchestra, Mr. Bernstein most eloquently proved that the interval is the heart and soul of music. How right he is, since melody, harmony, and counterpoint are derived fundamentally from intervals in combinations, just as words, thoughts, and sentences are formed by combinations of letters.

The students' understanding of intervals will make their understanding of harmony more perceptive. So it is the teacher's responsibility to begin to intellectualize on the patterns governing the construction of major scales, upon which both the general and specific analyses of intervals are based. Thus, the students will be able to recognize the qualities inherent in major, minor, diminished, and augmented triads, as well as the qualities inherent in the various types of chords of the seventh and ninth. Modality, consonance, and dissonance now should become household words in their vocabulary.

With this background achieved, the teacher can introduce the students to the functional approach of chord progressions, according to accepted practical standards. Students, to reach their creative objectives, must assume the responsibility for understanding the following: four-part harmony (soprano, alto, tenor, bass) governed by the established rules of proper doubling in triads in root positions and inversions; the involvement of chords of the seventh and ninth; the principles of good voice leading; and the usual restrictions and disciplines which can be relaxed under justifiable circumstances. Strict four-part harmony will graduate into the more elaborate use of melodic, harmonic, contrapuntal, and rhythmic structures, thus opening up unlimited avenues of creativity.

Melodies may be suggested by harmonic progressions in relation to the major scales; the simplest are:

$$
\begin{array}{cccccc}
 & & & \text{I} & \text{V (or V}^7\text{)} & \text{I} \\
 & & \text{I} & \text{IV} & \text{V (or V}^7\text{)} & \text{I} \\
 & \text{I} & \text{IV} & \text{ii} & \text{V (or V}^7\text{)} & \text{I} \\
\text{I} & \text{vi} & \text{IV} & \text{ii} & \text{V (or V}^7\text{)} & \text{I} \\
\text{I} & \text{iii} & \text{vi} & \text{IV} & \text{ii} & \text{V (or V}^7\text{)} & \text{I}
\end{array}
$$

In relation to the minor scales—harmonic form—melodies may be suggested by harmonic progressions; the simplest are:

$$
\begin{array}{cccccc}
 & & & \text{i} & \text{V (or V}^7\text{)} & \text{i} \\
 & & \text{i} & \text{iv} & \text{V (or V}^7\text{)} & \text{i} \\
 & \text{i} & \text{iv} & \text{ii}^\circ & \text{V (or V}^7\text{)} & \text{i} \\
\text{i} & \text{VI} & \text{iv} & \text{ii}^\circ & \text{V (or V}^7\text{)} & \text{i} \\
\text{i} & \text{III}^+ & \text{VI} & \text{iv} & \text{ii}^\circ & \text{V (or V}^7\text{)} & \text{i}
\end{array}
$$

Harmonic progressions in the various modes may be constructed according to standard procedures.

All of these chordal progressions could very well be played by the teacher to help the non-piano students derive melodic ideas aurally. The students who may have acquired some piano technique extracurricularly have an advantage, as they will be able to perform these chordal progressions themselves.

Melodies can be conceived in several ways. For example, in the key of C-major, I V (or V⁷) I can be used as a basis for a melodic motif. If the note "C" of the I chord is selected as a melody note, it may progress to the next nearest note in the V chord. There are two choices. It could progress to either "D" or "B." Let it be assumed that the former is selected. By continuing the same procedure, the next nearest note to "D" in the I chord could be either a return to "C" or a rise to "E." If the choice were the former, the motif would appear as:

EXAMPLE II-18

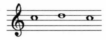

If the latter:

EXAMPLE II-19

By arranging either rhythmically, the result would be:

EXAMPLE II-20

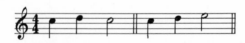

Either could develop into a 4-measure phrase and eventually into an 8-measure musical sentence by using devices of repetition, variation, transposition, sequence, and others referred to previously.

Applying this approach to any of the progressions listed above will help the young composers on their way to some rather elaborate conceptions. Introducing secondary dominant chords could increase color and interest. For example, in the progression:

I   iii (or iii⁷)   vi (or vi⁷)   ii (or ii⁷)   V (or V⁷)

by raising the thirds of the secondary harmonies, the progression
would be:

I	III (or III⁷)	VI (or VI⁷)	II (or II⁷)	V (or V⁷) I
	or	or	or	
	V (or V⁷)	V (or V⁷)	V (or V⁷)	
	of	of	of	
	vi	ii	V	

In all the progressions the first inversions of the IV and II chords may
be used, as well as the I$_4^6$ before the V (or V⁷). Experimentation at
the piano, employing the trial and error method, could very well produce unorthodox as well as contemporary progressions.

As the young composer becomes more acquainted with harmonic
concepts, he may usefully be apprised of the importance of all types
of foreign tones, which increase melodic, harmonic, and contrapuntal
interest, spicing the work with the important element of dissonance.
With more understanding of rhythm and meter, he can then benefit
from learning the basics of conducting, no matter how many instruments are used in his particular piece. Only in this way will his music
receive the proper interpretation when it is performed. (Fundamentally, beating time is a simple, geometric experience; the student,
however, must learn and experience that interpretation goes far beyond
mechanical gestures.)

At this time, with exposure to all approaches, the students may be
qualified enough to create pieces that have the necessary melodic,
rhythmic, harmonic, and emotional ingredients. The attainment of the
constructive principles of music must always be the goal of the student-composers.

The personality of a piece should suggest its appropriate medium
of expression, be it vocal or instrumental. With a piece of great propor-
tion, the importance of its motif becomes more significant in relation
to the piece as a whole. The proper use of the motif will insure unity.
For contrast, new material demands new ideas, changes in tempo, keys,
mood, and instrumentation. Very often a principal motif, announced

at the beginning of a work, is the unifying force of the entire piece. For example, in Beethoven's *Symphony No. 5*, all the themes are formed from the same pattern and nucleus as the opening theme. Although themes may appear to be different on the surface, there may be a common bond between them. An analogy may be made to members of a family who seem different but have a common denominator by virtue of a family resemblance.

However composers approach creativity, previous experience in listening, playing, and singing, whether in school or at home, together with instinct and common sense, will exert some influence on their work. Man is not an island unto himself. His exposure to environmental influences is inevitably reflected in his outlook, behavior, and creative orientation. Along with the encouragement of creative spontaneity, young composers should be taught to exercise control and discipline through proper guidance, so their compositions will have musical meaning, and so they will derive gratification from their accomplishments.

3

Teaching the Essentials

As the student is introduced to the fundamentals involved in the creation and development of a musical piece, he should be encouraged by the teacher to listen to examples of compositional techniques used by established composers. In this chapter, the basics of composition are discussed with reference to suggested listenings in the standard musical repertoire.

STRUCTURAL ELEMENTS

The basis of any piece is the *motif*. *Repetition* is a common device used to aid in the development of motifs. The works of any great composer will corroborate the importance of repetition as a tool to impress a musical idea on the listener, enabling him to follow its organic growth throughout the piece. Examples of the use of repetition are found in: the openings of *Symphony No. 40 in G minor* by Mozart; *Symphony No. 1* ("Spring") by Schumann; and *Symphony No. 5* by Beethoven. In these the initial motif and its many repetitions are made very clear. In the Mozart symphony, the motif of the first movement plays an important part throughout the exposition, development, and recapitulation. In the Schumann symphony, the motif of the introduction is the germ of the principal theme of the exposition, which is carried through the

31

entire movement. In the Beethoven Symphony, the famous four-note motif is the basic idea of the first movement and also appears literally or with variation in the subsequent movements. Among the devices used in the development of a motif are: *imitation,* the motif is simply repeated either literally or freely in another voice; *inversion,* the motif is turned upside down, according to either a literal or free interval relationship; *transposition,* the motif is placed either at a higher or lower plane according to an interval relationship; *sequence,* the motif is used with a minimum of two transpositions; *modulation,* the motif is placed in related or remote keys; *variation,* the motif is modified; *augmentation,* the notes of the motif are usually twice as long as the original; *diminution,* the notes of the motif are usually one-half as long as the original. Excellent examples can be found in the *Inventions* and the *Well-Tempered Clavier* by Bach.

Beyond the motif is the section that conventionally consists of two measures, and which, with the addition of two more measures of complementary material, becomes the 4-measure *fore-phrase* containing the motif and its repetitions, or several motifs. Its objective point is the *half-cadence,* usually dominant, sometimes tonic. The 4-measure *after-phrase* follows, leading into the *authentic cadence.* The fore-phrase and after-phrase establish the 8-measure sentence.

Phrases, of course, may vary in length, consisting of either two or eight measures, depending on the tempo. Phrases may be irregular, consisting of three, five, or seven measures. Examples of the conventional 4-measure fore-phrase and after-phrase consummating in a sentence of eight measures may be found in: *Annie Laurie,* and *Rondo a Capriccio* by Beethoven; the introduction of Haydn's *Symphony No. 94* ("Surprise"); the third movement of Mozart's *Sonata in C,* K.545; *Aase's Death* by Grieg; the first theme of the fourth movement of Brahms' *Symphony No. 1;* and the first theme of the second movement of Beethoven's *Eroica Symphony.*

FORMS

With the establishment of the motif, phrase, and sentence, form becomes the next consideration. Sentences, when combined with other sentences containing either repeated or new material, graduate into pieces.

Two-part form in its simplest structure consists of two complete 8-measure sentences. Each sentence may be repeated and contains the same material, making it a form in which there is one fundamental theme. The first sentence, after starting out in the home key, can modulate to a related key at its final cadence. The second sentence, which would start in this key, will modulate back to an authentic cadence in the original key. Although there is a change in tonalities, the fundamental musical material is the same. In this form designated by A, A', unity is achieved by repetition, variety by the inclusion of new tonalities, and coherence by the clear relationship of the tonalities. With each sentence containing eight measures, there is a perfect balance in length. Examples can be found in *Prelude No. 7 in A* by Chopin and *Waltz in A flat* by Schubert. This format very often is altered by the extension of either or both sentences, or by the inclusion of modulations into other keys, related and remote. Such examples are the *Inventions* and *French Suites* of Bach and *Prelude No. 1* by Chopin.

Two-part form may also contain two different musical sentences, each eight measures long, represented by the format A, B, as in Brahms' *Lullaby* and *Prelude No. 20* by Chopin.

Three-part form, which goes beyond two-part form, involves, after the completion of the first part, the addition of new material in a new key, preferably, followed by a return to the first part. The format appears as A, B, A in which the constructive principles are clearly delineated: unity by repetition of A; variety by the inclusion of new melodic, harmonic, and contrapuntal material of B, which can be in a new key with different meter, tempo, mood, register, location, and change in vocal and instrumental forces; and coherence by the clarity of the tonalities and the cohesiveness of the structure. The return of A can be literal or varied. Thus, restatement is established after contrast. Three-part form is basic to all structure. For example, a human's arms represent A, which flank his body B, or, to use a plebeian but practical analogy, a sandwich consists of two slices of bread, A, enveloping the food spread, B. Very often a *coda* or tail piece is added, which may be an extension of the final A. Examples of this form are legion: *Nocturne Op. 37, No. 1, Mazurka Op. 33, No. 3,* and *Waltz Op. 64, No. 1,* all by Chopin; the third movement of *Symphony No. 3* by Brahms; second movement of *Sonata Op. 27, No. 2* by Beethoven; sixth movement of Handel's *Water Music;* "Lift Thine Eyes" from *Elijah* by Mendelssohn; and "The Swan" from *Carnival of the Animals* by Saint-Saëns. In the classic minuets and scherzos, three-part form is used in which each part is in either two-part form or *three-part song form expanded,* as in the third movement of Haydn's *London Symphony No. 104* and the third movement of Mozart's *G minor Symphony No. 40.* Each part is not necessarily restricted to the 8-bar sentence. Extensions and developments are quite obvious.

Three-part song form is represented by A, A, B, A. Many folk songs and show tunes have this construction, such as *Home on the Range, Drink to Me Only with Thine Eyes,* and *Smoke Gets in Your Eyes.*

Rondo form, an extension of three-part form, is characterized by a principal theme that keeps recurring after intervening contrasted material. The simplest type containing two themes has the format A, B, A, B, A, which, upon examination, is a coupling of three-part form, in which the second A functions both as the third part of the first three-part form and the first part of the second three-part form:

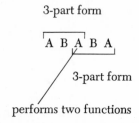

3-part form

A B A B A

3-part form

performs two functions

A good example is *Les Moissoneurs* by François Couperin. The sandwich analogy can be applied here as being a three-decker, in which are enveloped two bits of the same food spread, the three A's representing three slices of bread with the two B's representing two bits of the same food spread.

A more common rondo form is the type in which there is a main theme with two contrasting themes, A, B, A', C, A''; the primes indicate a variation rhythmically, harmonically, or contrapuntally that does not obscure the essential characteristics of the main theme. This could be analogous to a three-decker with two different bits of food spread in between. The A' and A'' each could be a different type of bread with the B and C each representing two different foods.

Examples are many: the rondo of *Sonata in C, K.545* by Mozart; *Polonaise in A,* and *Mazurka in B flat* by Chopin; *Rondo in C* by Beethoven; *Rondo Capriccioso* by Mendelssohn; *Till Eulenspiegel* by Strauss; and *Symphony No. 1,* third movement with its two trios by Schumann. Rondo form may be extended to any length by including even more contrasted material: *Musette en Rondeau* by Rameau, and *Rondo a Capriccio* by Beethoven. Chopin has incorporated unorthodox formats such as A, B, C, B, A, B as in his *Waltz in C-sharp minor.*

The *rondo-sonata,* which contains the elements of both, began with Beethoven and is used in the last movement of *Sonata No. 8*

("Pathétique"), in which the C portion is akin to the development in a sonata.

In *variation form,* a theme, after its initial presentation, may be presented differently. In the early days of instrumental music, a simple tune was varied by rhythmic and melodic embellishments, as in the works by Byrd, Bull, Couperin, and Rameau. These works are not necessarily very inspiring or challenging. However, *Les Barricades Mystérieuses* by François Couperin is a fascinating piece. The *Harmonious Blacksmith* by Handel contains variations all of which are in the same key of E-major with the basic harmony unchanged.

With Haydn the form improved. Witness the five variations of the "Austrian Hymn" from the *Kaiser Quartet in C-major,* each individually treated, and the variations in *Sonata in A-major, K.331,* by Mozart and the second movement of Haydn's *Symphony No. 94* ("Surprise").

The variation form became more advanced with Beethoven and subsequent composers through the nineteenth century. New keys, mood, meters, tempos, harmonies, rhythms, and counterpoints were involved in the process of varying the theme. Classic examples are: Beethoven's *Variations on a Theme by Diabelli,* the second movement of his *Appassionata Sonata,* and the second movement of his *Symphony No. 5;* Brahms' *Variations on a Theme by Haydn;* Schumann's *Symphonic Etudes, Op. 13;* Franck's *Symphonic Variations;* Strauss' *Don Quixote;* and Britten's *The Young Persons' Guide to the Orchestra.*

Sonata form has been used in the first and very often last movements of every conceivable symphony and sonata.

The *concerto,* a piece for solo instrument and orchestral accompaniment, consists of three movements: the first in sonata form with two expositions, the first, abridged, played by the orchestra, and the second, by solo instrument and orchestra; the second movement in three-part or sonata form; the third movement in either rondo or sonata form. These concertos are in abundance.

The *fugue,* the most highly developed of all forms, requiring both a mathematical and emotional understanding, can be best learned by analyzing the bible of all fugal literature, *The Well-Tempered Clavier* by Bach.

MELODIC TREATMENT

As a melody is conceived and developed, its wave-like structure, resulting from its ascending and descending motion, its step-wise and skip-wise structure, its elements of unity and variety, its activity and stagnation, should be salient considerations. These help toward *climax* and *anti-climax*, both of which should be inherent in a melody.

Examples of climax, usually in the middle of a melody, are found in: the slow movement of Schumann's *Symphony No. 2;* Tschaikowsky's *Symphony No. 4,* first movement; and Brahms' *Symphony No. 3,* second movement.

The *contour* of these melodies contributes a great deal to their vocal character. Many melodies exist that are essentially instrumental, and which are not intended to be sung, and whose range extends beyond the accepted vocal range of an interval of a tenth. Yet their intrinsic value is readily perceived in their contour and melodic line. Take for example: the horn theme in *Till Eulenspiegel;* the introduction of Beethoven's *Symphony No. 9;* the "Witches' Dance" of Berlioz's *Fantastic Symphony.*

In contemporary music, the following stylistic elements possess a well-delineated contour distinctively their own: non-vocal melodies; chromatic melodies based upon expanded tonality and free tonality, where the tonic exists, while the other eleven notes are equal and free (Hindemith's *Piano Sonatas*); melodies constructed in intervals of fourths known as quartal tones (Bartók's *Concerto for Orchestra*); the cycle of perfect fifths (the introductory theme of Berg's *Violin Concerto*); and, of course, the twelve-tone technique of Schoenberg and his disciples, where the sequence of notes appears distorted and disjointed.

RHYTHMIC TREATMENT

Changes in *meter* within a piece create a feeling of excitement, stimulation, and animation. Examples of change in meter are apparent in: the third movement of the *Eroica Symphony* by Beethoven, where the ¾ alternates with ¢ only briefly; *Symphony No. 1,* third movement, by Schumann, where the Scherzo ¾ alternates with the first trio in ²₄; and Stravinsky's *Rite of Spring,* which is rampant with changes of meter.

Rhythmic styles can be associated historically with idioms. For example, the baroque style of Bach's *Brandenburg Concertos* and *Suites* and Handel's *Concerti Grossi* is clear, conservative, concise, vibrant, and moving.

With the advent of the classical period, rhythm became less rigid with a preponderance of the Alberti bass accompaniment found in the instrumental works of Haydn, Mozart, and early Beethoven.

Syncopation, shifted rhythm, and complicated metric groups became more apparent in the nineteenth century Romantic style as, for example, in: the *Leonore Overture No. 3* by Beethoven; the first movement of *Symphony No. 1* by Schumann; the last movement of *Symphony No. 3* by Brahms. The concept of rhythm became more expanded in the twentieth century in: the ballets of Stravinsky; Bartók's *Concerto for Orchestra;* and the *Five Pieces for Orchestra* by Schoenberg.

INSTRUMENTAL AND VOCAL TREATMENT

As pieces are being conceived, it may be well for the composers to keep in mind the media for which they are intended. Accordingly, an understanding of the nature of these media is important. If possible, arrangements should be made within the curriculum for students to attend rehearsals of instrumental groups. Nothing is more valuable than a live performance. Attending concerts by professional groups in the local area, listening to recordings of chamber music, performed by trios, quartets, quintets, and ensembles, composed to represent every style, will acquaint the students with the sounds of the principal instruments and their uses. Listening to the orchestral works of composers of baroque, rococo, classical, romantic, impressionistic, late romantic, and the various contemporary periods will educate students in the evolutionary growth of the symphony orchestra. Suggested listenings include:

Baroque: Bach and Handel

Rococo: Couperin, Rameau, and C. P. E. Bach

Classical: Haydn and Mozart

Romantic: Beethoven, Schubert, Schumann, Mendelssohn, Berlioz, Liszt, Strauss, Wagner, Verdi, Puccini, Sibelius

Late Romantic: Bruckner and Mahler

Impressionistic: Debussy and Ravel

Contemporary: Barber, Stravinsky, Schoenberg, Fine, Milhaud, Hindemith, Piston, Bartók, Berg, Webern, Shostakovitch, Prokofieff, Copland, Berio, Stockhausen, Boulez, Cage, and many more

The recording of *The Young Person's Guide to the Orchestra* by Britten presents an excellent demonstration of every instrument used individually and collectively in the orchestra. For both a visual and aural experience, the film produced by Alexander Shaw, featuring the

London Symphony Orchestra, conducted by Sir Malcolm Sargent, is invaluable. The *Encyclopaedia Britannica* has issued a film, with narration, of the Vienna Symphony Orchestra, directed by Hans Swarowsky, which is most informative. Also recommended highly are the recordings, *Instruments of the Orchestra,* by the National Symphony Orchestra of Washington, Howard Mitchell, conductor, and the *First Chair Instruments of the Orchestra,* by the Philadelphia Orchestra.

The same approach should be used for vocal creativity—listening to live performances and recordings by soprano, contralto, tenor, baritone, and bass soloists, and also mixed voices in choirs. Here, too, it would be advisable for the composers to visit voice classes and rehearsals and to attend live performances by professional groups. Many recordings are available by renowned artists, such as Bjoerling, Pierce, Merrill, Price, Anderson, The Mormon Tabernacle Choir, The Robert Shaw Chorale, The Abbey Singers.

Before they begin writing, some student-composers with previous exposures may have particular media in mind. They should direct their pieces toward them, realizing what the possibilities, problems, and limitations will be. Other student-composers, inexperienced in media exposure, should question themselves, as they are writing or after they have completed their pieces, about the medium to which their pieces will be most adaptable. Can they best be used by a symphony orchestra, a chamber music ensemble, a vocal group, a solo instrument? To answer this question, students, by following the listening procedures I have mentioned, learn: the characteristics and qualities of all the instruments and voices, their timbres, their ranges, their relationships to one another individually and collectively in all kinds of combinations, their differences in sound and color, and their mixtures; the techniques for orchestration and arranging; and the setting up of an orchestral or vocal score. When a musical phrase or theme is assigned to an instrument, the student-composers are taught to cue that material in on the part of another instrument, which can then take over the solo if necessary; for example, a bassoon solo may be cued in on the cello staff, or an oboe solo on the clarinet staff. Very often the cue may occur in several parts, in order to assure the performance of a particular passage should any emergency arise in performance. Students learn the same fundamentals of all the voices and the techniques of writing for them individually, as soloists, or collectively in groups. The same instrumental principles are also applied to compositions for stage band and jazz combos. In all cases, extracting individual instrumental parts from orchestral scores, a laborious but essential job, is a requirement for preparing for a performance.

PROCEDURE FOR RHYTHMIC NOTATION

Before discussing compositional techniques in detail, I would like to help solve a problem that is a bugaboo and sometimes a frightening experience for the potential composers who have never had any experience with writing even a single note on paper. Very often I have been approached with a statement common to many—to quote typical youths and even adults, "We know what we want, but we can't write it down." This at first appears to be a formidable dilemma which can be dissipated if the composers will subject themselves to certain disciplinary procedures. Assuming that they understand the significance of simple meter, let them consider the quarter note as the one-beat unit. Establish a continuity of beats, each persisting for a duration of one second or more, whatever is comfortable for the individual. Let them then play their melodies on a keyboard instrument, preferably as they continue the beat by counting aloud. In this way they will be able to relate the value of each note to the established beat they are counting. If a pitch is held for two counts, they will know that it will be a half note; if it is held for half a count, it will be an eighth note, etc. If necessary let them isolate small units of the melody, until they feel they have recorded the values of the notes correctly. Then they should proceed to the next unit. To assure that they have the correct continuity, performing both units then is advisable. The units will accumulate gradually; repeating them as often as is necessary, the students will gain confidence, knowing they have done their job clearly and correctly. The primary requirements for such a project are patience, persistence, and tenacity. What if the students don't play a keyboard instrument? Whatever their instrument, be it singing, or playing a wind or string instrument, the same disciplinary procedure must be followed. If the instrument used makes counting aloud impossible, they can count mentally, or tap their foot, or both. In the final analysis, it is important to relate the value of the pitches to the established beat.

COMPOSITIONAL TECHNIQUES

There are certain fundamental compositional techniques that are paramount and that will help the students toward the development and fruition of their creative concepts. It is assumed that they will record their initial ideas, which will eventually expand into a full musical opus. Here time is inconsequential. Though every moment of work is important, they may concentrate for a long time on a particular section, only to decide to scrap it, because the results do not meet the standards they have already established for themselves through experience, growth, and dedication.

Time is never wasted; every effort is an experience and a guide. As Walter Piston used to say, "Spend five hours writing, composing, and the next four hours erasing." Working by trial and error, students are constantly learning. They write a motif, phrase, sentence, or section instinctively, with natural taste and discrimination; only later, will they learn by analysis the musical vocabulary, which they have unconsciously utilized. Gradually, they become acquainted with terms and technicalities as they learn traditional music techniques in theory class. Again, their first lesson is learning by doing.

The order in which the following techniques are discussed is arbitrary. Every one is equally important. Assume that the students are asked to create melodies. Let them create whatever they feel are acceptable melodies. With their completion, analysis follows. They should be asked to evaluate them in terms of style, contour, structure, rhythmic character, unity, and variety, all of which will condition and influence the type of *harmony* and *counterpoint* expected in support and for development. By exposure to literature in which these elements appear and with proper guidance by the teacher, the composers will feel confident in adapting harmonies and counterpoints, which would be most appropriate, logical, and justifiable for the character of the melodies.

Tempo is most important. The faster the tempo, the fewer the punctuations of harmony and the more economical the counterpoint. The slower the tempo, the more the number of harmonic punctuations and the more elaborate the counterpoint. This is based on the theory of *activity* and *stagnation*. The more active the melody, the more stagnant its support harmonically and contrapuntally, and vice versa.

How are the proper harmonies and counterpoints decided upon? Simply by *melodic synthesis*. The chords to be used will be determined by the arrangement of the majority of the notes according to interval construction in a melody within a phrase or section, again depending upon the tempo. For example, assume that the following phrase in fast tempo in C-major is to be harmonized:

EXAMPLE III-1

By synthesizing all the notes of measure 1, obviously the proper harmony is the tonic chord. Similarly in measure 2, the chord suggested is V⁷.

However, if the tempo were very slow, a diversity of chords (represented by Roman numerals) and subsequent counterpoint is expected:

EXAMPLE III-2

An eighth note counterpoint may be easily derived from this harmonic pattern:

EXAMPLE III-3

Of course, previous knowledge of harmonic structure will be an advantage for the composers. But what about the ones who have never had this instruction? Let them experiment at the piano to try and find combinations of notes that, according to their instinctive musical sense, will fit the melodic structure. Should they have difficulty, the teacher must orient them to the construction of chords in relation to the notes of the scale in question. Their understanding of the scale pattern, whether it be major, minor, or modal, should precede the building of triads on each degree of the scale. Then, it would be relatively easy for them to find the proper chords for each note or group of notes depending on the tempo of the melody. In the final analysis, the selection and placement of the proper harmonies and counterpoint, as well as the inclusion of foreign tones, will be based on instinct, taste, experience, and logic. The composers must avoid arbitrary acceptances. They must evaluate, accept or reject, always with a proper perspective in mind. Sometimes deciding on the proper harmony and counterpoint is difficult. An understanding of the style of the melody will suggest the proper harmonic structure. Both must conform to make the piece intelligible. The harmony will be stark and orthodox if it is baroque or classical. If it is romantic, it will be lush and sensuous, incorporating more chromatics, dissonance, and foreign tones. If it is impressionistic, the harmony will be suggestive and subjective with increased color, sonority, and dissonance. If it is in the atonal style employing the twelve-tone technique à la Schoenberg, the harmony will conform to the structure derived from the notes of the tone row. If it is neoclassical, it will contain unorthodox progressions and strong rhythms.

Since melody and its supporting harmony must aim toward consistency and conformity of style, student-composers must become acquainted with the particular style in which they wish to write.

How then is melodic style taught? In the same way that an understanding of different medias was achieved—by as much exposure as possible to different musical styles. Urge the composers to listen to, to analyze, and, if possible, to perform the works of the great masters, saturating themselves with the repertoire of the particular master whose style they wish to simulate. Have them study the various techniques the master uses in thematic quality, substance, development, thematic unity, and contrast. For example, if a student wishes to write in the style of Robert Schumann, he should concentrate on a certain number of his piano, chamber, orchestral, and vocal scores and recordings. By exposure to a representative number of pieces in these areas, he will subconsciously assimilate the lyrically melodic, the lushly harmonic, the transparently contrapuntal, and the syncopated rhythmic characteristics, along with the freedom of form. If he wishes to adopt the atonality of Schoenberg, by studying his works and those of his disciples, he will discover that the twelve tones are arbitrarily arranged in a row. Considered as the original, the row will be treated in inversion, in retrograde, and in inversion of the retrograde. With every appearance of the row under the conditions above, the rhythmic patterns can be flexible. The obvious dissonance and distortions resulting from this treatment can open up new areas of explorative creativity. If his bent is the musical theatre à la Broadway, he will want to acquaint himself with the music of Gershwin or Rodgers, whose inspiring, refreshing, and subtle creations are exemplary.

An understanding of proper *voicing* and *doubling* is most important for harmonic balance. If, for example, a piece is being arranged for four voices, the regulations concerning spacing in open and closed forms must be applied. This is fundamental even for instruments. As the number of voices or instruments increases, the distribution of notes must be kept in mind, though flexibility of treatment may be accepted if justifiable, depending entirely on the style, mood, and design of the piece. The student-composer should understand the mechanical structure of consonant and dissonant harmonies, as well as their inherent psychological and emotional values. His use of *consonance* or *dissonance* will be consistent with the message he wishes to convey.

_ Historically, the use of dissonance becomes more and more obvious after the eighteenth century. This is not to say that dissonance does not exist in music of the eighteenth century, as well as in the music of previous centuries. As the harmonies became more complex in the romantic music of the nineteenth century and especially in the music of the twentieth century, dissonance increased progressively. A favorite and most effective device that injects a biting and spicy flavor into the comparatively consonant music of the baroque and classic eras is the *pedal point*, which unobtrusively keeps repeating itself as the harmonies, with which it is used, keep changing. Its function, too, is to consolidate the section where it appears. Examples of its use are legion, as in the *Well-Tempered Clavier* and the *Passacaglia and Fugue in C minor* by Bach. Mostly used in the lower parts, it can be very impressive if used in the middle voice, with changing harmonies above and below it, and in the high voice, with changing harmonies below.

Placement of harmonies in relation to melody is flexible. Since the soprano voice, vocally or instrumentally, is the most prominent, one is likely to assign melody to it with harmonies below. This is not always true. A melody can be very useful if it is placed in the lower parts with harmonies above, or in the middle part with harmonies above and below. When it is used in the latter two instances, the dynamic level must be above that of the accompanying harmony so its function will not be obscured. In all cases of harmonizations, proper voice leading, especially in the inner parts, must be observed. This facilitates performance especially of vocal music.

Motion in music has a most significant function. The three types of motion, parallel, contrary, and oblique, have their appropriate place in a piece. Too much of each is obviously devastating and unimaginative. A reasonable balance of all three constitutes a well integrated and developed opus. Each should be used with discretion and understanding, always in relation to the piece as a whole.

Reference was made earlier to the devices that can be used to help develop a motif. These may be applied to themes in general. Examples of repetition, imitation, inversion, transposition, sequence, modulation, variation, augmentation, and diminution are found in: the *Inventions* and *Fugues* by Bach; Handel's *Messiah;* the *Requiem* by Mozart; the *Requiem* by Fauré; the *Elijah* by Mendelssohn; and the symphonic literature I mentioned before. Especially obvious in the *Messiah* is the use of *stretto* where the entrance of the imitation occurs before the part imitated completes its statement. This creates excitement and agitation. The fascination of shifted rhythm, where the statement enters on a beat other than the original, is rhythmically intriguing. Use of this device may be found in the *Well-Tempered Clavier*.

Antiphonal treatment of voices and instruments is a most logical and accepted method for musical development and for contrast and color. Witness again the *Messiah,* the development of the fourth movement of *Symphony No. 40* by Mozart, and the second theme of the first movement of *Symphony No. 4* by Tschaikowsky. *Recitatives* both vocally and instrumentally are effective as dramatic interludes. Again, the *Messiah* is replete with them. The recapitulation of the first movement of Beethoven's *Sonata in D minor, Opus 31 No. 2* begins with the piano pouring out in recitative form its message of warmth and sensitivity, a complete contrast to the busyness and activity preceding and following it.

Extensions of melodic material contribute to further development, as in: the minuet of the *Symphony No. 104* ("London") by Haydn; toward the end of the development of the first movement of *Symphony No. 40* by Mozart; the first movement of *Symphony No. 3* by Brahms; and the first theme of the first movement of *Symphony No. 4* by Tschaikowsky.

The device of *augmentation* is useful; the rhythmic values of the notes of a theme are multiplied usually by two, proportionately in length, as in the beginning of the recapitulation of the first movement of Schumann's *Symphony No. 1*. Similarly useful is *diminution,* in which the values are decreased usually by half proportionately, as in the "Fugue No. 9 Part II" of the *Well-Tempered Clavier*.

The selection of the proper *accompaniment* must be considered seriously. An accompaniment in a contemporary style would be incongruous to a melody in a classical style. Here again, the necessity for a composer to acquaint himself with every ingredient of a particular style—melodically, harmonically, contrapuntally, and rhythmically—becomes more significant and meaningful as he realizes his responsibility. Should he wish to write in the style of Chopin, a figurative accompaniment consisting of extended arpeggios, which reinforce the harmonies above the fundamental, would, ideally, support the romantically passionate melody. The Alberti bass would be most appropriate for a sonata or sonatina in the eighteenth century style. Block chords with added 9ths, 11ths, and 13ths in whole tone formation would suggest the subjective impressionism of Debussy.

Involved with accompaniment selection are demands made on the pianist and the popular and jazz combos as they improvise accompaniment to a singer or instrumental soloist. Although the talent for improvisation is usually innate, it can be developed by study and listening. The former will sound more spontaneously creative, while the latter might sound contrived or stereotyped. As the soloist is performing the melodic line, the accompanying instruments should make a serious attempt to avoid melodic duplication. The accompaniment should be harmonically and rhythmically contrapuntal, but not obtrusive or overbearing. The soloist and instruments should complement one another whenever possible. In this way, the spark of spontaneity can never be extinguished.

As students become acquainted with the sounds and ranges of instruments, and differentiate between those that are non-transposing and transposing, they will learn that the use of an instrument or instruments in combination must be appropriate to the piece, generally and specifically. The following techniques will contribute to good orchestration: instrumental contrast; antiphonal treatment; the addition and subtraction of instruments for crescendo and diminuendo purposes respectively, their function to increase resonance, color, and brilliance; the effective use of horn and bassoon on pedal points; the use of pizzicato, bowings, and other techniques on strings for rhythmic punctuation and support, the warmth and variety of tone color of the woodwinds; the brilliance of the brass; and the versatility of the percussion.

TWENTIETH CENTURY IDIOMS

Since many students today have been conditioned by music of the eighteenth and nineteenth centuries, it is important that their ears become attuned to music involving twentieth century techniques. Such techniques are: styles which are multiple harmonically, melodically, contrapuntally, and rhythmically; and styles in which conventional restrictions have been relaxed considerably with increased amounts of dissonance harmonically, expanded freedom melodically, more complexity contrapuntally, and greater flexibility rhythmically. Familiarity with modern giants from Debussy to Berg, with electronic and aleatoric avant-garde composers, with works influenced by the medieval modes, which have been enjoying a vital revival and have injected inspirational and refreshing elements into our contemporary repertoire, will expose the students to a totally new musical milieu. Suggested listenings include:

La Mer: Debussy
Five Pieces for Orchestra: Schoenberg
Wozzeck: Berg
Six Pieces for Orchestra: Webern
Symphony No. 5:   Prokofieff
Symphony No. 7:   Shostakovich
Concerto for Orchestra: Bartók
Rite of Spring: Stravinsky
Mathis der Maler: Hindemith
Suite Française: Milhaud
Appalachian Spring: Copland
Adagio for Strings: Barber
Age of Anxiety: Bernstein
Symphony 1962:   Fine
Seven Studies on Themes of Paul Klee: Schuller
Time Cycle: Foss
Symphonies: Ives
Piano Music: Cowell
Déserts: Varèse
Gesang der Jünglinge; Kontakte: Stockhausen
HPSCHD: Cage and Hiller
Free Jazz: Coleman

Induction into these media may be somewhat traumatic at first; those unused to them may rebel, cringe, wince, or possibly all three. Never mind, for it must be remembered that the twentieth century composer expresses his feelings and thoughts in accordance with the world in which he lives. To do so, he must resort to the techniques and disciplines of harmony, melody, counterpoint, and rhythm which have gone through extraordinary and significant stages of development in the last fifty years. For an art to remain healthy, such change is necessary, otherwise it may become stagnant and sterile. Learning contemporary techniques, which to the uninitiated seem strange and often unintelligible, is wholly justified. Students should experiment with sound clusters. Let them open their minds to new effects, to new visions, to new attitudes. Those who have been brought up in the baroque, classical, and romantic tradition may be immediately prejudiced against twentieth century music conceived according to twentieth century technique, for they expect to receive from it the same type of musical satisfaction they receive from the works of earlier composers.

Given the chance to broaden their understanding of the twentieth century idiom, however, and to listen to more twentieth century products, they will react positively before long. Not only will they derive pleasure musically from this new idiom, but they may also be inspired to attempt creations of their own based upon novel techniques that they find unexpectedly natural. Such explorations may one day make *them* the innovators, for example, in the area of electronic music, which has had great impact in recent years on musical creativity. After World War II, the Germans concentrated on pure synthesized electronic sounds. The French dealt with musique concrète using natural sounds. The Americans merged both.

Electronic music contains natural sounds, including voices, which can be distorted electronically and blended with electronic bleeps, beeps, gonks, and bonks. It can be either stereotyped or adventurous, depending on the ability and imagination of the electronic manipulator, as well as on the quality of his ear. Unfortunately, there are no critical standards with which to discriminate between good and bad. There is no rule of what is right or wrong. The sky is the limit.

It is a fallacy to believe that expensive equipment is required to write electronic music. Tape recorders can produce many sound mutations. When a normally recorded sound is played back at a speed faster or slower, changes will be obvious. A change in pitch can also result by resting a finger on one of the reels. Recording *sound-on-sound* at a different pitch level by using two tape recorders helps to produce different timbres and wave forms.

With a stereo-machine that has half-track heads, different sounds can be recorded on each track; with one that has quarter-track heads, two recordings can be made in one direction. With the tape turned over, two other recordings can be made in the other direction. All four sounds can then be heard at the same time on a two-channel machine.

Reverberation can be easily achieved by using a button provided on most modern stereo machines. *Canons* can be created by running a tape from one machine to another, by synchronizing the two machines and then by recording the same material on both machines simultaneously with a wye connector. *Ostinato rhythmic patterns* can be recorded on a tape loop which is passed through two empty reels. Speed changes result in new sound. The recording on the tape loop can be mixed with other sound material and then recorded on a second tape machine. Contact mikes cause a mutation of the original sound of an instrument when it is recorded on tape. *Percussive rhythms* can be produced by tapping on the mike. These can be set up on tape loops and superimposed upon each other. *Feedback* can be gotten by arranging patch cords between two tape machines. By patching from output to input on one machine, recordings can be made if the signal is directed to a second machine. *White noise* is a roar resulting from tuning the TV or FM radio off of a station. If the circuits of the white noise are interrupted, rhythms of all kinds can be used with tape loops.

In recent years the advent of the *Syn-Ket* and *Moog Synthesizer* has opened up new channels for creativity in the electronic area. The Syn-Ket is provided with several generators, a keyboard, dials, buttons, and switches, all of which can reproduce not only the sound of any conventional musical instrument or any type of noise, but also sounds that cannot be obtained on any instrument. It can also create many kinds of tone colors and rhythmic effects. The Moog Synthesizer is provided with amplifiers, mixers, filters, and voltage-controlled oscillators, as well as with an organ keyboard. Raw sounds, white noise, vibrato, and echo effects are easily produced. It has been used by avant-garde composers to produce themes for commercial television, and recently to electronically orchestrate pieces by Bach.

Students with the resources and equipment mentioned should have carte blanche for the expression and development of their ideas.

DEVELOPMENT OF STYLISTIC INDIVIDUALITY

I do not want to appear necessarily as a devotee *only* of twentieth century music. Certainly we have much to learn from the giants of past centuries, and it will be greatly to the student's advantage to listen to examples of all music—from Biblical times to the Middle Ages, the Renaissance, and finally the traditional baroque, rococo, classical, and romantic eras. One never knows when the students' work will benefit from any one of these influences. For example, Wagner was an eclectic whose music showed traces of Bach, Beethoven, Schumann, and others. From this tradition, he introduced personal characteristics and a style which inevitably mark his music as Wagnerian.

By experimenting in as many different idioms as time will permit, as well as in those in which the students comfortably write, they will evolve their own personality and style within the general framework defined by great composers, both past and present. In this way, they will mature and become more objective in all their creative efforts.

4

Establishing a Creative Climate

My experiences with young composers of middle and junior high school age at the Creative Arts Center proved most successful. Although this program lasted for only five weeks each summer, the teaching procedures in this type of program could obviously be used in a creative music course extending through a full academic year. This program can apply to children of all backgrounds and environments, not only to those who have had previous musical experience. The teacher, as always, will find that individual advising and counselling of each child will be necessary; time should definitely be set aside for this. As in all private consultation, much can be accomplished in an atmosphere free from the tensions of the classroom. Students should be expected to work consistently and independently on their own compositions at home or whenever convenient. In this way, their material, which will always be available for evaluation by teacher and colleagues, will develop gradually into the final fulfillment of an accepted piece.

The home, the administrators, and the music educators could all well implement the program by cooperating in the establishment of a healthy music listening environment. What a blessing this would be, not only as a cultural enrichment program, but also as a stimulant to the creative imagination of our young people generally.

At Newton High School, where I have taught for many years,

the same type of procedures that were used in the five week Creative Arts program are used, but in greater depth, in music courses extending throughout the academic year. Original compositions are created by students in the Theory I and II classes. Each class meets four times a week and offers five credits, thereby classifying the courses as major subjects.

The purpose of theory classes is to give the students a fundamental concept and secure understanding of the construction of music per se, which, in itself, is an inducement toward creativity. Performing a piece of vocal or instrumental music without this understanding leaves a void in its complete appreciation and enjoyment. Besides the cultural value of the courses, music theory teaches discipline, organization, and mental alertness.

Since relativity plays an important and vital part in any creative work, students should realize that notes in a piece are not isolated entities. Each note has a significant relationship to notes preceding and following. This melodic function conditions the harmonic, rhythmic, and contrapuntal structures.

Understanding the construction of the chromatic scale is the basis for understanding the major and minor scales and modes from which spring forth all the chord structures: primary, secondary, secondary 7ths, altered, chromatic, and modulatory, as well as non-harmonic or foreign tones.

Both Theory I and Theory II are designed for vocalists and instrumentalists as well as for the inexperienced. The great majority of students enter the class with a reading knowledge of music. For those who are completely inexperienced, a little tutoring helps them adjust and learn quickly.

In Theory I, all the major and minor scales and the modes are taught with a great deal of emphasis on the singing experience, with or without the syllable methods, as well as the application of scales and modes to the piano keyboard. The principle that the written note symbolizes a sound, and must be heard and felt, is stressed continually. In this way, the singing experience helps considerably in developing the sensitivity of the ear. The primary chords—tonic, dominant, dominant 7th, and sub-dominant—in root position and inversions, form the vocabulary in Theory I. Here again, the singing experience is constantly used. The chords are sung in arpeggio form in unison and then concerted with the class divided into the necessary parts.

Knowledge of the ranges of soprano, alto, tenor, and bass is required for the voicing of these chords in four parts in open and closed positions. This is followed by the progression of chords in cadences ac-

Members of a Theory of Music I class at Newton (Mass.) High School viewing introductory material of a composition by one of their colleagues, with the help of an overhead projector. A significant harmonic structure is being pointed out by the author.

51

cording to accepted procedures. All progressions are sung and played at the piano.

As the students do their work, they are urged to do it independently of the piano at first, in order to help them develop a sense of hearing mentally before they perform their work. "See with your ears; hear with your eyes."

The Color-Basic principle, actually first species counterpoint, is then taught; a soprano is harmonized with an economically, well-disciplined bass line using root positions and inversions. Again, they must be sung and then played.

With all the above as a foundation, the students proceed to the harmonization of 4- and 8-measure sopranos to be sung and played with an understanding of the following functions: section; phrase; sentence; half- and authentic cadences; harmonic rhythm; use of inversions and root positions, with the economy of the primary chord vocabulary to create bass line interest; proper doubling, spacing, and voice leading, employing principles of stagnation and activity in relation to tempos; the three principal motions; and avoidance of the traditional errors of cross parts, tritones, consecutive fifths and eighths.

Analysis of intervals and construction of intervals above and below a given note, significance of consonance and dissonance in relation to intervals and chord construction are gradually taught. Ear training, melodic, rhythmic, and harmonic dictation are an important part of the course too. Figured bass in relation to the primary chords is presented, as well as elementary analysis of materials within the vocabulary.

From the first day of school in September, students in Theory I are encouraged to create. Their first assignment is to go home and compose, as little or as much as they want, without becoming concerned about the merit of the piece. By so doing, they have a chance to break down the barriers that have often existed for years as a result of inhibitions and fears instilled in them as youngsters—the imagined difficulties and hardships they thought they would encounter without the benefit of courses in theory, harmony, counterpoint, orchestration, and so forth. How many music teachers echo the feeling, "Of course you can't compose unless you have gone through the mill, preparing yourself for the formidable task of composition by taking all kinds of courses that will give you the proper background and equipment." How we sell these students short! Perhaps conservative educators forget that one of the least schooled classical composers was Franz Schubert, who decided to study counterpoint shortly before his death.

To return to the first assignment in the Theory I course—students are asked to compose a piece in any style or idiom of any length. They may wish to experiment with a jingle, a couplet, or a quatrain, for which they write music according to the procedures outlined previously. This is perfectly all right, except that we are now dealing with high school students who have generally had some functional musical experience, instrumental or vocal or both, and whose age and practice warrant a more advanced approach to composition. Though designed for younger students, the jingle approach does have merits, especially for those who feel insecure and for those whose confidence might be more firmly established by using the jingle and its rhythmic essence as an initial guide.

In their early efforts, students are urged to "live dangerously," not to be too concerned about quality or the manner in which a piece will be received. This emphasis tends to lessen fear of rejection and helps students toward an attitude of relative abandon. It is exciting to see the variety of material produced at home by this initial experiment, all of it reflecting the heterogeneous character and experience of the group. After hearing each piece played on the piano, fellow composers evaluate and criticize it constructively. Weaknesses are pointed out, as well as strengths; nothing is berated, even if it does not measure up to accepted standards; errors are always explored and explained so that they can be avoided in the future. The students are asked to focus their attention on what they think is vital and relevant to the development of their compositions. With this step, they begin to develop confidence in their ability and talent and the faith in themselves to work toward real musical accomplishment. Since no demands are made on them to compose in a certain style, the students select, on the basis of past experience and exposure, the style in which they feel most comfortable. How exciting it is for them to realize that something significant *can* result!

Throughout these beginning stages, the use of material which may appear to be trite is called to their attention, and if such a passage cannot be entirely scrapped, the students attempt to improve upon it through a more subtle approach. How do they know what is trite? Listening to all sorts of music, good and bad, is helpful. So is reading musical criticism to develop standards of comparison. Before long they will begin to mature in both their sense of appreciation and in their conception of music. In the end, their sense of taste and discrimination will be the final judge. Despite inevitable errors, it is important that standards always be kept high. If a great deal is expected from these young people, they will produce; it is the teacher's job to spur them on constantly and religiously. Resolute and sincere in his demands, the teacher must, at the same time, remember that his students have other commitments besides composing. They have obligations to other courses and to whatever extracurricular activities they are engaged in. In exercising his demands, therefore, the teacher must be both patient and understanding. Given this approach, and in spite of a heavy academic schedule, the students will usually find the time and wherewithal to create, often slowly at first, but intensively and sincerely.

Inevitably, students do many things by instinct in their creative work long before they use them in daily harmonizations in theory class. And why *should* they wait for the textbook to spell out a particular principle before expressing it freely in a composition? For many weeks the students will harmonize 8-measure sopranos. Does this mean that they cannot advance beyond eight measures in their creative work? How restricted they would be if this were mandatory! It is far more rewarding for them to be free to write what they want, as extensively as they feel necessary and in any form, be it three-part, rondo, variation, sonata, fugue, etc. To help in this exercise, the teacher can guide his students in the application of these forms by earlier composers; together they can usefully analyze selected pieces.

I cannot stress this exposure to great musicians enough. Students will learn either by academic application, by osmosis, or simply by exercising natural good judgment if their work is developing correctly.

Throughout, a climate of constructive criticism should be encouraged. Each student should feel that it is to his own benefit, in terms of future growth, to subject his work to the critical faculties of his colleagues. Welcoming objective viewpoints from both teachers and students needs high priority, with criticism always given in a spirit of helping, rather than in censure. To suggest where improvements can be made, rather than to belittle or decry what one person thinks is inferior, is most important. It must be remembered that we are dealing with human beings, each with his own feelings and emotions, each needing encouragement regardless of extent of development. Student-composers will naturally feel sensitive to both acceptance and rejection, and because of the existing vulnerability inherent in creative work, it is especially important not to injure what confidence they do have. As sociologists have always said, there is good in every bad boy; likewise, there is good in every piece of music, no matter what its weaknesses, which can be converted to strength. Even the simplest tune has a particular quality in its curve, its climax, and its form, and the smallest child who has created it needs encouraging applause. I am not beating the drum for a mutual admiration society. What we do need is objectivity and serious criticism given in a benevolent way.

Whether melodies are to be revised and a final version accepted will depend upon individual composers. Here again patience and perseverance enter in. Students must, by either instinct or study, recognize the contour of a melody. They must be able to strengthen parts that are weak, prune wherever necessary, and achieve unity, variety, and balance. They must also attempt to reach a happy medium in the final selection of melodic material and its development, neither overdoing, nor underdoing. Who is to evaluate what is right or wrong? This will depend upon the past experience of the composers, their exposure to music already considered good, their sense of taste, and above all an objective evaluation coupled with their own judgment in which, it is hoped, they will constantly gain confidence.

As in the Junior High School program, it is important for the administration to schedule time for private consultation and counselling if free tutorial periods are not available for both students and teacher. Since the works of high school students will be more extensive and detailed than those of younger composers, individual attention will be that much more necessary. As I said earlier, both teacher and students should above all be patient so far as time is concerned.

In Theory II, the foreign tones are first taught in relation to the primary chords learned in Theory I. In this way, the students learn to do a great deal with a minimum of harmonic equipment. Then all the remaining chords, mentioned earlier, through modulation are taught. Throughout the year everything harmonized for four parts must be sung and played.

All the disciplines mentioned in Theory I are continued through Theory II. More extensive ear training and dictation, a broader concept of the use of harmony vertically and horizontally, more analysis of form, structure, and standard literature are included, as well as figured bass coinciding with the material that is progressively learned. Occasionally, a student has qualified for advanced placement in Theory II by virtue of his previous instrumental experience, which is usually pianistic and thus related to harmonic, contrapuntal, and rhythmic concepts, and by his exposure to the many fundamentals taught in Theory I. After several private orientation sessions, he will take a rigid and comprehensive examination, which is the determining factor for promotion.

Texts used in both Theory I and Theory II are: *Applied Harmony* by Carolyn A. Alchin, which teaches the immediate harmonization of sopranos based upon the principle of soprano activity and stagnation to stimulate a contrapuntal treatment in the lower parts; *Harmony* by Walter Piston; and my own supplementary material. (Other references are included in the Appendix.)

In the classroom, all the disciplines of proper harmonization are respected and followed. However, the students, in their creative work, are permitted to break rules justifiably, provided they do so with taste and judgment. As a result of the restrictions placed upon them in their academic work, the students find themselves, as they compose, in an atmosphere of freedom tempered with control and restraint.

Generally, the students have the advantage of tutorial sessions in the music room during a free period or in an after school session, in which several composers participate. Each observes what the others have been doing, usually in home preparation, and each is free to criticize. Beyond the four periods a week during which the theory classes meet, composers have been known to have had as many as three individual tutorial sessions a week. Frequently the pieces, either in the process of being composed or when fully composed, will be demonstrated in the regular class period for purposes of discussion, so there is integration between the tutorial sessions and the classroom. This arrangement of tutorial sessions with subsequent class discussion has proven most successful and indeed is most desirable.

As the piece is being fashioned, the composers learn what they have done in terms of melodic, harmonic, contrapuntal, and rhythmic construction as well as form. The mechanics of scoring are taught through relevant questions by the teacher. The students bring forth their own ideas of arranging for voice or voices, instrumentation and orchestration. If the teacher should have any reservations about the composers' suggestions, these ideas are temporarily held in abeyance pending further consideration by the composers. When the students realize that their subsequent thinking has more substance than their original thoughts, they know that they have climbed up another step toward maturity. At all times, the teacher must constantly be vigilant to maintain an atmosphere of freedom with restraint.

Very often it will be necessary to perform examples of the musical style in which the composers are writing. With the piano, tape recorder, and record player available, this is easily possible. Students learn by imitation, and the more they are saturated with the repertoire of composers they are simulating, the more authentic their pieces will be. From this should come germs of individuality, which they should seek to discover. True, there is nothing new under the sun. Yet new personalities can emerge in any art form if the individual artists are stimulated and determined to find it.

Each year at Newton High School, it has been traditional at the final concert of the Music Club, an extracurricular organization open to all students, to present a program of original compositions by members of the theory classes, who have created, orchestrated, and arranged their own pieces. What a new and thrilling experience it becomes for these embryonic composers, with a minimum of creative experience, to hear their own works actually performed! Because instrumental and vocal groups are more available at the High School, the musical possibilities are correspondingly greater. Students have at their disposal a symphony orchestra, usually adequate in size and quality and consisting of instruments representing each of the four choirs (although there have been years without an oboe, a bassoon, or a French horn). Students may write for the complete orchestra or for chamber music ensembles of all types. Vocal groups include an A Capella Choir, as well as a Madrigal Group and other choral organizations, each featuring proficient soloists. There is also a stage band and a jazz band combo. All these musical groups serve as a laboratory for the high school student. It has been a rich experience for all concerned—the composers; the performers, who are exposed to manuscripts conceived in a great variety of styles and idioms; and the listeners, whose cultural enrichment is surpassed only by their admiration for these unexpectedly youthful composers.

In the past, special rehearsal schedules have been arranged either after school hours or during a homeroom period if previous commitments did not permit the performing groups to be available during regular class periods. In recent years, school time has been made available for a period of two to three weeks before the annual concert. This is the ideal situation.

Creative writing cannot be rushed or pressured. More important is a consistency and devotion that will see an initial effort grow gradually in strength and intensity into a work of fulfillment and maturity.

5

Middle and Junior High Schools

Let us examine some of the pieces representing the creative efforts of youngsters from 11 to 14 years of age, grades 6 through 9. The experiments that resulted in these pieces were conducted during several consecutive summer sessions in the Newton Creative Arts Program. I have analyzed each piece in terms of style, form, phraseology, development, construction—melodically, harmonically, contrapuntally, and rhythmically—and for performance-medium. Each can serve as an example to be used by the student composer for his own creative efforts.

The first selections are exclusively vocal; the rest are instrumental, orchestrated for instruments available at the time. All were performed by the students. It was impossible to have the ideally-balanced choir and orchestra, but usually there was a variety of voices and instruments, which provided a good workshop for the composers.

The pieces in each area are arranged according to age group. A comprehensive analysis follows each piece. Again, we must remember that all are first experiences by neophyte composers, average in ability, who were initially exposed to the jingle and tone row, as well as the rhythmic and melodic approaches. As they became more experienced, they realized that their freely created ideas needed to be conditioned by restraints and disciplines to assure their proper development.

In both vocal and instrumental scores, the analyses are indicated wherever feasible: harmonies by Roman numerals, large for major and perfect, small for minor, small with added "o" for diminished, small with added "ø" for half-diminished, large with added "+" for augmented; 7th for a seventh chord, 9 for a ninth chord, 11 for an eleventh chord, 13 for a thirteenth chord; Arabic numbers determine inversions, 6 for first inversion triad, $\frac{6}{4}$ for second inversion triad, $\frac{6}{5}$ for first inversion of 7th chord, $\frac{4}{3}$ for second inversion of 7th chord, $\frac{4}{2}$ for third inversion of 7th chord; and the abbreviations of foreign tones are indicated wherever feasible.

The individual instruments of the pieces for orchestra are notated in the condensed scores by abbreviated labels. Other material applicable is also indicated by abbreviation. The following are the abbreviations used:

Instruments

Bass, Basses: *CB, CB's*

Bass Drum: *BD*

Bassoon: *B'n*

Cello, Celli: *Vc, Vc's*

Clarinet, Clarinets: *Cl, Cl's*

Cymbal, Cymbals: *Cym, Cym's*

Flute, Flutes: *Fl, Fl's*

Horn, Horns: *Hn, Hn's*

Oboe, Oboes: *Ob, Ob's*

Snare Drum: *SD*

Strings: *Str's*

Suspended Cymbal: *Sus Cym*

Timpani: *Timp*

Triangle: *Tri*

Trombone, Trombones: *Trb, Trb's*

Trumpet, Trumpets: *Trp, Trp's*

Tuba: *Tba*

Viola, Violas: *Va, Va's*

Violin, Violins: *V, V's*

Wood Block: *WB*

Xylophone: *Xyl*

Foreign Tones

Anticipation: *ant*

Appoggiatura: *app*

Auxiliary Tone: *aux*

Cambiata: *camb*

Changing Tone: *ct*

Chromatic: *chr*

Echappée: *ech*

Free Tone: *ft*

Passing Tone: *pt*

Pedal Point: *pp*

   (Tonic, Dominant): (T–D)

Suspension: *susp*

Upward Suspension: *upw susp*

Miscellaneous

Major: *maj*

Perfect: *perf*

Minor: *min*

Diminished: *dim*

Augmented: *aug*

Cross Relation: *C.R.*

Subject: *Sub*

Counter-Subject: *C.S.*

Free Part: *F.P.*

Divisi: *Div*

Unison: *Unis*

Dominant Harmony

  over Tonic Pedal Point: $\dfrac{V}{I \text{ or } 1}$

The Animals' Discussion

Linda Tufts

The ze - bra and el - e - phant did dis - cuss why stripes and
co - bras and rat - tle - snakes did dis - cuss why fangs and

trunks could be use - ful to us. The sword - fish and min - nows
poi - son weren't giv - en to us. The moths and the bee - tles

did dis - cuss why swords and tails are not use - ful to us.
did dis - cuss why wings and shells are not use - ful to us.

The ea - gles and the pa - ra - keets did dis - cuss why weight and

THE ANIMALS' DISCUSSION   Linda Tufts, Grade 6

The text of this song is indeed imaginative and reveals Linda's knowledge of animals and fish and the physical characteristics common to
both. The verse creates a triple flowing rhythmic pulse. Musically, the
piece is in three-part song form, A, A', B, A. The rhyme of the verse is
economical, using only the words "discuss" and "us" in both parts A and
B. This repetition is not disturbing because of the activity and variety
of the text; it becomes accepted almost as a necessity. Notice that "discuss" and "us" in part A appear at the ends of their lines or phrases.
However, to get variety in part B, the composer clearly planted the
word "discuss" directly before the ends of the lines in which it occurs.
"Us" remains at the ends of the lines. In spite of the irregular use of
"discuss," which on the surface would be likely to precipitate a rhythmic disturbance, the rhyme is still felt.

In the fore-phrase or question, the first motif of A:

EXAMPLE V-1

The   ze - bra and

after the anacrusis or upbeat ascends stepwise and is followed by a
measure of repeated notes. The second motif:

EXAMPLE V-2

did   dis -

appears in measure 3, continuing upward and reaching a climax in
measure 4, where the half- and quarter-note rhythm is repeated. The
after-phrase or answer begins in measure 5 with the rhythm of the
second motif, its objective seeming to be a gradual descent to the
masculine half-cadence in measure 8. Rhythmically, measures 5, 6 and
7 are a reversal of measures 1, 2 and 3 of the fore-phrase.

    A rhythmic plan of the first eight-measure sentence reveals the
following subtle organization:

EXAMPLE V-3

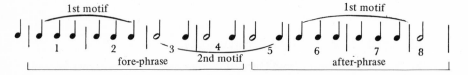

    One would expect that the after-phrase would repeat the pattern
of the fore-phrase rhythmically. Instead, it begins with a continuation
of the second motif rhythmically for one measure, delaying the appearance of the first motif until the following (sixth) measure. Measures 6 and 7 balance measures 1 and 2, while measures 3, 4 and 5, all of
one common rhythmic motif, serve as a balance between those measures which flank them and contribute variety and contrast. At the same
time, unity and coherence are achieved through repetition of the
rhythmic patterns of both motifs. The A' section adheres to the same
format as A, with the exception of measure 10, where the word "min-
nows," with its two syllables, requires the use of the second motif, that
is, the half- and quarter-note. A' ends with the masculine authentic

cadence in measure 16 and the necessary note from the tonic chord, serving as a pivot chord—I in "F," IV in "C."

Section B offers variety by changing the key to C-major and introducing a new theme. The first two measures of fore-phrase B and B' give the illusion of $\frac{2}{4}$ rhythm, without the text, through a feeling of shifted rhythm, creating drive and excitement:

EXAMPLE V-4

The   ea - gles   and the   pa - ra - keets

(B and B', as written)

EXAMPLE V-5

(give the illusion of $\frac{2}{4}$ rhythm)

The rhythmic patterns of theme A are quite obvious in B and B', measures 19 and 20, 27 and 28 respectively of the fore-phrase and throughout the after-phrase. This is another example of unity and coherence within theme relationships. In measure 24, the masculine half-cadence appears in the key of E-minor, while, in measure 32, C-major is the tonality of the authentic cadence.

Throughout A and A', a tonic pedal point, with moving harmonies of tonic, subdominant, and dominant 7th above, is used in the bass accompaniment. Dissonance is created in measures of dominant 7th harmony, especially in measure 15 where both dominant 7th harmony and the appoggiatura of "A" in the melody are used. In B and B', the bass takes on a descending diatonic step-wise motion, in contrast to the previous stagnation of the pedal point in the A section. Above the moving bass, notice that the C-major chord is sustained for four measures, performing a function similar to the pedal point in section A. In the after-phrase, the relative minor of C-major (A-minor, or the submediant chord, VI) and the subtle modulation in measures 23 and 24 from C-major to the mediant chord E-minor (iii $^6_4$ through V of iii) contribute both melodic and harmonic variety. With an immediate return to C-major, B' begins and repeats B, except for the expected authentic cadence in C-major approached by the subdominant 7th. The style of the harmonic accompaniment, with its appropriate bass lines subordinate to the melody, is ideal. It allows the vocal line to proceed without duplication of the melody by the right hand in the piano part. This duplication happens in music too frequently, interfering with the real function of the solo line.

The alto part in section A is based generally on the pattern of parallel 6ths, and occasionally 5ths and 3rds, with evidence of oblique and contrary motion. In section B, there is oblique motion between the repeated alto and the moving soprano in the first two measures. The unison in measures 19 and 20 is quite effective, followed by well-chosen contrary motion for two measures, then oblique and contrary motion approaching the modulation to E-minor. In the corresponding spot in B', this contrary and oblique motion continues to the end of the section to the tonic of C-major, the pivot chord acting as the dominant of F-major. The DS al Fine, which ushers in the return of section A, completes the three-part form, giving the piece unity in the final repetition of section A.

The melodic line, well wedded to the substance of the text, gives evidence of the kind of rhythmic wave motion so important to the construction of a good melody. The range of an 11th is not objectionable, since the high "F" in section A is approached by step-wise motion. There is ample use of foreign tones (the passing tone, free tone, echappée, appoggiatura, auxiliary tone) to spice up the melody. All of these are indicated in the score. Dynamically, the rise and fall of the melody invites the use of crescendo and diminuendo. Care and judgment must be exercised to avoid making the interpretation too mechanical. Conservative use of upward suspensions at the cadences, too, should be executed with discretion.

We find in "Animals' Discussion" many interesting developments in vocal composition:

1. Original text in which the composer's interest in animals and fish is revealed, making possible the integration of a scientific area with a musical interpretation
2. Only two rhyming words throughout
3. Three-part form; evidence of unity, variety and coherence not only between themes, but also within themes
4. Fore-phrase question balanced by after-phrase answer, with use of both masculine half- and authentic cadences
5. Balance, contrast, and unity resulting from a subtle rhythmic plan, consisting of two patterns within two phrases (fore-phrase and after-phrase)
6. Theme B more exciting with suggestion of shifted rhythm
7. Harmonic structure made interesting by the use of pedal point, a

moving bass, active and sustained harmonies as accompaniment to the melody, and modulations

8. Alto part significantly contrasted to the soprano in terms of harmony, through use of parallel, contrary, and oblique motions

9. Appropriate agreement of rhythmic wave motion of melody with words

10. Range of an eleventh justified

11. Melody, and therefore its related harmonies, spiced up by foreign tones

12. Exercising discretion important in the interpretation of the song involving variance of tempo

Books

Marjorie Kaplan

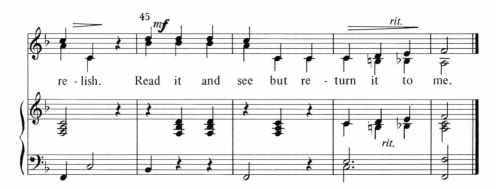

re - lish.   Read   it   and   see   but   re - turn   it   to   me.

BOOKS   Marjorie Kaplan, Grade 6

The ingenuity of this young composer is evident in her descriptive text. Philosophically, the idealism of this youngster is expressed by her admiration for books. She recognizes their importance in affording pleasure and as sources of knowledge. Her respect for books is indicated by her desire to repossess them after giving others an opportunity to experience their value.

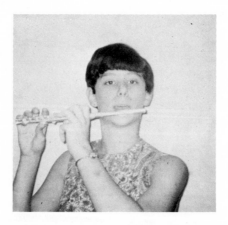

It now would be advisable to examine the content and treatment of the stanzas. In the first stanza the rhyme falls within the lines:

Line 1:   treasure _____ measure
Line 2:   see _____ me
Line 3:   story _____ glory
Line 4:   see _____ me

The above words fall on the strong beats of the even measures of each phrase. The first two lines form a couplet, as do the last two lines, with each couplet associated with eight measures of music.

In the second stanza, the rhyme falls within the first and third lines, while lines two and four rhyme at their ends:

Line 1:   pages _____ ages
Line 2:   _____ ago
Line 3:   chapters _____ factors
Line 4:   _____ know

Obviously this was aimed as contrast to the first stanza.

Again the words forming the rhymes coincide with the strong beats of the even measures of each phrase, while the arrangement of the couplets is parallel to that of the first stanza.

The third stanza follows the same format, rhyme-wise and couplet-wise, and the same structure as the first stanza with the rhymes:

Line 1:   pleasure _____ leisure
Line 2:   see _____ me
Line 3:   cherish _____ relish
Line 4:   see _____ me

Musically, the piece is arranged in clear-cut, three-part form with each part, consisting of the customary orthodox eight measures repeated, A, A, B, B, A, A totalling forty-eight measures. If the simple ABA form were used, twenty-four measures would result. If the three-part song form A, A, B, A were used, thirty-two measures would result. However, the composer chose to extend the form by repeating the B and A as indicated. Compare this plan to that of an eighteenth century minuet:

Three part song form expanded

||:A:||:BA:||

or

||:A:||:BA':||

Form of "Books"

||:A:||:B:||:A:||

Notice the same number of letter appearances in both (four A's and two B's), but the order of these letters differs.

Obviously, in the latter the repetition of B, measures 25 through 32, is expected because the words used in this stanza fit those of the previous stanza, measures 17 through 24. Repetition of two A's follows to balance the first two A's.

Unity is effected by the repetitions of the A section; variety results by introducing B, which gains its own unity by repetitions. Each section is logically consistent. Coherence is achieved.

The musical construction is logical. In the fore-phrase or antecedent, the first motif:

EXAMPLE V-6

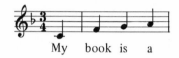

consists of the anacrusis and the notes in the first measure which proceed diatonically upward. This is followed by the second motif:

EXAMPLE V-7

characterized by an octave jump downward. Both motifs appear frequently throughout the piece.

The second motif is used with the words "treasure," "measure," "story," "glory," "pleasure," "leisure," "cherish," "relish." The first syllable of each word is associated with the upper note of the octave, giving these important words the emphasis required. Each word is preceded by a skip of a minor third which also helps to emphasize it.

The after-phrase or consequent always begins with a note higher, which stresses the significance of the reading function. This is followed by what seems to be an afterthought, but one that is so important to the composer, "but return it to me." It is ushered in by the downward octave jump followed by the diatonic rise, a transposition of motif 1. The downward and upward motion of this material are both related to the motifs of the fore-phrase. In the B section, the fore- and after-phrases are actually the same and so serve as a contrast to those in the A section.

The staff, which accommodates the vocal line with the lyrics below, is combined with the piano part, which serves as the accompaniment. In its upper staff, the melody and the harmony are integrated without being obtrusive, so that the vocal line can predominate. On the lower staff, there appears simplicity itself using the root notes of the harmonies. With an active melody, the entire accompaniment should function only as a support. Before Marjorie attempted the piano part, the three principal chords, I, IV, and V, were taught. Everything in the vocal line had been created instinctively, free from association with any harmonic structures. By using the synthetic method of associating each of the melody notes with chords that agreed, she selected the proper harmonies.

The authentic cadence, consisting of V progressing to I appearing at the end of each eight-measure period, creates the feeling of ending. In this piece, there was no opportunity to apply the half- or rising cadence at the end of the phrases, since the melody at these points did not require the V chord. However, often a half-cadence can demand the tonic harmony in either root position or first inversion. In the former, the third or fifth may be in the soprano; in the latter, the root or fifth may be in the soprano. In either case, one gets the impression of temporary cessation with the desire to continue.

The composer felt that the piece could be more effective if written for soprano and alto. Throughout the A section, the alto harmony to the soprano melody is simple but effective. The occasional unisons between both are balanced by harmony in parallel and contrary motion. In the B section, the melody is assigned to the alto for the sake of variety and also to give the alto a feeling of responsibility. The soprano sings a counterpoint of sustaining notes in parallel motion with the alto. The motif of the alto in measure 17:

EXAMPLE V-8

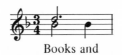

Books and

is developed by a downward sequence in the following three measures. Although this format occurs four times through the entire B section, the repetitions are not objectionable because the word "books" keeps appearing. This invites the use of the same musical material for emphasis. The melody curves, assuring a good line. The range is conservative, only a major 9th. There are no syllables in the words which would create any singing problems.

Generally, this song is a happy wedding of words and music, and, for Marjorie's first attempt, it is most laudable. It could have been treated differently in some aspects. For example, the melody of the final cadence could have descended to serve as contrast to the previous corresponding cadences. The B section could have appeared once, ending with a half-cadence on the dominant, again seving as a contrast to all the tonic cadences before and after. The form of the piece could have been A, A, B, A. However, Marjorie had more to say in her story requiring the repetitions.

This song offers many opportunities for dynamic contrast by the nature of the melodic direction—crescendo for upward motion, diminuendo for downward motion.

In "Books," observe the following:

1. Creation of a text in which the composer's love for books is dramatically presented
2. Rhyme in the A section abundant, while rhyme in the B section conservative
3. Three-part form with each part repeated, resulting in unity, variety and coherence
4. Meaning of words enhanced by appropriateness of motifs with which they are associated
5. Piano accompaniment, integrating melody and harmony, subordinate to vocal parts; use of primary chords discreet
6. Interest of song increased by incorporation of harmony by alto; use of chromatic and diatonic passing tones and auxiliary economical
7. Dynamic effect and ease in singing made possible by comfortable melodic line and range

The Swing

Words by Robert Louis Stevenson
Music by Betsy Banks

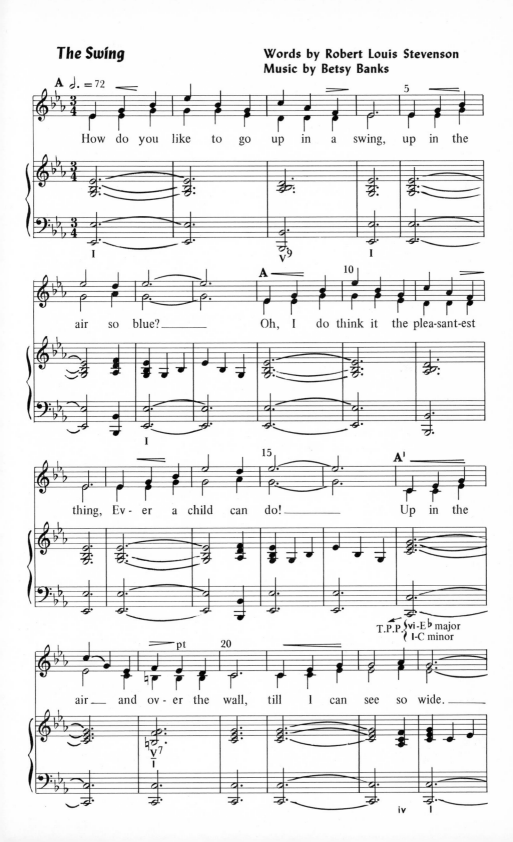

Riv - ers and trees_ and cat - tle and all, ov - er the

coun - try side._____ Till I can look down on the

gar - den green; Down on the roof so brown._____ Up in the

air I go fly - ing a - gain. Up in the air and down._____

THE SWING Betsy Banks, Grade 7

"The Swing," with words from a poem by Robert Louis Stevenson, is
most suggestive of the swaying of a swing. Lyrically, the stanzas rhyme
at the ends of lines one and three, and two and four. Musically, the
piece is in unitary form in which one theme is used in repetition and in
variations, A, A, A', A", A, A'''. With this format, unity is achieved
through the literal repetitions of the principal and only theme, not
only in E-flat major, but also in C-minor. Variety is obtained by the
change of key, as well as the occasional differences in melodic treatment.

The swaying motion is depicted ingeniously by the choice of
notes in the melodic line, fundamentally the arpeggio pattern. This
pattern begins in the first two measures outlining the tonic chord,
followed in measure 3 by the outline of the dominant 9th. The principal motif:

EXAMPLE V-9

How do you

is the arpeggio, ascending, descending with occasional step-wise motion at the various cadences where this treatment seems to be expected
in contrast to the arpeggios. The composer exercised her instinct and
imagination well in describing the sensation of a swing. Analyzing the
components of an arpeggio, she realized that using alternate notes
successively in the chords was the ideal way to depict her intentions.
This indicates that an inexperienced composer can successfully create
an effect or an image by utilizing his instinctive powers without necessarily knowing the technical or scientific aspect inherent within the
music—again the application of the organismic and experimental philosophy of creativity.

The first eight-measure sentence, A, is repeated exactly. The use
of the tonic cadence, appearing at the end of each four-measure
phrase, does not become monotonous or obtrusive because of the
melodic line preceding each tonic harmony. The fore-phrase ends on
the low tonic, while the after-phrase ends on the octave tonic.

The same melodic material is used for the next sixteen measures
beginning in measure 17. Because these eight-measure sentences are in

the relative minor key, and since each is treated differently, the use of A′ and A″ is justified. In the fore-phrase, the arpeggio, based on the C-minor triad, which is the pivot chord vi in E-flat major, i in C-minor, rises and falls followed by a downward step-wise motion to the tonic cadence. (Notice the similarity of this direction to the third and fourth measures of the piece in E-flat major.) In the following after-phrase, the treatment differs. The rising arpeggio is not completed. After one measure, the upper note is repeated and concludes with a plagal cadence harmonically. If both phrases had paralleled those in E-flat major in the A section by literal transposition, monotony would have resulted. Somehow the instinct of the composer urged her to change at these points. She did so wisely and logically. This urge was continued into the fore-phrase of the next sentence, A″, in measure 25, where the arpeggio motif in the first two measures is treated in inversion, again to avoid monotony. However, the next two measures repeat the notes of the corresponding two measures in the fore-phrase of A′. The after-phrase continues as did the previous after-phrase of A′. At the cadence of the after-phrase of A″, the melody note necessarily changes, because of the modulatory return to E-flat major at A. The note "F" will demand the use of the dominant harmony of the original key, effecting the only dominant half-cadence in the piece. By resolving to the tonic in E-flat major, the original A reappears in measure 41. With its repetition, the piece is concluded. In the final cadence, the "F" in the melody is optional if "D" should be slightly uncomfortable for the average voice.

The harmonies are fundamentally tonic and dominant in both A and A‴ sections in E-flat major and in the A′ and A″ sections in C-minor. Notice the predominant tonic minor pedal point throughout the C-minor parts which creates a delicious tang of dissonance when used with the V⁷ chord above it. Toward the end of A″, the pedal point must change because of the approaching half-cadence modulation back to E-flat major. How convenient is the use of the chromatic C-flat in measure 30, leading from the "C" to its objective B-flat, ushering in the dominant of E-flat!

The stagnant nature of the accompaniment has been wisely chosen to contrast with the activity of the soprano. In order to relate the melody to the accompaniment and thereby add to unity, the accompaniment motif has been included in the cadences at the ends of the sentences. The incorporation of an alto harmony is very effective in its simplicity and supporting role to the soprano. Parallel, oblique, and contrary motion are used, as well as occasional unisons. Voice leading is impeccable, conducive to comfortable singing. The melodic line continually waves. The range of a minor tenth, if the optional note at the end is to be ignored, is acceptable. Except for two passing tones and the use of the tonic pedal point against the dominant harmonies, the piece is free of dissonance. In spite of the consonant nature, it has a quality of warmth and childish innocence. Opportunities for dynamic contrasts are intrinsic in the character of the piece.

The salient features of this piece are:

1. Creation of song inspired by pleasurable childhood joys so beautifully expressed by a great poet
2. Rhythmic flow of music with lines rhyming alternately
3. Unity and coherence through constant repetition of the same theme; contrast by obvious variations of theme
4. Swaying of swing dramatically suggested by appropriate rise and fall of arpeggio motif
5. Simplicity of childhood consistent with simplicity of harmonic vocabulary; restlessness of childhood conveyed by tonic pedal point in minor section creating dissonance
6. Accompaniment, obviously conservative, consistent with its proper function—to be subordinate to melody
7. Simple and effective treatment of alto with good voice leading and interesting motion paramount
8. Assurance of good performance attributed to comfortable range and dynamic character

Travel

Words by Robert Louis Stevenson
Music by Guila Dulfano

1. I should like to rise and go where the gold-en ap-ples grow.
4. There I'll come when I'm a man with a cam-el ca-ra-van.

Where be-low an-oth-er sky par-rot is-lands an-chored lie.
Light a fi-re in the gloom of some dust-y din-ing room.

2. Where in sun-shine reach-ing out east-ern ci-ties miles a-bout
5. See the pic-tures on the walls, he-roes, fights, and fes-ti-vals and

are with mosque and min-a-ret a-mong sand-y gar-dens set.
in a cor-ner find the toys of the old E-gyp-tian boys.

Fine

3. Where the great wall round Chi-na goes and on one side the__ des - sert blows.

And with bell and voice and drum cit - ies on the oth - er hum.

TRAVEL   Guila Dulfano, Grade 8

Selected stanzas from Robert Louis Stevenson's "Travel" inspired eighth grade Guila Dulfano to create music to this immortal poem, fascinating in its description of distant and exotic lands. Lyrically, in all the stanzas rhyme occurs at the ends of lines one and two, and three and four.

Musically, it is in three-part song form extended, A, A, B, A, A. Unity is attained through the repetitions of A; variety is obvious in the variations in A and the use of B, new material, all of which contribute to coherence.

Stanzas 1, 2, 4 and 5 share the same music labelled A. The material of the fore-phrase, the first 4 measures, and that of the after-phrase, the second 4 measures, is the same except for slight changes in the latter, obviously for the sake of variety. Motifs 1 and 2 consist of:

EXAMPLE v-10

I should like to

EXAMPLE v-11

rise and go

and are developed by a rhythmical relationship, while the pitches, by their step-wise motion and direction, take on a new guise as if to assert their independence of the original motifs.

In the B section associated with stanza 3, the traditional 8-measure sentence, in which the material of the fore-phrase differs from that of the after-phrase, is used. What a nice contrast to the material of the other stanzas, which resemble one another. The $\frac{4}{4}$ meter is a welcome diversity to the $\frac{6}{8}$ of the other stanzas, a procedure well-taken by Guila. The first motif in B:

EXAMPLE v-12

Where the great wall

is developed rather freely, especially in rhythm with the eighth notes falling on different beats of the measures, affording rhythmic variety and excitement. In most cases, the eighth notes are used with monosyllabic text, since the composer felt the eighth note doublets would increase interest. In the after-phrase, motif 2 becomes simplified, using only quarter notes:

EXAMPLE v-13

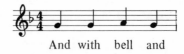

And with bell and

Little did Guila realize that she had composed her melody in both the Mixolydian and Dorian modes, which express the exotic character of the story so well. Until an analysis had been made, which helped her to understand the idiom, she had not known of the existence of the modes. To her, everything was either in a major or minor modality. She realized that the focal point of the A melody was the note "C," because it kept recurring at the cadences. This note is called the final. The scale on which this melody is based consists of the following notes consecutively:

$$\text{C} \quad \text{D} \quad \text{E} \quad \text{F} \quad \text{G} \quad \text{A} \quad \text{B}\flat \quad \text{C}$$
$$1 \quad 2 \quad \underset{\tfrac{1}{2}}{3 \quad 4} \quad 5 \quad \underset{\tfrac{1}{2}}{6 \quad 7} \quad 8$$

Because the half steps occur between 3 and 4, and 6 and 7, it could be neither major nor minor. It is Mixolydian.

She realized that the focal point of the B melody was the note "G," the final, because it kept recurring, not only within the entire melody, but also at the cadences. The scale on which this melody is based consists of the following notes consecutively:

$$\text{G} \quad \text{A} \quad \text{B}\flat \quad \text{C} \quad \text{D} \quad \text{E} \quad \text{F} \quad \text{G}$$
$$1 \quad \underset{\tfrac{1}{2}}{2 \quad 3} \quad 4 \quad 5 \quad \underset{\tfrac{1}{2}}{6 \quad 7} \quad 8$$

Because the half steps occur between 2 and 3, and 6 and 7, it could be neither major nor minor. It is Dorian.

This experience was an invitation to acquaint her and the other students with the modes used in music of the medieval period derived from the ancient Greeks.

In order for Guila to select the proper harmonies, she constructed the triads on every degree of both modes. Then, the choice of chords was determined by the quality of chord suggested by the note of the melody occurring on the strong and medium beats. In the Mixolydian mode the triads were:

C	E	G	on the first degree
D	F	A	on the second degree
E	G	B♭	on the third degree
F	A	C	on the fourth degree
G	B♭	D	on the fifth degree
A	C	E	on the sixth degree
B♭	D	F	on the seventh degree

In the Dorian mode the triads were:

G	Bb	D	on the first degree
A	C	E	on the second degree
Bb	D	F	on the third degree
C	E	G	on the fourth degree
D	F	A	on the fifth degree
E	G	Bb	on the sixth degree
F	A	C	on the seventh degree

In the first measure of the piece, the melody note "G" is a member of the triads on the first, third, and fifth degrees of the mode. The triad on the first degree was selected, since the root of the chord is the final or tonic. Beginning on this triad gives the piece security. How then is the following note "D" to be explained? This could be either the ninth of the tonic chord or a foreign tone, used as an anticipation of the "D" in the following triad. The process of selecting chords throughout the piece by relating the notes of the melody to the beats referred to before was applied. Whenever there was a multiple choice, the decision was based upon the propriety of the progression from the chords preceding. Through this kind of experimentation, one's eyes and ears are opened to the use of alternate harmonies.

The modal idiom offers a freedom of harmonic structure and progression to avoid the stereotyped progressions of chords associated with traditional major and minor scales. Therefore, the composer should select the triads which would be appropriate not only in their own individual use, but also in relation to the rest of the piece.

The chordal accompaniment with punctuations occurring mostly on the strong and medium beats in both the $\frac{6}{8}$ of the A section and the $\frac{4}{4}$ of the B section is logical and gives impetus and momentum rhythmically. Occasionally, this pattern will deviate, as in measure 4 of A where the composer felt one punctuation was sufficient because the cadence wants less movement in the accompaniment. In measure 19 of B, the ascending voice wishes to be free of overactivity in the accompaniment. The natural feeling of harmonic stress demands an economy of punctuations on the beats specified above. In this way, the composer has avoided the pitfall of getting in the way of the melodic flow by punctuating every note with a chord. Observe the wave motion of the melodies in which the motives maintain their rhythmic identity but alter their pitches primarily by inversion. A skip becomes a step, and vice versa.

In Chapter 3, I stated that vocal melodies should be written in ranges that are comfortable for singing, seldom to exceed a tenth. In "Travel," the composer has gone beyond this limit, using the interval of an eleventh—the lowest note "C" in the A section to the highest note "F" in measure 19 of the B section. However, the "F" can be justified because the upward step-wise motion that gradually precedes it facilitates its execution. Immediately following "F," a descent occurs step-wise which is musically effective, since the voice wants to go down after it has ascended.

Generally, the notes occurring on the weak beats are foreign tones, since they are not members of the harmonies used. As marked, they are either passing, auxiliary, appoggiatura (on medium beat in measure 5 of A) or echappée. On the third beat in measure 18 of B, the melody note "D" (on the medium beat) forms a ninth with the C-major triad, increasing intensity by its dissonance. This is the function of all foreign tones, especially those on strong parts of beats. The composer's defense of this choice is justified because she wanted this sound. It fits. It is unobtrusive.

All the words in the song are easily singable. The "s's" in the words "heroes" and "fights" in the A section of stanza three may create a sibilant sound, which can be overcome by clear articulation.

With the rise and fall of the melodies, interesting dynamic levels can be attained to help the interpretation of the piece.

These observations about "Travel" will be of interest to the student composer:

1. Availability of many fine poems by recognized poets for creative compositions evidenced by Guila's use of "Travel" by Stevenson
2. Variety achieved by using $\frac{6}{8}$ and $\frac{4}{4}$ rhythm, the former in the A section, the latter in the B section, resulting in a ratio of rhythm and musical material— $\frac{6}{8}$:A $= \frac{4}{4}$:B; occurrence of rhyme on adjacent lines
3. Use of the classic three-part song form extended, A, A, B, A, A; the constructive principles, unity, variety, and coherence, achieved
4. Prevalence of the rhythms of the motifs in the phrases and their development throughout the A section, while their pitches change; in the B section, difference in phrases both rhythmically and melodically; again, the constructive principles evident within all the phrases
5. Evidence that the composer was free from the influence of major and minor scales, a common practice for the last three centuries; instead, use of modes
6. Selection of proper harmonies, rather demanding in a mode, made

with discretion and perception based upon logic, taste, experience, and instinct

7. Obvious understanding of rhythmic punctuations accompanying the melody

8. Wave-motion of the melody produced by the rhythmic character of the piece

9. Justifiable use of the range of an eleventh

10. Moderate number and variety of foreign tones, which increase the interest of the piece melodically, rhythmically and harmonically

11. Dynamic contrast, for proper interpretation, inherent in music

Summertime

Words and Music by
Stuart Glazer

Sum - mer - time is lots of fun for all the fam - i - ly.
It's out - door liv - ing in the sun; there's al - ways lots to see.
We love to run and play on a ve - ry warm day, but when the day
is bad, we sit and just look sad. Some flow - ers in the sum - mer
are red; but there is more___ to be said, for the ones___ that are
ve - ry blue are the ones that are so pret - ty, too.

SUMMERTIME   Stuart Glazer, Grade 8

Stuart's philosophical message is so true and genuine. Obviously, his
own experiences are depicted in the piece—the fun of summer activities,
which, at times, are disturbed by expected changes in the weather. His
appreciation encompasses the extremes in color. Blue and red are
beautiful in their contrasts. How profound for the thinking of a boy of
thirteen! His love of nature is readily reflected in the simplicity and
warmth of his romantic conception of the music.

In this piece, rhymes occur between lines one and three, and two
and four in the first stanza, and between one and two, and three and
four in the last two stanzas. This piece is another example of unitary
form, A, A', A", with variations. Unity is established by the constant
use of the same material either literally or in variation. Variety is
achieved by the ways in which variations are introduced. All of this,
of course, aims toward coherence. The entire piece contains twenty-

four measures—three musical sentences, each eight measures in length.

In the first four measures of the fore-phrase, the general melodic plan of the motif:

EXAMPLE V-14

Sum - mer - time   is

is based on the arpeggio of the tonic harmony including step-wise motion. A dominant half-cadence is suggested in measure 4. In the after-phrase beginning in measure 5, although the motif begins in the same way as the original, the melody continues mostly by step-wise motion down and up, interrupted only by an interval of a third, whose purpose seems to be an assurance that the arpeggio-like character of the original was not to be completely discarded. A tonic authentic cadence is suggested in the 8th measure. The material of A returns as A′ in its arpeggio form in variation. The number of notes in measures 10 and 14 is abbreviated. The full meter at both these points is preserved by the sustaining function of the notes, which substitute for the syllables of the text in the corresponding measure, 2, in A. Notice the resemblance between the treatment in measures 3 and 4 of A and 3 and 4 of A′ (measures 11 and 12). The latter necessarily adds a note, because the word "very" contains two syllables. Also, the wider skip of the major sixth to the word "warm" reaches a climax melodically. This is followed by the repetition of the "D" in the next measure, as though to emphasize the already consummated climax on "warm." The step-wise descent, already established in the parallel spot in measures 5 and 6 of A, then appears in measure 13 at a step transposed higher as if wanting to develop the motif. In contrast, there is an upward ascent by step in measures 7 and 8 of A′ (measures 15 and 16), a temporary modulation to the dominant key by virtue of the B-natural. This is the traditional technique used in modulation—use of the secondary dominant chord, V of V, progressing to V.

In A″ (measure 17), the first four measures are similar to the corresponding measures of A except for the added note in the second measure needed for the added syllable. In measure 4 of A″ (measure 20), there is continued activity in place of the corresponding dominant half-cadence pause in A. Measure 5 of A″ (measure 21) resembles measure 5 of A′ (measure 13) effecting the principle of unity within the variation treatment. In measure 22, there is no stopping; for emphasis, a skip to the original high point seems to reiterate this objective. Then the descent, leading to the final cadence, appears. The characteristic descending step-wise motion is already established.

This piece, in the monophonic style, is to be performed either in unison or as a solo piece a cappella. There are no parts or harmonic accompaniment. Such additions are possible and could serve as a project for the student. With no harmonic structure as a guide, no foreign tones exist. However, if harmony were to be created, there would be no difficulty in ascertaining the foreign tones, provided the harmonies and their punctuations fitted the proper character of the piece.

The song offers singing ease, because the melodic line waves well. The range is within an interval of a ninth, all of which helps toward dynamic interpretation.

In "Summertime," text and music bring out the following:

1. Reflection of a young boy's love of nature and appreciation of summer in the purity of his music; inner feelings delightfully expressed by melodic contour, range, and interpretation
2. Rhyming lines differ in stanzas
3. Theme with variations; motif subjected to several variations in an uncontrived and natural manner
4. Unity, coherence and variety achieved by similarities and differences in treatment
5. Opportunity and challenge for the student to supply harmonic structure and accompaniment, making foreign tones functional

You Can Always Tell the English

Words and Music by
Judy Alexander

thought with-out me, he could not go wrong.

Poor man was ne-ver found a-gain, _____ for he was just too stub-born. _____ That goes to show you, _____ that he'll not give in. _____ He is proud to be a Yan-kee, and he has ev'-ry right, but he seems to go too far, _____ when he puts up such a fight.

YOU CAN ALWAYS TELL THE ENGLISH   Judy Alexander, Grade 8

The inspiration for this jingle came from a couplet Judy discovered in *A Treasure Chest of Humor for Boys and Girls*, compiled by Jason C. Mellon. The couplet, which Judy uses for her first stanza (without crediting the author), moved her to create a catchy, repetitious verse and song with appropriate music.

The substance of the text, in which the Yankees are the target of censure, is somewhat satirical. The author praises them for their courage and tenacity, but warns that these traits, if carried too far, could bring unpleasantness.

In sections A and B rhymes occur at the ends of lines two and four, while in section C rhymes occur at the ends of lines one and three. Musically, each section is in two-part form with the entire piece outlined as:

Themes	AA′	AA′	AA′	BB′	C	AA′
Keys	C	D♭	D	D	E min.	F

condensed into A, B, C, A. Unity by the many repetitions, variety by using new keys and material, and coherence are very evident.

In the A section, the motif:

EXAMPLE V-15

You can

is developed in an upward melodic sequence in the fore-phrase, and then a motif of downward eighths:

EXAMPLE V-16

You can al - ways tell the

completes the after-phrase. This leads to the half-cadence with the dominant harmony in measures 7 and 8. The rest in measure 5 is particularly interesting, because its silence creates a syncopation on the weak beat. Ordinarily, one might have used the same rhythmic pattern as in the first measure:

EXAMPLE V-17

instead of:

EXAMPLE V-18

This would have resulted in dullness and monotony. The rest causes a feeling of suspense which invites the rhythmic surge of the eighth notes that follow, thereby bringing about excitement. A' follows in measure 9, indicating that the material of A is used, but with variation occurring in the after-phrase. This is introduced very subtly with the note "A," after which the descending interval of the minor third is transposed downward leading to the authentic cadence.

In the following two stanzas, which parallel the first stanza in both material and meter, monotony is avoided by subtle transpositions chromatically upward to the keys of D flat and D.

The next section, B, measure 49, in the key of D major, is a welcome contrast for 16 measures. The motifs:

EXAMPLE V-19

EXAMPLE V-20

are used throughout, treated more or less in melodic transposition and
in free rhythm. B′ follows in measure 64 for 16 measures. At the conclusion, a return to the initial theme of the jingle is expected. But no!
The final note "D" serves as the dominant of "G," the first note of the
C section. In this section, a new theme and thought enters in the key of
E-minor. This material, music and words, is recitative—a free type of
musical declamation. All the motifs, of which there are several, are
conditioned by the free rhythm of the text:

EXAMPLE V-21

Poor   man   was

EXAMPLE V-22

Never found a

EXAMPLE V-23

For   he   was

The final note "E" in measures 94 and 95 can be considered the leading
tone of the key of "F," whose tonic (F) follows melodically with the
return of the original theme. The choice of F-major as the highest
tonality is a fitting musical climax for the text's statement of the
Yankee's prowess and courage.

Foreign tones and harmonic support may be supplied for this
unison a cappella song in the same manner as suggested for "Summertime."

The melodic line waves throughout. The range is exactly a major
ninth, presenting no problems. Interpretively, the piece could very well
begin pianissimo. As the theme rises chromatically, the dynamic level
can increase gradually with each transposition to the B section. Because
this section serves as a climax both musically and verbally, it can be
sung fortissimo. A sudden contrast is appropriate for the C section
where despair is delineated musically and verbally. Pianissimo would
be most suitable.

The final stanza, which can return to a normal level of dynamics, possibly mezzo-forte, is a lasting and fitting tribute to the dauntless qualities of the Yankee.

In summarizing the features of this piece, notice the new areas explored:

1. Creation and development of a pure jingle both lyrically and musically with substantial philosophical evaluation

2. Hybrid form conception using transpositions of original material with the incorporation of contrasted themes—an excellent lesson of unity, variety, and coherence

3. Interest and excitement musically, as well as lyrically, induced by devices such as sequence of motif, syncopation, transpositions of material, treatment à la recitative, logical use of notes in key relationships, and rise of themes

4. Opportunity available to supply a harmonic structure for this monophonic piece

5. Excellent possibility to experiment with dynamic interpretation of the piece, which constantly builds with a melodic wave-line and comfortable range

Thoughts of Spring

Words and Music by
Jonna Amicangioli

95

THOUGHTS OF SPRING   Jonna Amicangioli, Grade 9

"Thoughts of Spring," with words and music by Jonna, is a song appropriate for a musical revue or musical play, because of its light, romantic, and refreshing quality. Jonna makes spring synonymous with fragrance, happiness, beauty, love, ecstasy, prayer, and joy.

The construction of both the verse and music is a bit unusual, but most interesting. Generally, the rhyme of the lyrics is unorthodox. Rhyme exists between the first lines of stanzas one and two, within the second, third, and fourth lines of stanzas one and four, and within the second, third, and fourth lines of stanza two. In stanza three, lines two and four rhyme; there is no rhyme between lines one and three, where "springtime" is emphasized by its own repetition.

Musically, the piece is in three-part song form, A, A', B, A', in which an extension occurs to allow for more emphasis on the word "springtime" and another climax. The constructive principles of unity, variety, and coherence are evident.

Observe that the first section, or musical sentence, consists of seven measures divided into a 3-measure fore-phrase and a 4-measure after-phrase. In the fore-phrase, the motif:

EXAMPLE V-24

is followed by the second motif:

EXAMPLE V-25

which takes precedence over the first by virtue of its several appearances throughout the sentence. It ascends as an arpeggio; each note is repeated consecutively, followed by a chromaticism leading to the section cadence in the form of a whole note. Then, in the after-phrase in measure 4, a quarter note motif appears descending step-wise:

EXAMPLE v-26

True love's sweet sound

This descending treatment is then developed both by a rhythmic variation based on the rhythm of the second motif of the fore-phrase and by a melodic transposition leading to the half-cadence in measure 7. In measures 13 and 14, the treatment is similar, except for closing on the tonic in the authentic cadence.

In the B section, measures 15 through 22, the release or bridge— to use the accepted jargon of the popular music industry—is the conventional 8-measure structure. The second motif of the fore-phrase of A is very predominant, made more emphatic by added repetitions of notes and by transposition.

Notice the high point in measure 20 that becomes the climax of the piece. It is approached by step-wise motion, an appropriate procedure for the climactic effect. In the form of a musical after-thought in the next two measures, the motif is in a lower register, as contrast to the preceding climax, ending on the dominant half-cadence.

In the final section, nine measures appear instead of seven because of the insertion of the 2-measure extension in measures 28 and 29. The emphasis on "springtime" is achieved by using half notes, which serve as contrast to the predominance of eighth notes throughout the piece.

All the following combine to make the harmonic structure rich and colorful: the primary harmonies I, IV, and V; the secondary harmonies ii, iii, and vi; the secondary dominant chords V^7 of vi, V^7 of iii; altered chords; the ii^7 and vi^7 chords with raised root and third, thereby becoming diminished seventh chords acting as appoggiatura chords to the I and V^7 respectively. Especially noteworthy are the chords on the last two beats in measure 6 into measure 7 in which the bass progresses chromatically.

The use of pedal points adds to the attraction of the piece: the tonic pedal point in measures 4 and 5; the sub-mediant pedal point in measure 20 below the progression V^7 of vi to vi, an excellent example of the deceptive cadence; and the "F" pedal point in measure 21.

The V^7 of iii in measure 29 progresses well to the super-tonic chord in the following measure. The half-cadences occur in measures 7 and 22, while the authentic cadences naturally fall in measures 14 and 31.

The piano arrangement, fashioned after the conventional standard format, may be performed exactly. However, if there is a pianist available with the creative and technical ability to improvise upon it artistically with discretion and taste, much can be added to the effect of the performance.

The interval of the third is used mostly for the alto harmony in support of the soprano. Occasionally a unison with soprano or the interval of a second, fourth, fifth and sixth are for variety and for conformity with harmonic requirements.

The melodic line throughout creates interest in its low and high points and in its general contour. The range of an eleventh can be justified by the step-wise approach to the climax.

With the rich harmonic structure contributing much to the delight of the piece, foreign tones supplement by adding spice and interest. Appoggiaturas, auxiliary tones, suspensions, a cambiata, an echappée, and passing tones are used well.

Interpretation for this song may be most flexible. It may be sung as a commercial ballad in which liberties of tempos, involving tempo rubatos, would play a significant part. It may be performed in strict tempo, making it suitable for ballroom dancing. Both styles may be combined; one chorus can be sung completely ad lib, followed by a second chorus in strict tempo for the A sections, followed by ad lib in the B section, and, finally, strict tempo for the final A, culminating in a dramatic upward suspension in approaching the cadence. Experience, taste, and theatrical know-how will help the performer make an interpretive decision.

The technique and style of musical comedy writing is fully explored in this piece:

1. Original text, romantic and delightful in quality, with a philosophical message describing spring in all its glory; the music most expressive of the text
2. Three-part song form containing a subtle extension for emphasis; an unusual phraseology containing 7 and 9 measures—a rather refreshing technique
3. Constructive principles very evident not only in the form, but also in the use of the eighth note motif either literally, varied, or transposed. In works of the masters, the prominence of a secondary motif is com-

mon; very often it may be more important than the principal one, and consequently makes more of an impression

4. Interpretation enhanced by use of: rich harmonies, pure and altered; pedal points; freedom for improvisation in the piano arrangement; soprano and alto harmonies; melodic line and range; foreign tones

5. Flexibility of interpretation dependent on musicianship, experience, and taste

Trial and Error No. $\frac{3}{4}$

Words and Music by
Audrey Shafran

or may-be sing of some love-ly day. ———————— These

cra - zy —— poets rave on and on, —— and they ne-ver will

stop to think ——————— of do - ing some - thing down—

—————— to earth, like clean-ing the kit - chen sink. ——————

102

They all have things to write of earth shak-ing im-por-tance; at least that's what they think, _____ but when it's seen in print, there's one thing we must do, ___ is pray it's all o-kay. _____ He'll write all the

TRIAL AND ERROR NO. $\frac{3}{4}$ Audrey Shafran, Grade 9

"Trial and Error No. $\frac{3}{4}$" is an experiment in sophisticated popular song writing. In her text, Audrey initially apologizes for not writing about clichés, such as "birds," "May," "lovely day," which usually find their places in pop tunes. The song is a subtle, cynical, and tongue-in-cheek creation in which idealistic poets are satirized for their fantasy and their impractical philosophy; their feelings of importance are taken with a grain of salt. However, Audrey regrets that poets are appreciated when it is too late for them to enjoy the fruits of their labor.

Metrically, the text is replete with syncopations. In stanza one, rhyme occurs at the ends of lines 1 and 2, and within line 3. All the other stanzas, arranged in couplet form, follow the standard form of rhyme at the ends of the lines.

Musically, it is in free rondo form, A, B, B', A, B'', C, C', A, B'''. The constructive principles are very obvious.

In this piece, there is a great deal that can be of value to the neophyte composer, especially in the area of rhythm. Audrey could have made the melody a rather "sing-songy" rhythm, but, in studying the relationship between the words and the music, she chose syncopation. For example, the first motif:

EXAMPLE V-27

I'm   not   ve - ry   good

could have been written conservatively:

EXAMPLE V-28

I'm   not   ve - ry   good

Audrey chose the former because of the rhythmic interest expressed in syncopation. Notice that the pattern with an added tie for further syncopation:

EXAMPLE V-29

is carried throughout the piece as if it were a rhythmic leitmotif. Vitality, excitement, verve, enthusiasm, and drive result. Commercially, this song would be an excellent production opener for a musical, or a topical number in a revue, musical comedy, or musical play.

At the end of A, a tonic cadence appears in measures 7 and 8; it is imperfect, because the third of the chord is in the soprano. Consequently, continuity of movement is felt leading into B with the motif:

EXAMPLE V-30

To   write   a   piece   of   junk

Compare the melody of measures 9–16 with measures 17–24. The almost literal repetition seems appropriate. Notice the similarity melodically and rhythmically. However, compare the differences between measures 14, 15, and 16, and measures 22, 23, and 24. In the former, the harmonic progression gives the impression of continuity, that more is to come. The notes preceding the melody note "E" are necessarily placed a bit higher to allow for descent to the "E." In measures 22, 23, and 24, the melody ends on "D" in the V chord. This implies a half-cadence, which progresses to the note "C," the anacrusis of the next section, actually a repetition of the original theme. Since the "D" is lower than its corresponding "E" in measure 14, the two notes preceding the "D" are lower than the corresponding notes preceding the "E."

Compare now the next section, a recapitulation of the A theme. In measure 33, the phrase enters as B″; changes begin to occur. From measures 37–40, the notes are different, but the rhythms are the same as the corresponding rhythms in measures 13–16. In the former, a perfect authentic cadence, with the root of the tonic chord in the soprano, is the objective. So the notes preceding must necessarily approach the final note in the cadence as indicated.

The new material, C and C′, the so-called release or bridge between measures 41 and 56, makes for a refreshing contrast. The motif:

EXAMPLE V-31

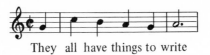

They all have things to write

is free of syncopation, a welcome relief, although the entire section is
not without some semblance of the syncopated motive. The half-
cadence in measure 56 leads into the final recapitulation of A. Here the
first 8 measures are exactly the same as the original. With B''', beginning in measure 65, the changes in the melodic treatment create a desired contrast and lead to climax. The rise of the soprano step-wise to
the high "E's" invites a new harmonic dressing that helps crystallize
this climax and the finality of the piece.

When Audrey first outlined her V and I chords, she used them in
alternation, fitting them to the melody notes accordingly. Occasionally,
she would include the super-tonic chord. The use of this limited vocabulary tended to make the harmonic scheme rather dull and conservative. It was necessary to establish a pattern of harmony that would
dress-up and excite. For example, in measure 1, instead of using V,
which is suggested by the synthesis of the soprano notes "D" and "G,"
she experimented with the sound of super-tonic 7th below the "D."
She then continued it through the "G," which virtually made it an eleventh chord or a ii⁷ with added 4th. In the next measure, the "E" suggested I, but since ii was used in measure 1, and since ii progresses
normally to V, she tried V below the "E" but with added foreign tones,
making the chord a V⁷ with 9th, 11th, and 13th:

EXAMPLE V-32

Actually, the "E" in the soprano may be analyzed as the added 6th of
the V⁷. In either analysis, a most exciting dissonance is created. At first
Audrey resisted its usage. Eventually, she realized it made the harmonic scheme more interesting, and so she accepted the technique. As
a result, not only did she improve her composition, but she also added
a new twentieth century concept to her musical vocabulary.

In measures 3 and 4, she uses fundamentally the same harmonic pattern, which appears whenever the melody demands it. Measures 7 through 16 are orthodox in progression and present no problems. Note the chromaticisms in the bass, which color what could very well have been conventional harmonies. For example, in measure 12 the tonic chord could have continued from the previous measure without disturbing the continuity. The change of harmony to the chromatic C-sharp diminished seventh chord as vii^{70} of ii increases the color and interest leading to the super-tonic in measure 13. Measures 13 and 14 could have been harmonized with the super-tonic throughout, followed by tonic in measures 15 and 16, causing dullness and stagnation. This is avoided by the inclusion of the chromatic descending bass line, which suggests the chordal changes as indicated. The release follows the orthodox pattern of harmonization including some chromaticisms in the bass. In the final statement of the A theme, the direction of the melody leading to climax suggests the harmonies, as pointed out previously.

The style of the piano accompaniment is simple yet adequate. The right hand chords punctuate and enhance the syncopated style of the melody throughout, while the left hand bass unobtrusively confines itself to the root notes of chords, generally punctuating the first and third beats of the measures:

EXAMPLE v-33

Notes indicating the inversions of chords are used when expedient. These contribute to a bass line which assumes a chromatic line:

EXAMPLE v-34

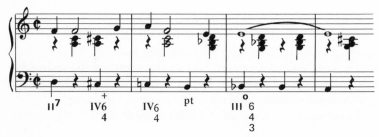

At times they assume a diatonic line:

EXAMPLE V-35

Notice the effective contrary motion between soprano and bass.

Again, this piano arrangement follows the standard format. When played exactly, it could be adequate. However, in a piece of this type, an improvisation by the accompanist done with taste and discretion can enhance a solo singer. If performed amateurishly or in an exaggerated style, it could over-shadow the singer and spell doom.

The melodic line with its syncopations and the range of the piece, a major tenth, produce a piece exciting and comfortable to sing.

Foreign tones per se are non-existent if absorbed as components of chords considered legitimate in twentieth century technique. For example, the "E" and "C" in measure 2, as explained earlier, are the 13th and 11th respectively of the V chord. However, theorists may argue that the "E" is an unresolved appoggiatura and the "C" is an appoggiatura resolving to the "D" in the next measure; that the "G" in measure 1 is an anticipation of the "G" in the V chord in the next measure. The "G" in measure 3 can rightfully be a free tone. Legitimate foreign tones do exist, however, such as the appoggiatura "A" in measure 12 and the passing tone "B" in measure 20. What does it matter how a note is classified as long as one understands its function?

Since the piece is rhythmic throughout, it would be folly to take liberties with the tempo in its interpretation. This is definitely a sophisticated rhythm tune and must be moving at all times to be completely effective.

This song is certainly unusual because of the following characteristics:

1. Subtle, cynical, and satirical text—characteristic of a young adolescent?
2. Use of syncopation metrically and musically, showing composer's maturity
3. Three-part song form extended, creating unusual rhyme scheme in which the constructive principles are inherent
4. Value of this type of piece commercially high

5. Unity obtained by repetition of material; monotony avoided by varied treatment of material toward the end of sections, which, if repeated literally, would be frustrating (compare the last four measures of B (13–16) and B″ (37–40); also measures 10–16 and 66–72)

6. Use of more progressive harmonies

7. Understanding of the idiom solo-wise by the singer and a flexibility of improvisation by the accompanist required for a consummate performance and interpretation

CONCLUSION

All the preceding examples show the possibilities of coordinating vocal music with texts. As has been pointed out, it is always important to impress upon the student that speech patterns are the basis of rhythm, which in turn is the basis of melody. In early experiments, the student should confine himself to strict metric patterns in either duple, triple, or quadruple time—patterns that are consistent throughout any given section. As he gains experience, he will be able eventually to modify this pattern, provided the flexibility of the text allows it. (The following examples also apply to instrumental compositions.)

For example, rhythm may be altered by shifted accents:

EXAMPLE v-36

which simulates duple time by considering the accent to be the first beat of a measure (the dotted line is the imaginary bar line):

EXAMPLE v-37

which simulates triple time in the same way:

EXAMPLE v-38

Asymmetric divisions such as 2+3+3 in one measure, or 3+2+4 in one measure, or asymmetric meters such as $\frac{5}{8}$ or $\frac{7}{8}$, or changes in meters in consecutive measures such as $\frac{3}{4}$, $\frac{3}{2}$, $\frac{4}{8}$, $\frac{7}{8}$, etc., can all effect rhythmic interest.

These constructions would naturally be reserved for the experienced or more advanced student whose conception of rhythmic complexity allows such exploration.

All the above information also applies to the following compositions in the instrumental areas.

Piece for Flute

Joanne Sapers

PIECE FOR FLUTE   Joanne Sapers, Grade 6

"Piece for Flute" was an interesting experiment, which Joanne performed with piano accompaniment. The piece was written in three-part form, A, B, A, with B repeated as B'. The contrast of material between A and B is evident not only in the rhythm, but also in mode. Joanne was unaware as she wrote the piece that she used the Aeolian and Dorian modes.

The A section begins with an activated motif of eighth notes:

EXAMPLE V-39

The repetition of the "E's" is followed by a down and up motion, which ceases on the dotted half note in measure 2. The motif is repeated in the next two measures. It develops into an arpeggio figure in measure 5 and is repeated in measure 6. An interval skip to a climactic height in measure 7 leads to the feminine cadence in measure 8, characterized by the appearance of the tonic chord on the weak second beat.

Fundamentally, the initial motif is used throughout the fore- and after-phrases, establishing unity. The wave-like motion makes a good melody.

The contrasting B section consists of the motif starting in measure 9:

EXAMPLE V-40

Note that the motif is followed by a reverse treatment of the quarter notes melodically, going up by step, and then the dotted half note. In the next four measures, the procedure is similar with a melodic change approaching the cadence in measures 15 and 16.

In the repetition of the eight measures, B', the last two measures are simplified by a prolonged authentic cadence on the tonic. Here too, in B and B', the wave of the theme contributes to good melodic quality. The return to A completes the three-part form, and the constructive principles of unity, variety, and coherence are established.

Section A is written in the Aeolian mode, while B is in the Dorian by virtue of the F-sharp. The entire piece has an Eastern quality most appropriately assigned to the flute, though an oboe would probably have been more desirable if it were available.

Before constructing the piano accompaniment for A, Joanne was presented with the triads built in the Aeolian mode. She was asked to find those which would fit the melody through the synthetic method. Realizing that the activity in the soprano demanded stagnation in the accompaniment and vice versa, she found that the tonic chord would be appropriate throughout the first four measures. This selection is determined by the majority of notes in measures 1 and 3 that relate to the tonic. Those in the minority are foreign tones. In the first measure, the harmony is sustained under the active soprano. The opposite was applied in measure 2 where imitation of the flute in the piano part would be more interesting. Thus, the principle of antiphonal treatment or musical conversation was applied. Joanne thought repeating the piano imitation of measure 2 in measure 4 would be too monotonous. She was asked to determine the motion of the melody thus far. It was observed to be downward generally. She was asked, "How could contrast be achieved motion-wise?" The answer was obvious. This resulted in the bass figure (measure 4), which actually is an inversion of the motif.

In the fifth measure, the majority of the notes suggests a G-major chord, which is VII in the Aeolian mode, and also suggests the traditional treatment of having the chord follow the tonic. Because this harmony is suggested for three measures, the composer was asked about the advisability of retaining the G-chord throughout. She reacted negatively, claiming monotony would result. Using the pattern of tonic descending to VII, as in measures 4 and 5, it was suggested that the adjacent chord below VII be experimented with in measure 6. The F-major chord on VI with appoggiatura "E" to the "D," the sixth of the chord, created a dissonance with the soprano, which at first she was reluctant to accept. Actually it was classified as an eleventh chord because of the "G" and "B" compounded by the aforementioned analysis. Another approach would be to consider it as polytonal, G-major in the melody, F-major in the accompaniment. She was asked to be sympathetic, to be open-minded, and to postpone her final decision until the entire phrase was consummated harmonically. Continuing the downward pattern diatonically, the next obvious chord to be tried was the E-minor v chord in measure 7. This was satisfactory with the melodic line, which was virtually a G-major arpeggio because of the common notes between the melody and harmony. The "D" made it a v⁷ chord. Note that one harmonic punctuation suffices in measures 5, 6, and 7 because of the continued activity of the soprano.

Finally, in the cadence, VII to i completed the phrase. When the after-phrase was played in continuity, the F-major chord in the sixth measure seemed to belong and added spice and excitement to the music.

This experiment teaches that the whole is greater than the sum of its parts; each part is mutually dependent. Play the sixth measure out of context and it means little; play it in relation to what precedes and follows, and an entirely new sound results. Joanne liked and accepted the change.

Next, the triads of the Dorian mode were presented to help Joanne write a piano accompaniment for the B section. The same procedure of fitting the melody through the synthetic approach was used. The principle of stagnation and activity presented more opportunities for the accompaniment. In the first measure of the B section, the dotted half note, "D," in the soprano invites activity in the accompaniment. Compare the bass line here to the soprano in the next measure. The question was asked, "How can the accompaniment be made more significant?" By using antiphonal treatment and inversion, the composer filled in the bass part in measure 9 with the inversion of the motif of the soprano in measure 10. Writing the bass in measure 9 exactly as the soprano in measure 10 was considered and attempted, but discarded in favor of the inversion, which seemed to be more interesting, offering more contrast. Again, in the following measures, antiphonal treatment and inversion were used between soprano and bass in piano accompaniment. In measure 16 at the cadence, Joanne felt no activity was necessary, since a feeling of rest was desired.

The theme repeats itself except in the last two measures of the score. Since the soprano holds throughout, it was felt that something of interest should occur in the piano part. (Notice the changing tones "G" and "B.") This was a golden opportunity to teach this contrapuntal device by asking the composer what notes exist that are foreign to the A-minor chord in the direct vicinity of the note "A." The answer was as expected. After the "G" and "B" were inserted between the extreme "A's," she was delighted with the results. She had learned a contrapuntal device practically.

Passing, auxiliary, and changing tones and appoggiaturas occur throughout. Dynamically and interpretatively, this piece has much to offer. Tempo is moderate. B section could be played slightly faster than A, which returns to complete the three-part form.

The following observations are of interest:

1. The composer's use of Aeolian and Dorian modes indicating the learning by doing approach

2. Three-part form in which the motifs are presented clearly, developing logically and contributing to the constructive principles; qualities of good wave-like motion in both themes

3. With the acquired knowledge of chords associated with both modes, proper harmonic progressions, suggested by the synthesis of the melody, accepted

4. Obvious understanding of activity and stagnation in creating a piano accompaniment based on the chords selected; antiphonal treatment, imitation, and inversion

5. Unorthodox areas explored to avoid repetitions of the same harmony; dissonances and foreign tones, at first appearing out of style with the idiom, incorporated because of their value

String Quartet

Beverly Gerson

117

STRING QUARTET   Beverly Gerson, Grade 6

This piece, a string quartet of sheer simplicity, is written in a typically juvenile eighteenth century classical style. The piece is in three-part form—a short 6-measure A, followed by an 8-measure B, developed into an 8-measure B', and finally a return to the original A. From this, the constructive principles may be easily determined.

The motif:

EXAMPLE v-41

is used throughout the 6-measure phrase of A. The motif and its upward transposition, a major third, are repeated an octave lower followed by step-wise motion leading to the authentic cadence. Immediately, B follows containing the first motif:

EXAMPLE v-42

leading to the second motif:

EXAMPLE v-43

This material is repeated for the next four measures. The second motif, beginning in measure 15, is developed by inversion with a sequence of three transpositions, all represented by B', leading to the half-cadence on V in measure 22. The A section then appears again for six measures.

After writing the melody, Beverly wanted to harmonize it. By employing the method of melodic synthesis, she was able to determine the fundamental harmonic structure. The primary chords I, IV, and V and the secondary triad ii were the prevalent chords. Open position is used in the first two measures, both in tonic root position, giving dimension of breadth. In the repetition an octave lower, closed position of the first inversion and root position were expedient because of the lower register of the melody. In the fifth measure, the third inversion of V^7 leading to the first inversion of the tonic, which is traditional, appealed to Beverly.

In the B section, the dotted half and quarter note motif in the soprano for two measures invited motion in the bass, according to the principle of activity and stagnation. With the inner parts sustaining against the parallel moving soprano and bass, oblique motion results. In the next two measures, parallel motion with unisons between the upper and lower parts contrasts with the preceding style. To complete the B section, these four measures are repeated. In B′, motif 2 of B continues in sequence toward the half-cadence for eight measures with concerted treatment of the quarter and whole notes; the upper voices are in unison in contrary motion to the lower voices in unison. In this way, more contrast is achieved.

It might have been more advisable to have sustained the harmony in the lower two voices in measure 13 of B, while the upper two voices functioned. In measure 14, while the upper three voices sustained their notes, the bass voice could have moved in imitation of the quarter note motif, possibly in inversion. This procedure could have continued throughout the first six measures of B. In this way, there would never have been a dull moment. However, the composer felt that her approach was satisfactory. As long as the tempo remained bright and avoided any potential inactivity, her approach was logical and justifiable.

The A section resumes the original harmonic style, a contrast to B′. Since the piece is generally consonant in nature, foreign tones, auxiliaries and passing tones are at a minimum.

Beverly expressed a desire to orchestrate the piece for string quartet. To do this, she had to learn the ranges as well as the quality and timbre of each instrument. Each of the strings performs its own function. The first violin is the soprano; the second violin is the alto; the viola is the tenor; the cello is the bass. Writing in the C-clef for the viola, a completely new experience, was fascinating for her. By relating to middle C on the piano, there was no problem assigning notes to the viola.

To write this piece for instruments, Beverly had to develop her listening powers. Before she orchestrated the piece, the instruments existed for her in name only. She now had to relate each one to the other, to distinguish each one individually, and she had to become conscious of the blends and mixtures of colors. Her ears began to listen to the instruments in a different way, a more intellectual way, with a more active attitude. Her listening powers became more acute; she orchestrated the piece; the theory of learning by doing was proven again.

In her first experiment, Beverly maintained the distribution of the strings, as explained before, throughout the piece with the understanding that in future works, she would resort to antiphonal treatment between the instruments where possible. In this way, she would fulfill the objective of string quartet writing by making each part equally important. The unison of the violins against the unison of the viola and cello, to be sure, is elementary. It creates a contrast, peppering up the piece, which has had a sustained harmonic style in the lower three instruments up to this point.

The dynamics and tempo changes, which help toward the interpretation, are logically placed according to the character of the music. The gradual crescendo and accelerando in B is most dramatic and reaches its climax with a natural upward suspension before the resumption of A.

On the surface this piece is brief, but it contains much of value:

1. Simplicity and transparency in eighteenth century style; three-part form easily delineated
2. Development of motifs in a natural, uncontrived manner, creating unity as well as variety by employing the devices of transposition and inversion
3. Use of primary chords and the super-tonic made possible by the synthesis approach; examples of open and closed positions, use of parallel, contrary and oblique motions, concerted harmonization and unison obvious throughout
4. Foreign tones at a minimum
5. Superficial understanding of the ranges and the timbre and qualities of each instrument required
6. Indications of dynamics and tempo changes most important in the interpretation of the piece

The Playful Pup

Michèle Cooke

THE PLAYFUL PUP   Michèle Cooke, Grade 6

"The Playful Pup," written for violin, cello, clarinet and flute, is rightfully named because of its sprightly, frivolous and gay character. It is a piece in two-part form repeated, A, B, A, B'. Repetition is necessary in order to exploit instrumental uses. The first eight measures represent the A theme, while the next eight measures represent the B theme.

In the beginning, the motif of the fore-phrase in the first measure:

EXAMPLE V-44

is repeated for emphasis and unity. This is followed by a downward step-wise diatonic scale passage for the next two measures, a contrast to the somewhat stagnant first motif. The after-phrase in measure 5 is a transposition of the original motif of the fore-phrase leading to authentic cadence in measures 7 and 8.

The fore-phrase of B in measure 9 is a combination of an arpeggio figure:

EXAMPLE V-45

developed slightly upward in measure 10. This is followed by a descending scale derived from the second motif of the fore-phrase of A, leading to cadence in the key of the dominant in measure 12.

In the after-phrase beginning in measure 13, it seems as though the four-note descending motif is interrupted after the second note and then repeated. In the next measure, a complete transposition would be a natural procedure, but instead a surprising skip of a third appears and repeats itself. Then the descending motif from the fore-phrase of A appears as if in reminiscence, finally leading to half-cadence in measure 16, again creating a feeling of continuity.

One could call the entire B section a variation of A because of the predominance of the quarter notes and especially the descending scale figure. The several intervals of the third also can be related to those thirds that appear in A. It would be justifiable to analyze it as such. In any case, unity as well as variety is evident throughout. A is then repeated followed by B, considered as B' because of the change in the final tonic cadence, to give a feeling of completion.

After the composer finished writing her melody, she felt that more was needed. She began by adding the counterpoint in the bass. Because of her lack of exposure to anything resembling late nineteenth and twentieth century procedures and because of her elementary knowledge of music in general, she was prone to adhere to strict consonant tonal conceptions. She experimented with notes that would fit well with those in the soprano. It was not surprising to find her selecting the notes "E" and "G," the components of the C-major triad. Past experience taught her that these notes would fit even without any scientific analysis of simple triads. Their inclusion throughout the measure made everything consonant—elementary, colorless and unchallenging—since it did not describe a playful pup programmatically. The repetitions of the "C's" in measure 1 suggested some kind of motion in the bass. She started with note "C." "E" was the target. She observed by trial and error that "E" could be approached step-wise by "D":

EXAMPLE v-46

The combination of both parts now began to say something. The sound of the minor seventh on the second beat evoked images in her mind consistent with her objective. However, when she heard the "G" in the bass in combination with "E" in the soprano, the saccharine sound slightly deflated her image. It was not in character. Because of the nature of the melody in relation to her conception of the playful pup, it was felt that a touch of twentieth century sound would be most effective and descriptive. In other words, a cute, biting, poignant sound was envisaged. She tried every conceivable possibility. Some of the combinations irritated her at first, but as her ear became accustomed to the dissonances, she began to realize that her original choice of the note "G" was completely out of character. She finally accepted the F sharp as the most desirable note to help describe her pup. She realized, too, that the oblique and parallel motion in the first two measures welcomed the use of contrary motion in the next two measures. Originally in measure 3, she had all parallel motion between soprano and bass in sixths. Her decision for the contrary motion was so much more effective. It, too, was a contrast to the previous measures. To be consistent with the style already established in the first two measures, the notes in the bass were accepted by trial and error. When she arrived at "B" in the fourth measure, she felt that activity should cease temporarily, a point well-taken. A part sometimes becomes more effective if its continuity is interrupted by rests or inactivity. When activity resumes subsequently, the music is enhanced and becomes more significant.

In the after-phrase, just as the soprano part was a transposition of the fore-phrase, the same procedure was applied to the bass, except for the unison on the authentic cadence. Then in the B section, the counterpoint, which originally had been completely consonant, was changed to the way it appears now. Michèle employed the procedures of exploring, evaluating, deciding, and accepting, making possible an effective expression of her "Playful Pup."

For the first six measures of B, her counterpoint is based on chromaticism, which, when combined with the melody, produces characteristic intervals that help to convey her concepts. Dissonant intervals such as the augmented 4th, the major 2nd, the minor 7th, the major and minor 9th, and their relationship to all the consonant intervals before and after them help spice up the music. The cross relations between A-flat in the bass and "A" in the soprano in measure 11 of B and between "F" in the soprano and "F-sharp" in the bass in measure 15 of B contribute vitally to the overall picture of gay frivolity and refreshing poignancy.

A judicious use of all three motions—oblique, parallel, and contrary—activates the piece in the delineation of the pup. Unity occurs at the end of B in both parts; the melody has the descending scale passage from A, while the counterpoint uses the figure, note for note, from measure 1 of A. So in B, there is variety as well as unity. The appearance of the F-sharp in the bass creates modulation to the key of G, justifying the tonality of G-major in the next measure. Because I in "G" is V in "C," functioning as a pivot chord, it forms a perfect modulation back to C-major with the reappearance of the A section.

Because of the linear character of the piece combined with the use of chromatics, harmonic analysis must be streamlined. Nevertheless, the progression of I, IV, V, ii, V, and I are apparent in A. In B, one's imagination feels that I, iv (parallel minor), V and vi in C, which is the same as ii in G, as a pivot chord, are the basic harmonies. Foreign tones cannot be easily determined because of the contrapuntal and chromatic style. However, passing tones and an isolated anticipation are indicated.

After completing the composition, Michèle wanted to orchestrate it. She felt that the "Playful Pup" would require the violin, cello, clarinet and flute. After learning the necessary facts about their ranges and qualities, as well as the technique of writing for clarinet in B-flat, a transposing instrument, she proceeded to score.

Use of the violin and cello in the first eight measures with alternate down and up bows is contrasted with the slurs and the pizzicatos in the next eight measures. On the repeat of A from 17–24, Michèle assigned the melody to the violin an octave higher and the flute an octave higher than the violin, thus reinforcing the octave harmonics of the violin. She maintained cello loco with clarinet an octave higher. For contrast, the next four measures, 25–28, were assigned to the clarinet on the melody and the cello on the accompaniment. The last four measures in a tutti again present the strings in pizzicato, flute an octave above clarinet, with all ending on the tonic in octaves.

By scoring in this way, a richness and resonance results, which seems to emphasize the importance of our little character, the Playful Pup, showing how a theme presented with a variety of instrumentation can dress itself in a different garb. To describe the Playful Pup, dynamics and a feeling of buoyancy are expected, as indicated in the score. The tempo should maintain itself evenly throughout.

This piece, though brief in content, has much to contribute in various areas:

1. The first instrumental piece that is programmatic in content and in instrumentation describing the subject concisely and clearly
2. Existence of relationship between A and B obvious in terms of material effecting the constructive principles of unity, variety, and coherence
3. Use of counterpoint in a contemporary idiom à la Prokofieff in the delineation of the subject most impressively; chromaticism consistent with this approach
4. Existence of wave-like motion in the soprano and bass parts contributing to climaxes and anti-climaxes
5. Dynamics and proper tempo to be observed for an adequate interpretation

Píece for Instrumental Ensemble

Donna Meyers

PIECE FOR INSTRUMENTAL ENSEMBLE   Donna Meyers, Grade 7

This piece is written in the classical Haydnesque style, a strict rondo
form, A, B, A, C, A, with introduction, orchestrated for flute, clarinet,
timpani, piano, violins I and II, viola and cello. It is interesting to note
that Donna composed the introduction *after* the main body of the piece
had been completed. She felt that starting the work at section A
seemed a little abrupt and that something prior was needed to help
launch the theme. The first motif of section A appeared to impress her
with its importance. Like many composers who use the main motif in
their introduction as an identifying mark and to establish unity, Donna
felt it would be effective to do so in her piece. Realizing that antiphonal
treatment between voices and instruments is used to heighten contrast
of color, she applied the device in her music. She had a superficial
auditory and visual acquaintance with the instruments she was plan-
ning to use. Teaching her the ranges of each instrument and orienting
her to the quality and character of each made her feel more confident
as she began to orchestrate.

The main motif is announced by the flute, with imitative answers
coming consecutively from the first violin, viola, and cello, all in different registers, and finally from the piano. Next, all the instruments play
in unison, including a dramatic roll by the timpani at the masculine
half-cadence in measure 8. Asked why she did not include the clarinet
in this tutti, she said that she wished to reserve the timbre of this instrument for its solo function in section B—a rational, logical and commendable decision.

The two motifs of the A section:

EXAMPLE v-47

EXAMPLE v-48

occurring in the first two measures, are each transposed downward by
step. This concludes the fore-phrase at the masculine tonic half-cadence
in measure 12. The after-phrase begins with motif 3:

EXAMPLE v-49

made up of quarter notes. This motif is followed by the melodic trans-position of the second and first motifs of the fore-phrase, leading to the masculine authentic cadence in measure 16. It is remarkable how deftly these motifs are used throughout the section. They seem to fall in their natural places without being forced. Especially noteworthy is the way the composer has used motif 1 at the beginning and end of section A, thus balancing the two phrases. By treating the motifs in this way, the entire section takes on the desired wave-like motion. Within the A section unity (repetition of each motif), variety (use of the several motifs), and coherence are easily achieved.

In section A, the first violin bears the responsibility for the melody. Occasional slurs, in contrast to those notes individually bowed, add personality to the theme. Lightly accompanying the violins are the other strings. In the fore-phrase, punctuation of the harmonies is short, while in the after-phrase they are sustained as a means of contrast.

Asked why she was economical in her use of chord punctuation, Donna replied that she felt that any more than one to a measure would be top-heavy because of the light, fast character of the theme. Again, her logical evaluation is based on the theory that when a melody is active, the accompanying voices should be unobtrusively inactive or stagnant. By synthesizing the majority of melody notes in each meas-ure, the type of supporting harmony called for became self-evident. The decision on tonic and dominant chords was clear.

Attention should be called to the wave-like progression of the bass line obtained by using inversions of the dominant 7th chord. The importance of an interesting bass line such as this cannot be stressed enough. In relation to the harmonies used, foreign elements in the melody consist of several auxiliary tones and one passing tone, as indi-cated. On the repetition of this section at A', the strings, with the ex-ception of the cello, are raised one octave higher, with the first violin doubled by the flute. Clearly, the purpose here is to add more bril-liance, more resonance, and more color to the orchestration.

In section B, written in the key of A-minor, relative to C-major, motif 1 in measure 25:

EXAMPLE v-50

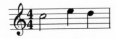

is followed immediately by motif 2 in measure 26:

EXAMPLE v-51

The rhythmic repetition and melodic variety of these motifs and their discreet placement within the section properly assure unity. The tonic half-cadence seems almost non-existent because of the way in which the fore-phrase, through the use of motif 1, measure 28, in melodic variation and inversion, melts into the after-phrase, concluding with a masculine authentic cadence in measure 32. By transposing these motifs, the entire section gains coherence and contour, and, again, the desired wave-like motion.

A new timbre is introduced. The clarinet in B-flat takes the solo part in a very legato style, in contrast to the spritely A theme. The whole piece is enhanced at this point not only because of this change in instrument, but also because the clarinet adapts itself well to the character of the melody. They are ably supported by an Alberti bass accompaniment given to pizzicato cello and viola. Notice that the cello punctuates on the first beats of each measure, while the viola carries the remainder of the measure—a traditional and very effective style. Both instruments finish the section with an arco, obviously to produce a feeling of completion. Simultaneously, the upper strings (first and second violins) maintain contrast with the pizzicato lower strings by sustaining, throughout each measure, the notes of the dominant and tonic harmonies obtained by melodic synthesis.

Upon close examination, every component of each tonic and dominant chord in this section is supplied by a different instrument at the beginning of each measure, assuring fullness of harmony and avoiding barrenness. The accompanying violin harmony is higher than the solo clarinet, thus allaying the old fear that a melody may be partially obscured if the harmony runs above it. Nothing could be further from the truth. To help bring out the melody in a situation like this, the dynamic level of the accompanying instruments should be slightly below that of the solo instrument. The flute is conspicuously absent, since the composer had used it previously and felt it would be out of character in relation to this particular theme. A counterpoint had been suggested, but she thought this would have an overbearing effect, because so many things were going on simultaneously in the accompaniment already. Her decision was honored. Throughout section B, anticipations, appoggiaturas and auxiliary tones are indicated. After repeating B, we come to section A′ again, but now with fuller orchestration, resonance and color.

Next we arrive at a brand new theme at C, written in F-major, which deserves scrutiny because of its complete contrast to the material preceding it. The difference lies in its martial character, delineated by the instrumentation, and the treatment of the accompaniment (concerted harmony and the running, step-wise bass line).

Phraseologically, the question-answer material in the first sentence is clear, leading to a masculine dominant half-cadence in measure 48. In the fore-phrase, the first motif (measures 1 and 2):

EXAMPLE v-52

suggests a trumpet call from its arpeggio-like construction. A relative high point is reached in measure 43, with motif 2:

EXAMPLE v-53

resolving in measure 44 into a repetition of measure 2 of the first motif. The after-phrase repeats motif 1 completely, followed by the melodic transposition of motif 2 at a lower level, leading to the half-cadence in measure 48. In the second sentence, the fore-phrase presents motif 1 of the first sentence literally in the first two measures, and motif 2 in measure 51, ascending to a climactic point in measure 52 with motif 1 material inverted. Through the after-phrase, motif 1 continues at this higher level until the end of the section and its authentic cadence in measure 56. This gives the entire theme a buoyancy and continuous rhythmic wave. Unity is achieved through the many repetitions and imitations of motif 1 and the imitations of motif 2. Variety is achieved by the appearance of these contrasted motifs. Coherence results from the discreet treatment of all the material.

In terms of instrumentation, the clarinet picks up the solo, with concerted harmonic support from the violins. Viola and cello in octaves, reinforced by the piano, engage in a martial step-wise figure:

EXAMPLE V-54

mostly down, down, up, down, etc. The timpani punctuates the initial strong beat of each measure, demonstrating its importance with emphasis and insistence. This construction creates naturally the feeling of a march; it is not a new approach, but was used most effectively by the composer. To maintain the resolute and decisive character of this section, slurring, which would, of course, have defeated the whole martial effect, was avoided.

Asked why the flute was tacit, the composer replied that since it performed in a solo capacity in the previous theme and was to return in the next section, its absence here would be advisable in order to bring a refreshing quality upon its return. The flute could very well have trilled a high "F" as a pedal point throughout, changing only once to a note of the dominant harmony on the half-cadence in measure 48. It could have performed an elaborate piccolo-type counterpoint as in "Stars and Stripes Forever," but this again would have made the flute solo in the next section less effective. The suggested trill or counterpoint could have been supplied by the piano. It would have been natural, too, to use a trumpet for the melody, with harmony supplied by the clarinet above. What could be more suitable than a trombone, sounding imposingly and massively on the step-wise accompaniment? Unfortunately, these vital and descriptive instruments were not available.

Harmonically, the three primary chords, tonic, subdominant and dominant, are all used by synthesizing the notes of the C melody. Unlike the vocal work, the theme and its harmonies contain no foreign tones whatsoever. This lack is compensated for by the inclusion of passing tones in the running, step-wise accompaniment. Finally, the return of theme A′ brings the piece to its conclusion. (An appropriate coda could effectively have been added, but time did not permit.)

In interpreting the "Piece for Ensemble," there is enough dynamic contrast to allow for variation of expression within each individual theme. The introduction maintains a mezzo piano until the unison, at which point an appropriate crescendo is made. During theme A, the dynamic level is subdued, but on its repeat at section A′, with the change in register of the strings and with the addition of the flute, the dynamic level is increased to mezzo forte. A slower tempo and resumption of the mezzo piano mark the appearance of the B theme, new in material, key and orchestration. A return to theme A' in the original tempo follows. With the entrance of the third theme at section C, the climax is reached with "all stops out," as might be expected. Recapitulation of the A' theme completes the piece. Here again, the basic principles of unity and variety are successfully carried out. The appearance of the principal motif of theme A in the introduction and its several repetitions insure unity, while the intervening contrasts of themes B and C contribute to variety. Through effective use of the motifs in each theme, the composer attains coherence.

A great deal can be learned from this original instrumental piece:

1. Good example of classical style in rondo form
2. Use of the main theme's principal motif in the introduction, imitated and treated antiphonally by the orchestra
3. Proper use of the motifs within a sentence for purposes of unity, variety, balance, contour, and coherence; for variety, different key for each theme
4. Importance of understanding the character of a melody in terms of its appropriate harmonic, contrapuntal, rhythmic, dynamic, and orchestral accompaniment
5. Method of determining the harmony of melody synthesis and incorporation of a good bass line obtained by using harmonic inversion
6. Applying the theory of stagnation and activity in relation to simultaneous use of two or more different voices
7. Use of foreign tones to increase melodic interest
8. Judicious and discreet use of instruments to achieve contrast in timbre, increased resonance and color, and suitability of theme to character; device of slurring for legato purposes (except for the martial C theme) and dynamics, all contributing to appropriate interpretation

Study in Jazz

Barbara Sandler

Snares as before

STUDY IN JAZZ   Barbara Sandler, Grade 7

This opus which "swings" is orchestrated for flute, clarinet, piano, snare and bass drums, and strings. Obviously, Barbara already had been exposed to jazz. This exposure combined with a natural feeling for the idiom resulted in a very commendable piece. It has all the earmarks to classify it as "swing"—syncopation used discreetly, the minor mode, rhythm.

The piece is in three-part song form, A, A', B, A, bound to satisfy the requirements of unity, variety, and coherence.

The motif of the 8-measure A theme is used in the fore-phrase in alternate measures 1 and 3:

EXAMPLE V-55

with the second motif in measure 2 being balanced by its abbreviation in measure 4:

EXAMPLE V-56

The after-phrase presents a new idea:

EXAMPLE V-57

leading upward diatonically to the appearance of the first motif in measure 7 (making for unity) into the half-cadence in measure 8. The section repeats, leading to the authentic cadence in measure 16.

The next section, B, beginning in measure 17, the release or bridge, employs two motifs used alternately, each time transposed twice in the form of a sequence:

EXAMPLE V-58

EXAMPLE V-59

After these six measures, the material in measures 23 and 24 leading to half-cadence seems to be an expanded use of motif 2 of B and motif 1 of A. Phraseologically, it seems that the fore-phrase of B is contained in its first six measures because of the continuity of the material, and the after-phrase in measures 23 and 24 functions as a conclusion or after-thought. Then follows the repeat of A.

Upon hearing the first theme, Barbara knew that she had written it in a minor key. Her previous experience and exposure to both major and minor modes had taught her to distinguish between the two. She could recognize the sounds of both merely by listening, without knowing technically the difference.

With a superficial knowledge of the major scales, she was taught that each major key has its own relative minor key built a minor third or three half steps below it. As an example, the keys of C-major and A-minor were used. The fact impressed upon her was that both used the same signature. Understanding this, she was ready to construct the three forms of the minor scale and to realize that the accidentals involved in the harmonic and melodic ascending forms did not affect the signature. She now knew that she had written her piece in the key of C-minor. To determine the relative major of C-minor in order to find its signature, she reversed the procedure of the interval relationship of relative major and relative minor. She found that E-flat was a minor third above "C."

She now knew that C-minor contained the three flats of E-flat major. The appearance of the A-naturals and B-naturals indicated to her that she was involved with the melodic ascending.

In measure 2 of A, these accidentals were logical because of the ascending step-wise motion. However, how could the A-naturals in measures 1, 3, and 7 be justified? She felt that the combination of A-natural with the tonic minor triad was in keeping with the exotic jazz sound, creating an atmosphere that was inherent in the art form. This conclusive argument could not be refuted.

With the outline of all the triads associated with the notes of the key of C-minor, she found that, harmonically by synthesis, the tonic and dominant chords were fundamental in A. The tonic chord "C, E-flat, G, A-natural," commonly called a minor 6th chord because of the interval of a major 6th from "C" to "A," was predominant.

After determining the type of chord to be used below each melody note, she simply built downward, supplying the remaining components of the chord. For example, the first note "G" is a member of the C-minor tonic chord, "C, E-flat, G." With "G" as the highest note, the remaining notes of the chord were placed directly underneath in close succession. With the next note, E-flat, the order of notes below resulted as indicated. Notice that the successive chords in the treble clef are arranged in close compact form, causing a tight and tense effect so appropriate to the swing idiom.

Especially exciting is the appoggiatura E-flat, on the fourth beat in measure 6, used closely against the V chord, causing a short, biting, effective dissonance. In the cadences, a V^9 flat also creates dissonance.

Throughout this section, the composer was careful to select, wherever possible, notes in the bass that would result in a melody line in contrary motion. Starting in root position, she experimented until she was completely satisfied. Occasionally, there is parallel motion which injects a bit of variety. Several passing tones are also present. All parts are now said to be in block formation, a concerted arrangement of vertical notes in chords proceeding successively.

By studying this section, the student will be able to learn the procedures outlined, but in the final analysis, his ear, taste, and experience will be the deciding factor.

In the B section, the harmonies of iv, iv^6, i and V^7 are used. The harmonic rhythm changes every two measures, except for the last two measures in which the tonic to dominant is used to allow for repeating the section and for resolving to the return of A. The theme is supported throughout by sustained chords.

After the customary indoctrination in the understanding of instruments used, Barbara was ready to orchestrate. In the A section, the flute and clarinet in B-flat, the latter a transposing instrument, were assigned the upper two parts respectively, in the treble clef, doubling the first and second violins. The viola, a C-clef instrument, took the next part below. In other words, all three upper voices had been accommodated. The cello was assigned the bass part. The drum part is simple, to be sure, but should offer opportunities for improvisation by an imaginative and experienced performer.

In the B section, the clarinet has the solo responsibility, while the flute and strings sustain the harmonies above and below, voiced in a way consistent with orthodox procedures.

The change to brushes for the drummer is effective because of the contrast of dynamics, the change in character of the melody and its assignment to one instrument. Here, again, is the possibility of improvisation by the percussionist.

This piece has the following items of interest:

1. Good commercial model of jazz in swing style
2. Three-part song form
3. Good development of the various motifs throughout effecting the constructive principles of unity, variety, and coherence
4. Structurally, use of 4-measure and 6+2 measure phrases
5. Theory and construction of the minor scales delineated
6. Melodically, good theme contour; harmonically, jazz idiom expressed effectively by chords; rhythmically, importance of syncopation, a vital ingredient of jazz; contrapuntally, the movement and excitement of the piece aided by melodic lines; and orchestrally, the blending and contrasts of color fully consummated with changes of dynamics in themes

Quintet for Strings and Flute

Daniel Starr

140

QUINTET FOR STRINGS AND FLUTE   Daniel Starr, Grade 8

This quintet for first violin, second violin, viola, cello, and flute, with the viola interchangeable with clarinet, is written in rondo form, with the plan, A, B, A′, C, C′, interlude, cadenza, A, B, codetta.

The beginning of A states the motif:

EXAMPLE v-60

This motif is predominant throughout the A and B sections, creating unity. After the motif is announced, it is transposed down by step, followed by a slight melodic development effected by transposition, repetition, and inversion. In the fourth measure, there is hardly any feeling of half-cadence because of the activity involved. The authentic cadence definitely occurs at the end of A in measure 8.

The B portion is actually an outgrowth of A, because of the continuous presence of the motif in transposition and inversion. The half-cadence of B ends in the fourth measure of the fore-phrase (measure 8) on the dominant minor triad. The authentic cadence occurs in the eighth measure on the tonic (measure 12).

After the repeat of A, a new concept appears at C in measure 25; the motif consists of sixteenth notes effecting variety:

EXAMPLE v-61

The motif is developed by transposition, inversion, repetition, and variation. Note that the fore-phrase of C, whose cadence ends on the subdominant, contains three measures, while the after-phrase contains four measures ending on the VII_6 chord (measure 24) which bears a relationship to the dominant. A 7-measure musical sentence results. The C′ section fore-phrase consists of three measures also, as if to balance with the fore-phrase of C. The appearance of 3-measure phrases gives the same feeling of intensity found in Hungarian and Scotch folk music. Sometimes this feeling is created with intellectualized intent, in which case it may sound contrived; it is better if it evolves naturally. This is the case here.

C′ is extended in the form of an interlude (measures 28–36), which is somewhat episodal, consisting of scale passages primarily developed in sequence upwards. After a violin cadenza based upon the previous episodes, the da capo restores A and B, followed by a final appearance of A abridged in the form of a codetta.

This piece is written in Mixolydian mode starting on "A":

EXAMPLE v-62

and generally bears a strong resemblance to the style of Bartók.

Harmonically, the piece is rather subtle and enterprising. The A section begins on the leading tone, which may appear rather unusual to the average layman or inexperienced musician. The progressions that follow throughout the piece, such as VII to IV to I, create a folk-like nostalgic sound. Upon examination, each of the above chords has a quartal relationship to the other; each progresses by the interval of the fourth.

In the C section, the sixteenth notes are a welcome contrast to the previous triplets, which have been used in abundance. An interesting tonic pedal not only serves as a support, but also creates a little dissonant flavor as well as color contrast. The interlude, based on the IV, VII, I progression, eventually ends on the minor dominant 7th chord leading to the cadenza.

The reason for doubling some of the thirds could be debated, since it violates orthodox harmonic procedures, such as the use of color tones in some of the major harmonies. Because these tones are brief in duration, due to the moving continuity of the music, the objection can be negated.

There is an abundance of foreign tones—passing tones, appoggiaturas, auxiliaries, echappées, anticipation and changing and free tones. Though these are all indicated, observe especially: the echappées in section A' (measure 16), notes "A" and C-sharp in the violins; the anticipation in C, measure 21; the fourth sixteenth note, "B," as well as the last one in the measure, C-sharp. Other points of interest are the C-sharp in the viola in measure 2 of A, which could be classified as the seventh of the IV chord. In the fourth measure, notice the biting and poignant sound of the melodic tritone between "G" and C-sharp in the viola, creating the interval of the augmented fourth. Technically the C-sharp should have continued upward by step, but this violation of the rule can be justified by the interesting effect obtained by jumping down a third. In C, the first beat in measure 23 contains the notes consecutively, "B," "D," and F-sharp, which can be considered the ninth, the eleventh, and the thirteenth in relation to the tonic chord. In the same measure, the F-sharp suggests a I^6 chord. In the final analysis, a polytonal sound results, an F-sharp minor against a B-minor. In the second beat in measure 27 of C', the free tone "G" is played by the cello.

Instrumentally, the composer has achieved as great a variety of orchestral sound as possible, varying the solos by switching instruments and by employing antiphonal treatment.

In the A section, the solo viola is ably supported by punctuated pizzicato chords in the other strings. This punctuation continues in B, but the flute has taken over from the viola the solo responsibilty in antiphonal treatment. Continuing on to the after-phrase of B, the flute invites the viola to join in harmony of sixths below. The punctuations of pizzicato strings, however, continue as before.

On the return to A, the first violin is soloist with the second violin in harmony of thirds, while the cello punctuates arco in double stops, involving a bit of interesting off-beat syncopation. Meanwhile, the viola sustains pedal points or simply harmony notes. In the after-phrase, the same appears, but with a reinforced sustaining quality produced by the flute, which duplicates the viola an octave higher.

At C, the viola returns in the role of soloist with both the flute above and violins below sustaining notes of the changing harmonies. The cello provides a tonic pedal. In C', the cello, which up to this time has functioned primarily as a harmony and rhythmic instrument, becomes the soloist, while the other instruments above provide sustained harmony notes.

Through the interlude, the cello continues, at first alone, but eventually joined in octaves by the second violin. Then the others continue with harmonically sustained notes above them rising in a concerted effort majestically to a climax. All instruments punctuate a minor dominant chord with a fermata which ushers in the exciting little cadenza featuring the violin. Here the soloist continues the episodic passage established in C'. The return to A and B follows, and finally comes the codetta where the viola begins the theme with punctuations pizzicato by the other strings while the flute sustains. On the cadence, the violins arco take over a sensitive throbbing diatonic run, while the others sustain notes of the final tonic chord.

Musical sensitivity is important in the interpretation of this piece. Many concepts in this piece can be invaluable to the student:

1. Written in the Mixolydian mode with Bartókian influence
2. Written in rondo form, including a rather episodic interlude used as an extension and a violin cadenza based on previous material

3. Fundamental motif predominant throughout much of the piece creating unity; variety obtained by a new concept at C; motifs developed through devices of transposition, inversion, repetition, and variation

4. Structurally, 3- and 4-measure phrases natural and uncontrived

5. Harmonically interesting due to: quartal progressions giving the piece a folk-like character; variety of foreign tones; suggestion of polytonality, though briefly; inclusion of pedal points above and below

6. Subtle variety of instrumentation in the solo parts well supported by appropriate accompaniment; harmony above solo parts used contrapuntally, causing frequent contrary motion, which creates excitement

7. Proper balance of melody and accompaniment to be observed for good dynamic interpretation

Frolic for Clarinet and Piano

Rosalie Phillips

FROLIC FOR CLARINET AND PIANO   Rosalie Phillips, Grade 8

This is an experiment in syncopated musical novelty. The material is particularly adaptable to the clarinet, which Rosalie played and for which she felt comfortable writing. The piano was used for accompaniment.

It is a written in three-part form. After the second theme is completed, it is presented again but in variation. The plan of the piece is A, A', B, B', interlude, A'.

In the A theme, the dotted eighth and sixteenth motif is immediately presented:

EXAMPLE V-63

followed by a second motif of simple syncopation:

EXAMPLE V-64

This leads to a transposition of both motifs in measures 3 and 4. As if in relief from the prevalence of the ♩. ♪ note motif, the after-phrase begins with motif 3 of quarter notes:

EXAMPLE V-65

repeated in transposition. This is followed by the return of the persistent ♩. ♪ note motif in an upward and downward arpeggio leading to a syncopated half-cadence in measure 8. After measure 14 of A', a 2-measure extension containing the ♩. ♪ note motif in transposition culminates in an agitated treatment of the same motif. If then descends as a tonic major sixth arpeggio to the authentic cadence in measures 17 and 18.

Section B in E-flat major begins with a very effective quarter rest followed by the ♪. note motif in a downward sequence. In the next measure, the ♪ rhythm carries through the syncopated character of the piece. These two measures are then transposed in the next two measures in a unique way. Compare measures 20 and 22. The rhythm is the same, but the notes and direction change for variety. Then, in the after-phrase, the ♪. note rhythm prevails, slightly abbreviated in every measure except in the authentic cadence, measures 25 and 26. Here the motif ascends diatonically in contrast to the descending arpeggio of the authentic cadence of the A' theme.

Thus far, one can readily appreciate the importance of the ♪. rhythm, characteristic of the piece and used as a unifying link between the two different themes.

At B' in measure 27, the variations of B are quite obvious in the triplet treatment. Take special note of the quarter rests in the fore-phrase which are used simularly in the fore-phrase of B. They are conspicuous by their absence in the after-phrase, again for variety and rhythmic excitement. Suddenly an upward chromatic flourish, not used before, leads to cadence. The chromaticism does not end here, but continues in the form of an interlude in measures 35 and 36, which brings us back to A' without the 2-measure extension.

Harmonically, the orthodox progressions in the piano accompaniment are a result of the melodic content. Opportunities for chromatic treatment are presented in various places, as in measures 2 and 4. In measure 5, the pivot chord allows for the progression into the key of D-minor. In the eighth measure, the V^9 flat of D-minor appears. This should, by all intents and purposes, resolve to the tonic in D-minor. Instead, the presence of the F-sharp in the soprano suggests the leading tone of G-minor, the relative minor of B-flat major. The expected tonic becomes the V^7 of vi in B-flat major, which progresses to V^7 in the original key. Chromaticisms continue to appear in the B section.

Harmonic analysis is clearly indicated throughout the piece. The student should particularly observe the use of the vi^7 and ii^7 chords with root and third raised (non-dominant diminished seventh chords) in measure 16 of A' and 19 of B, respectively, as well as other chords with alterations and progressions.

Foreign tones of all sorts, which have been identified, are of particular interest, because of the exciting and stimulating effect they offer.

The piano accompaniment serves a supporting role primarily punctuating in an "um-pah" format as well as sustaining and, at times, giving a rhythmic syncopated impetus.

In a category by itself, "Frolic" contributes the following:

1. Typically a novelty in which the clarinet frolics and capers about
2. Three-part form including rhythmical variations on the second theme
3. Persistence of the principal ♩. ♩ note motif developed by transposition and sequence; syncopation throughout
4. Inclusion of an interlude, which grows out of chromaticism used in the B′ section, deftly leading into the recapitulation of A
5. Use of harmony in the piano accompaniment embracing orthodox, chromatic, and modulatory progressions including secondary dominant chords; harmonic variety aided by the multiple foreign tones contributing to the creation of a picturesque quaintness effected by the combined forces of the clarinet and piano
6. Subordination to the soloist of the piano accompaniment, involving an economy of improvisation for proper interpretation with dynamic changes in both instruments

Concerto for Piano More or Less

Joey Singer

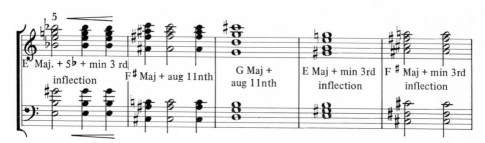

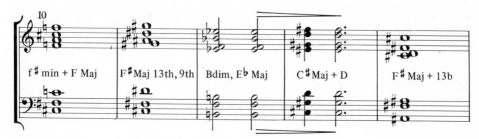

152

153

155

CONCERTO FOR PIANO MORE OR LESS   Joey Singer, Grade 9

For Joey, who had been nurtured on traditional music with no exposure to twentieth century styles and techniques, this opus, facetiously entitled "Concerto for Piano More or Less," is indeed commendable. He deserves great praise and credit for attempting a piece in the contemporary medium.

The creation of a motif and the understanding of the procedures involved in its development and fruition are most demanding and exacting, requiring the extension of imagination and the exercise of discipline. This is true even when composing in a familiar idiom. However, when the composer is creatively inexperienced in unfamiliar areas, how much more difficult it is to fulfill the requirements. When he accepts these responsibilities and when the results are exciting and stimulating, what a great accomplishment for the composer! What a fulfilling contribution to his listeners!

In the beginning, when the composer is first introduced to and experiments in anything relatively modern, his ears must become at-

tuned to the sounds which appear strange to him. He may become
hostile, intransigent, recalcitrant, and even rebellious. The first step
in getting him involved is to win his confidence. Sometimes this is
difficult and requires patience and understanding on the part of the
teacher, who must remain firm in his own conviction and dedication.
When a feeling of rapport gradually develops between the two, the
time has arrived for the composer to embark on his challenging project.

"Concerto for Piano More or Less" began as an improvisation in
the traditional, stereotyped, and unchallenging idiom to which Joey
was accustomed. Immediately, he was asked to "live dangerously" and
to inject into his musical ideas the element of the unexpected—to shock,
to surprise. "How was this to be done?" he asked. The obvious answer
was to escape from the tyranny of the expected and to use notes which
bore remote relationship to one another. In other words, inject a freedom from tonality, an expanded tonality, involving the ingredient of
chromatic and harmonic dissonance of all types. Joey's adventurous
spirit and sensitive musicianship prompted him to accept the challenge.
As he progressed, he was assured that the restrictions employed in the
harmonic practice of composers in the traditional eighteenth and nineteenth century styles are relaxed in the twentieth century style, that
harmonic progressions are more flexible today, and that the feeling of a
tonal center to which everything gravitates is no longer mandatory.

In this piece, Joey does not go completely off on a tangent. There
are evidences of tonalities, but at least he shows imagination along with
control and restraint when needed.

The composition is in three-part form with an introduction and a
coda orchestrated for flute, three clarinets, horn, trumpet, piano, violin,
and cello.

The andante $\frac{4}{4}$ introduction, which contains nineteen measures, is
divided phraseologically into two musical sentences, in which a fundamental motif:

EXAMPLE v-66

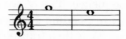

is explored and developed. The first sentence consists of eight measures
with two equal 4-measure phrases. The second sentence has an as-
symetric arrangement of eleven measures with phrases of 3+3+2+3
measures.

The harmonic structure is quite ambitious. The polytonality, the
chords of addition and omission of notes, the chords with the inflection

of the minor third over the major third, and chords with altered notes were all conceived simply by experimentation at the keyboard. It was a trial and error approach, to be sure, with a pre-determined attitude of complete abandon in order to arrive at combinations of notes whose sounds would establish the mood and tone of the piece. The results analyzed as individual chordal structures are justified by the philosophy expressed before concerning the relaxation of harmonic restrictions. The persistent and continuous tension suddenly abates at the end of the introduction with the pure unadulterated octave "G," which gives the impression that tonality, possibly the dominant of "C," had been achieved. Not for long.

Observe that the notes of the majority of the chords are of long duration, notated as whole notes. Occasionally, quarter and half notes creep in not only to prevent rhythmic monotony, but also to give a bit of motion, including syncopation. The ponderous quality of the chords is made more apparent by the tonal mixtures of woodwinds, brass, and strings.

The allegro section A in $\frac{2}{4}$ presents a motif primarily of eighth notes:

EXAMPLE V-67

These are combined with notes assigned to the piano bass line. The first 2 measures consist of three parallel perfect fifths followed by a major seventh. Establishing a mood of irony and satire, the motif is carried through in extensive wave-like development for twenty-five more measures, achieving unity. As it progresses, the pattern of the intervals changes to involve intervals of the major sixth, major seventh, and major and minor ninths.

The A section begins with a 4-measure phrase which is transposed twice upward in sequence. The A' section begins in measure 32, with a repetition of the corresponding 4-measure phrase of A, an octave higher. Its fourth measure, 35, is then transposed downward to measure 36 but freely by interval. Measure 36 becomes the first measure of the next 4-measure phrase. Here the interval pattern changes. The remaining three measures of this phrase are transposed downward freely in sequence. Then a 2-measure phrase, mostly chromatic, beginning in measure 40, appears three times ending in measure 45.

In this section the piano is featured as the solo instrument supported by chordal concerted punctuations in the ensemble. In measures 20–36, and from measures 37 through 45, the chords result from a synthesis of all the notes. In the latter group of measures, the chords may be considered hybrid in their construction, since they borrow from notes of each beat, which actually have little relationship to any chordal structure. The chords arrange themselves seemingly in a quartal series.

The harmonies, again indicated as individual chordal structures, are somewhat conservative in the early measures, but they become progressively dissonant from measure 36 on. In some of these chords, their sound still lingers on after they have been consummated, creating increased dissonance with the sound of the second beat where a major seventh or major and minor 9th interval exists, themselves dissonant. A sound results appropriate to the ironic feeling, which the music is meant to portray.

Because of the nature of the harmonic structure, every note has its significant function. Either it is a bona fide component of a chord or it is not. If the latter, it could be termed a foreign tone in relation to the chordal structure with which it is used. However, since each note belongs to a particular category of its own, in which it has a significant function, it would be safe not to term it a foreign tone.

Rhythmically, the chords occur on the first beat of every measure except in measures 23, 27, 31, and 35, where they enter on the last half of beat one, creating a rhythmical shock of unexpected syncopation.

Functioning on these chords are the three clarinets, trumpet, and violins divisi, while the French horn and cello sustain pedal points in unison. Cello and French horn change every four measures to notes that would be in agreement with the harmonies used. Only in three measures, 36, 37, 38, do they both join the other instruments in punctuating the chords with cello pizzicato.

A 10-measure interlude, 46–55, follows section A in which a persistent pedal point is successively interrupted by ascending consecutive major triads, as indicated, leading to a dramatic climax. All rhythms are now equal, the pedal point and each chord being a half note. The piano is supported on the pedal point by vibrant tremolo cello and violins and on each chord by the remaining instruments executing their notes incisively and emphatically.

For variety, a complete contrast in measure 56 unfolds with sections B and B′ in slow tempo giving forth a somewhat quizzical quality. The B consists of three 5-measure phrases. The fore-phrase contains four measures plus a 1-measure extension, as does the after-phrase. Finally, a 5-measure phrase, arranged as 3+2, acts as an anti-climactic codetta in which the music descends to an anticipatory resting point.

In B′, the first 5-measure fore-phrase of B in measure 71 is heard again. The after-phrase now graduates to six measures as the music rises toward climax in measure 81. This is followed by a descending codetta-like 6-measure phrase leading to another resting point before a return to the beginning of the piece.

The motif:

EXAMPLE v-68

which, on the surface, appears to be a rhythmically syncopated treatment of the B-flat minor arpeggio, is expanded into other seemingly legitimate tonalities, B-flat minor and B-major predominating. The analysis is indicated as chordal structures.

Especially effective is the swaying downward and upward motion of the motif as it develops both in its arpeggio and occasional step-wise format. The implied tonalities in the melody line combine with a harmonically unrelated basso ostinato to produce a polytonal trenchant effect. For the first 3½ measures, the C-major bass, alternating tonic and dominant in perfect fifth relationship, is used against the melodic line based on the B-flat minor 6th and B-major arpeggios. This treatment lays the groundwork for the desired quizzical atmosphere.

In measure 59, the bass line begins to break away from its ostinato format by developing upward and downward for two measures. The interval of the fifth predominates. Notice how it has borrowed from the B-major arpeggio material of the melody in measure 58. In measure 60, the tonality of A-minor, relative minor of C-major, appears, anticipating the A-minor basso ostinato in measure 61. This carries through most of the phrase by combining against the melodic line based on the B-flat minor and B-minor 9th arpeggios. In measures 64 and 65, the bass line functions similarly to the way it did in measures 59 and 60 of the fore-phrase. However, here the intervals used are more varied, including quartal progressions.

Finally on the first codetta in measure 66, the format of the moving ostinato terminates, obviously to help the melodic line reach the terminal resting point. Notice how it occasionally and unobtrusively supplies the melody with colorful chromatic harmony in parallel motion. A feeling of some tonality is sensed—a welcome relief from the polytonality that has persisted to this point.

In B′, measures 79, 80, and 81 of the after-phrase, polytonality becomes more dynamic as both voices begin their climactic rise. The upper voice uses a B diminished triad in measure 79, an F⁷ chord in measures 80 and 81, while the bass line in measures 79 and 80 employs notes of the A-sharp minor scale somewhat diatonically. In measure 81, the bass outlines the harmonies of G-sharp diminished 7th and D-major. Then comes the 2nd codetta phrase (beginning in measure 82) where again the bass terminates its basso ostinato format for reasons similar to those in B. It takes on the function of supplying the melody with colorful orthodox sounding harmonies in parallel motion. The presence of these harmonies dissipates the previous polytonality, but only temporarily. Again, the dissonance returns in the last three measures indicating that tonality was only ephemeral.

As the voices progress in measures 82–85, quartal relationships appear in measure 83, between B-flat diminished and F-major, and in measures 84 and 85 in the bass line.

Foreign tones function rather freely because of the polytonal character of the piece. They are indicated either as free tone, echappée, or appoggiatura.

Instrumentally, in B and B′ the clarinet assumes the solo responsibility accompanied by the piano and cello in unison. A second clarinet appears at the climactic point in B′ and continues briefly into the codetta. Especially effective is the dissonant clash with the first clarinet in measure I of the codetta.

The simplicity of the instrumentation in B and B′ is an excellent contrast to the tutti used in the introduction and A section and also delineates the quizzical character of the music.

After the return to the introduction and A, the coda appears in measure 133 where the piano continues the motif of A with its melodic major sevenths and parallel perfect fifths in a chromatic line. The coda, in 2-measure sections, is transposed up by step twice, making a sequence. A polytonal chord involving the tutti of the ensemble punctuates the beginning of each section. Two more measures follow in which the piano performs parallel octaves in perfect fifth intervals.

The piece ends with a powerful strident tutti, a final utterance of polytonality in which a quartal relationship of notes is supported by a B-flat augmented chord. Proper interpretation of the piece will depend not only on the adherence to metronome marks and dynamics, but also on an understanding of the idiom.

For a first attempt at musical creativity, this piece is certainly most ambitious, enterprising, and imaginative. For the student it offers a great deal:

1. Proves that with the proper attitude, success probable in any challenging venture
2. Maintenance of the traditional three-part form with introduction, interlude, and coda
3. Motifs explored and developed logically in waves through transposition and sequence in all sections of the piece, achieving unity; contrast attained by different concepts and tempos
4. Many twentieth century techniques producing dissonance arrived at by experimentation at the keyboard, such as polytonality, altered chords, chords of omission and addition, chromaticisms, quartal lines harmonically and melodically; tonality apparent at times; analysis of foreign tones relative; discreet use of basso ostinato
5. Imaginative and colorful orchestration; instruments used subtly to accentuate both the harmonic and rhythmic structures
6. Proper interpretation dependent on understanding, supported by adherence to tempos and dynamics

Neophyte Rondo

Ronnie Smoller

164

165

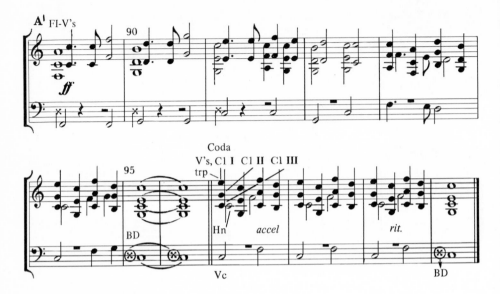

NEOPHYTE RONDO Ronnie Smoller, Grade 9

The salient features of this piece are transparency, simplicity, and lucidity. The directness and innocence of the themes are enhanced by the classic purity of both the harmonization and orchestration. It is orchestrated for flute, three clarinets, horn, trumpet, bass drum, violins, and cello. The piece is in rondo form slightly varied by the order of the themes. The plan is A, A', B, B', A, A', C, B, B', C, A, A', coda. After C appears for the first time, it is followed immediately by B and B' in-

stead of the expected return of A, which is further delayed until after the second appearance of C. The composer's reason for this treatment was justifiable. He felt that too many A's would sound stereotyped and even monotonous. Unity by repetition of themes and variety by using new material are achieved.

The fore-phrase of A consists of a bold, spirited, and military-like motif:

EXAMPLE V-69

which is transposed up by step in measure 2. In measure 3, the ♩. ♪ note rhythm appears again transposed up, but immediately it is followed by a downward step-wise motion leading to a tonic half-cadence in measure 4. Then in the after-phrase a new motif:

EXAMPLE V-70

is treated in upward sequence until another tonic imperfect cadence is arrived at. All the material of A is then repeated as A', inasmuch as the tonic cadence in measures 15 and 16 end perfectly. With the repetitions of each motif, unity is achieved. The use of two different motifs creates variety. The entire musical sentence progresses in good wavelike motion.

Instrumentally, the theme of the fore-phrase of A and A' is assigned appropriately to the French horn to portray the regality of the music. Surrounding the horn, the clarinets sustain open-concerted harmonies, while the cello supplies the bass line, and the bass drum punctuates the rhythm. In the after-phrase, clarinet I and trumpet take over the solo in unison supported by clarinet II and horn in open concerted harmony, while clarinet III and cello play a wave-like contrapuntal bass line in octaves.

Harmonically, the chords are determined generally by the synthesis of the melody. The progressions are quite orthodox, utilizing only the primary harmonies IV, V, and I.

Curiously, the piece begins on the sub-dominant chord giving the impression that it is in the key of F-major. If it were, the cadences on the fourth and seventh measures would be half-cadences; the C-major chord would be considered to be the dominant in "F," reinforced in the eighth measure by the dominant seventh chord because of the B-flat in the bass. However, the factor determining the tonality as C-major is the appearance of the C-major chord in the final authentic perfect cadence. One also could argue that the piece is in the Lydian mode with "F" as the final. If the B-flat did not appear in measure 8, this theory might bear some weight.

Foreign tones are at a minimum. The two passing tones are indicated.

The B section, beginning in measure 17, carries on the spirit of the A section though it appears to be lighter and almost carefree. The fore-phrase consists of two motifs:

EXAMPLE V-71

EXAMPLE V-72

They appear consecutively and are repeated. In the after-phrase beginning in measure 21, the motif is related rhythmically to those of the fore-phrase, achieving unity. The motif is repeated twice before it reaches the tonic authentic cadence.

In B′, the motif of the after-phrase is not repeated twice as it was in B, but is transposed upward twice, reaching the tonic cadence in an upper octave in measure 32.

Because of the lightness of B and B′, the instrumentation necessarily changes. Appropriately, the flute staccato and violin are used in unison. Ronnie felt that these instruments would not contribute to the regal quality of the A section. He reserved them wisely for the B section. Accompanying them are the horn on a dominant pedal point and the cello on a tonic pedal point. Occasionally, the latter progresses to the dominant pedal point in measures 18 and 20 where syncopation is created. To consummate the feeling of levity, no harmony is used. The bass line and the horn pedal are sufficient as support of the melody. Passing tones and auxiliary tones are used in moderation.

The slow C section reflects the Aeolian mode which is actually the relative natural minor form of C major, the tonality of the previous B section.

In the fore-phrase, the motif in measure 49:

EXAMPLE V-73

is followed by a slight elaboration rhythmically and melodically in measure 50. Measure 51 is reminiscent of the motif followed by a ♩. ♪ and ♩ note cadence on the subdominant in measure 52. The after-phrase is similar to the fore-phrase except for the authentic cadence where the ♩. ♪ note rhythm combines with the eighth note fragment of the motif. Throughout, there is a natural wave-like structure to the melody.

Instrumentally, clarinet I is the soloist throughout, supported below by clarinet II, horn, and cello in open concerted sustained harmony. The melody lends itself to beautiful chordal changes derived from the Aeolian mode.

Foreign tones are confined to simple auxiliary and passing tones. After the intervening contrast of B (measure 57) in the relative major key, the C section returns in measure 73, but in a new Aeolian tonality. The evolution of this change warrants an explanation. Rather than repeat this material as before, Ronnie felt that a new final would be refreshing. He justified using the key of F-natural minor (Aeolian on final "F") by considering the cadential C-major chord of the B section as a pivot chord in terms of V of "F."

Still maintaining the clarinet I in solo capacity, he surrounded it with concerted sustained harmony by using instrumentation different from that in the previous C. Trumpet is above, while clarinet II and III are below. Unity is obtained by repetition of a theme and by use of the same solo instrument. Variety is obtained by new tonality and new instrumentation arranged harmonically different from the first appearance of C.

With this section completed, the composer felt that the final cadential chord of F-minor would easily progress to the F-major chord, which begins the A section in measure 81. In other words, the transition from F-minor to the parallel major was a normal and simple one.

The final A is treated exactly as it was in the beginning, while in A' the instrumentation of the original A' is supplemented by the addition of a flute and a violin on the solo part to insure more resonance and brilliance.

A coda, added in measure 97, consists of three consecutive appearances of the third measure before the cadence of A'. This repetition before the final chord helps dramatically. The instrumentation of A' continues through the coda.

Observation of the proper tempos with an understanding of the character of the piece will contribute to proper interpretation.

The highlights of this piece are:

1. Conformity of harmonic and instrumental treatment with the character and personality of the piece

2. Free rondo form in which all the constructive principles are explicitly evident

3. Concise and unobtrusive use of motifs A and B

4. Strong relationship of C motifs to each other, thereby attaining unity; complete contrast of C to previous material in mood and feeling expressed instrumentally, harmonically, and by change of key; subtle contrast in the two C's, key-wise, and clever way they are approached and left in terms of key relationship to the other sections

5. Foreign tones not required for this pure abstract style, which can stand on its own, not needing the elaboration and ornamentation of these non-harmonic tones

6. Proper interpretation achieved by observation of dynamics, tempos, mood, phrasings, staccatos

6

Senior High School

Let us examine the creative output of students from the ages of 15 to 17. The composers in this group, older than those in the junior high school area, might be expected to be more experienced musically and technically and thereby capable of more mature creativity. This is not necessarily true. They certainly are older and could very well have been exposed to more musical activities, but without any creative experiences prior to their high school years, how could they be expected to compose freely? It is axiomatic that the earlier a child is exposed to creative experiences, the fewer will be his inhibitions and frustrations.

In my experiences with high school student-composers, everyone was a neophyte in creativity and each believed musical creativity was designed for the specialist. This, of course, is not necessarily true. To instill a feeling of freedom based upon the premise that everyone can write, every stumbling block to free creative activity, every restraint, every fear, every insecurity has to be broken down. Inspiration is the initial step. The result of this positive approach, assuring students that they can write, is now on record in the following analysis of selected pieces composed, arranged, and orchestrated by senior high school students who were completely inexperienced, average youngsters. Every piece is analyzed in detail. Each can be an inspiration, a motivation and a model for the student who, for a long time, may have had strong desires to compose, but whose fears have been a hindrance.

171

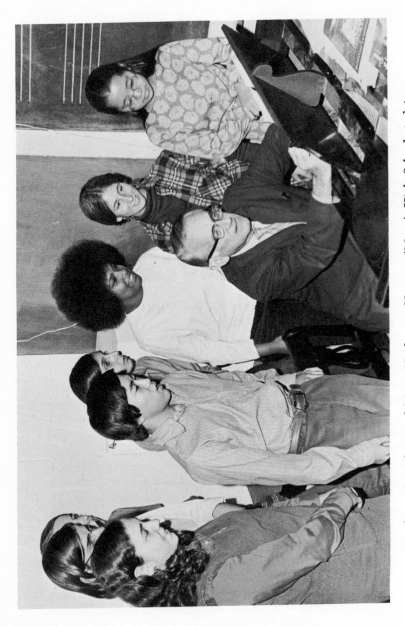

Members of a Theory of Music II class at Newton (Mass.) High School studying a composition by one of the students. The informal grouping of the class, with the author seated at the piano, contributes to an atmosphere conducive to objective analysis by everyone involved.

Dissipate those fears, and the student will feel free to write anything.

The first section contains pieces for madrigal singers and one piece arranged for mixed voices and woodwind, horn, harp and timpani. The second section comprises instrumental pieces, arranged for small chamber instrumental groups and symphony orchestra. All were performed by student musicians. Fortunately at Newton High School, the diversity of voices and instruments made it possible for the student composers to select whatever combinations they considered feasible for their pieces. These instrumentals are arranged according to style rather than academic grade.

Ne'er to Part

Linda Fisher

Sop. I re-call the day you left so long a-go.

Alto Ah — Ah —

Ten. Ah — Ah Ah

Bass

It was mid Sep-tem-ber and the sun was sink-ing low.

Ah — Ah —

Ah — Ah Ah

Here I am so all a-lone won-der-ing why.

Ah — Ah —

Ah — Ah Ah

175

lon - ger shine, my heart no long - er sings. When my love re -

turns to me ne'er more to part. Au - tumn's wind will

cease to blow, joy will fill my heart, la la la la la

177

178

la la la la la la la la la la la la la la

voom _____ voom ____ V

rit.

I I

A ♩ = 72

Peace - ful night creeps o'er the land, set - ting me free.

Ah _____ Ah _____

Ah _____ Ah Ah

While I wait for love to come, come back to me. You

Ah _____ Ah_____

Ah _____ Ah Ah

NE'ER TO PART   Linda Fisher, Grade 12

This is a romantic madrigal for SATB written in a 19th century style. Robert Dumm described it in *The Christian Science Monitor* as:

> . . . the sadness of distractable youth which changed to joy midway with hardly a turning light.*

A feeling of sadness is immediately established in the text. A young man reminisces about his loved one on the day of departure; after the brightness of summer, autumn is setting in and the sun is sinking, add-

---

* From a review by Robert Dumm in *The Christian Science Monitor,* June 2, 1961. Used by permission.

ing to the shadows. In spite of the loneliness, he feels optimistic about the eternity of his love, a perfect love because it comes from heaven, and he is confident that it will never leave him again.

In the text, rhyme occurs at the ends of lines 1 and 2, and lines 3 and 4 of each stanza. Musically, the form of the song is rondo, with the plan A, A', B, B, A, A', C, C', A, A'. A and A' each indicates a complete musical sentence of eight measures, each divided into two 4-measure phrases (fore-phrase and after-phrase).

The first motif of A, introduced in the fore-phrase:

EXAMPLE VI-1

I   re - call the day you left

consists of a series of ascending and descending eighth notes. This is followed by the second motif:

EXAMPLE VI-2

So   long a   go

which is less active and comes to a resting point at the cadence in measure 4. The after-phrase is similar to the fore-phrase except for the third measure, which is at a point melodically higher than the corresponding one (measure 2) of the fore-phrase. The material in the next eight measures, marked A', is similar to the first eight measures except that a climactic point is maintained which descends to cadence in measure 16. These two phrases form the A portion of the piece.

The B section, beginning in measure 17, contains a syncopated motif:

EXAMPLE VI-3

For   the night   comes nigh to

which gives rhythmic spice and contrast to the squareness of previous material. The motif predominates in the first two measures of both the fore- and after-phrase of B, while a whole note on the last two measures of the two phrases serves as an intermediate contrast. At two points, this syncopation reaches a climax at the authentic cadence in measures 23 and 31. After repeating A and A', a new section is introduced, C and C', beginning in measure 49. In both fore- and after-phrase, the composer alternates these two rhythmic motifs:

EXAMPLE VI-4

Measure 57 of the after-phrase reaches a climactic height, followed by a cadential pause. In C', measure 59, the dotted eighth and sixteenth rhythm predominates. With its final return to A and A', the piece completes the rondo form.

Let us examine the melodic line of the fore-phrase in both A and A' in terms of structure and harmonic treatment. Based on the F-minor triad, the soprano melody, supported by sustained harmony in the lower three parts all singing "Ahs," rises and falls in the first two measures, its arpeggio character interrupted by a B-flat passing tone. The next two measures begin with descending notes of a C-minor arpeggio, then rise up and resolve by step to the tonic. The minor dominant triad definitely places the tonality in the Aeolian mode, the natural minor scale so characteristic of folk songs. While the cadential point is being sustained, eighth notes in the bass imitate the motif of the soprano by inversion. Measures 7 and 8 of the after-phrase contrast to measures 3 and 4 of the fore-phrase through inversion. The notes ascend and descend, suggesting the arpeggio of the minor dominant 7th chord, and resolve finally to the tonic. At the cadence, the expected pause requires no imitative activity in the bass. The following diagram compares the four measures:

EXAMPLE VI-5

So long a - go   sun was sink -ing low

The result of this contrast is melodic interest. How boring it would have been had these measures repeated each other! In section A′, A is repeated except for the last three measures, where a climax is followed by a descent of the minor dominant 7th arpeggio, resolving to the tonic. In this way, more variety is obtained. Whenever the material is melodically the same in two 8-measure sentences, variations at the end of the second section are advisable; exact repetitions cause loss of interest. Repetition does contribute to unity, but variety is necessary not only for contrast, but also to enhance earlier material when it is repeated. Throughout section A′, the sustained harmonic character of the alto, tenor, and bass parts is quite evident.

Using this analysis for a foundation, evaluate the next 8-measure sentence, where repetitions and variations are easily detected. Certain special features ought to be pointed out. For example, in the fore-phrase, in measures 17 and 18, the soprano in subdominant harmony is imitated by the tenors in the next two measures by tonic harmony. Yet the notes are exactly the same. In measure 17, the note "C" in the soprano part, which feels as though it could be a passing tone to D-flat, is interrupted by the cambiata E-flat, creating a pleasant dissonance. The "C" eventually functions as a legitimate passing tone at the end of measure 18. In measure 19, the B-flat in the beginning of the tenor part is an upward suspension to the note "C." The E-flat may be considered the 7th of the tonic, returning by passing tone D-flat to "C." Then comes a B-flat, anticipating the note B-flat in the next measure.

In the after-phrase, the sopranos again have a slight variation in the second measure leading up to the tonic, at which point the basses imitate in inversion, using the note D-flat as a passing tone. B is repeated, leading to plagal cadence. Throughout both B's, except for imitations of the sopranos by tenors and basses, the sustained character of the harmony is maintained. The return to section A follows.

A completely new theme appears in A-flat major, section C:

EXAMPLE VI-6

la   la la   la la   la   la la   la

a contrast to the hitherto Aeolian mode. This theme is introduced in measure 49 through a drone bass sung by tenors on the dominant and basses on the tonic. The drone bass persists throughout, while sopranos and altos sing a joyful, carefree, and frolicking melody to appropriate "la, la, la's" in the text. In this way, the optimistic message is conveyed. The contrary motion between soprano and alto is most effective. The unisons and cross parts lead eventually to a cadence on the after-phrase in measure 58, giving the impression that more is to come.

This expectancy is realized in the next sentence, C'. Here, fore-phrase sopranos are answered in the after-phrase by altos who, at the end, make slight changes in notes for cadential purposes. Excitement is created throughout C and C' by combining occasional passing tones with the dissonance created by the tonic pedal point when the dominant harmony is heard above. A final return in measure 67 to section A follows with slight variations in thematic material. Throughout, the harmonic voicing is in closed form, except where the soprano reaches a height justifying open form. The tenor part is written in the treble clef with the understanding that it be read and performed an octave lower.

The following are the significant aspects of this madrigal:

1. Provides an excellent opportunity for expounding personal philosophy or observations about nature and the world by creating an original text
2. Rhyming of consecutive lines
3. Musically, fine example of the rondo form with: unity achieved by repetition; variation by inversion as well as by new material
4. Sadness of text expressed by melodic line and Aeolian mode; with change to A-flat major, happy optimism recorded melodically through a brisk freshness with vibrant and vivid rhythm; throughout, interesting wave-like motion of themes, indicative of good melodic writing
5. Folk song quality maintained by use of the tonic, dominant minor, and subdominant triads; creation of attention, contrast, and dissonance by use of drone bass in section C below the playful melody of sopranos and altos in counterpoint; throughout sections A and B, maintenance of the sustained character of the harmony by voices supporting the sopranos, except for occasional imitations in section B
6. Creation of excitement and interest by closing the rhythmic gaps in a voice by imitating previous material (as in theme A) and imitations between parts (as in theme B)
7. Use of passing and auxiliary tones, cambiatas, upward suspensions, anticipations, and appoggiaturas to create dissonance

8. Normal voice ranges, although the soprano is a little extensive ("C" to "F," an interval of an octave and a perfect 4th)

9. Contrast between sad and happy themes through proper dynamics and appropriate interpretation

The Land of Counterpane

Words by Robert Louis Stevenson
Music by Dottie Case

THE LAND OF COUNTERPANE   Dottie Case, Grade II

Dottie's song cycle of Robert Louis Stevenson's *A Child's Garden of Verses* is an accomplishment worthy of study. Of the six poems by Stevenson to which she composed music, one, "The Land of Counterpane," will be discussed. In "The Land of Counterpane," a sick child's imagination is extended into areas of fascination and fantasy. The music is appropriately and vividly adapted, depicting the nature and

content of the piece. The vocal resources of the SATB choir, for which the song has been arranged, are explored in every respect for musical variety, dramatic interest, harmonic and contrapuntal treatment, and adherence to the principles of good voice leading. In this type of piece containing odd intervals and dissonance, demands on the sensitivity and perceptivity of the ear are great. Care must be taken in achieving

voice leading, which is not too unorthodox and which still offers challenge.

The piano functions as accompaniment, harmonically and contrapuntally, and is coordinated with the voices to set the character and
mood. Throughout the piece, influences of twentieth century techniques
are quite evident.

Rhyme occurs between lines 1 and 2, and 3 and 4 of each stanza.
Musically, the piece is very free in form; each stanza is associated with
a different musical theme. The results are a rather unusual A, B, C, C′,
D, coda series, similar to the durchkomponiert or narrative type song.

The moderately-paced A section contains a musical sentence of
six measures. The fore-phrase consists of three measures, a rather unusual structure. The first motif:

EXAMPLE VI-7

When I   was sick   and

appears in the first two measures as a half-phrase. The second motif:

EXAMPLE VI-8

had two pil-lows at   my head

is self-contained in the third measure. It ends on a half-cadence, which
is in character harmonically with the piece.

In the after-phrase, which parallels the fore-phrase, the melodic
material is varied, achieving both unity and variety. It ends on a tonic
authentic imperfect cadence (measure 6) in A minor, which fundamentally is the tonality of this section. Notice that the rhythm signature
in this measure changes to $\frac{5}{4}$ to allow a feeling of complete pause before
B begins with its anacrusis or up-beat.

All the musical material for the A section is concerted, the SATB
chorus being duplicated in the piano accompaniment. The chordal
character seems to assert the dispelling of illness by the happiness
which toys can bring.

Harmonically, the section begins conventionally with an A-minor
7th chord in the third inversion, but immediately the next chord is V
with major 7th. The A-minor 7th returns, only to be followed by the

V $^7_{5b}$ resolving deceptively to IV in second inversion. From here on, the harmonies involve chords of addition in which 2nds, 4ths, 6ths, and 9ths increase the color element; altered chords as well as a quartal element converge to the cadence in A-minor. Because the chordal structure is in blocks, foreign tones are obviously absent.

In the B section in measure 7, the musical sentence of eight measures seems to have neither half- nor authentic cadence. The motif:

EXAMPLE VI-9

Some - times   for   an

is the basis of the entire sentence which is indeed a viably active one.

The fore-phrase consists of 3¾ measures, 7–10, while in the after-phrase, measures 10–14, the material differs slightly rhythmically, achieving unity and variety. At a faster tempo, the basses and tenors hold forth in unison with the piano duplicating them in the left hand, while the right hand punctuates harmonies built on intervals of perfect and augmented 4ths. A series of major and minor triads follow, all creating a polytonal situation. The B section begins in A-minor, staying in A-minor only briefly at which time the melody begins to wander involving chromatics, which vividly depict the movement of soldiers. Again, because of the polytonal character of this section, foreign tones are in the minority.

A feeling of cadence in A-minor is reached at the beginning of the C section in measure 15. The C section contains a sentence of eight measures followed by the C′ section, also eight measures.

This ¾ faster flowing portion, which covers the gamut of activity on sea and land, as expressed by the text, has as its motif:

EXAMPLE VI-10

And   some - times   sent   my

which is constantly being explored for unity. The motif starts in A-minor with excursions in consecutive measures through a multiplicity of keys, as indicated, for variety. The sopranos and altos combine in a duet as a contrast to the previous tenor and bass unisons. Orthodox key progressions are visible to the eye. However, the key situation changes

when the piano is engaged in accompaniment. The right hand duplicates the vocal parts; the left hand contributes to the metamorphosis of
keys by employing an active moving octave bass line both diatonically
and chromatically. Passing tones, appoggiaturas, and auxiliaries are
recognizable. Because of the juxtaposition of the many keys, analysis
of both harmonic structure and foreign tones is relative. It may be well
not to be too concerned about these matters, but to merely appreciate
the music in continuity. The ideas are the important issues. Execution
of the ideas harmonically and non-harmonically becomes easier with
more experience. The combination of voices and bass line creates an
expanded tonality causing tension and vitality. A surprise cadence in
A-sharp minor in measure 30 concludes this portion only to be followed
by A-minor which begins the final D portion.

    This majestic section of an 8-measure sentence has a 4-measure
fore-phrase whose motif:

EXAMPLE VI-11

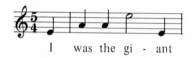

I   was the gi - ant

pervades the entire sentence for unity. The pattern of unison of the
four parts as well as harmony in four parts appears in $\frac{5}{4}$ and $\frac{4}{4}$ rhythm
alternately for variety, as the voices majestically proclaim the personi-
fication of strength and fortitude. The tonality of A-minor with interruptions of suggestions of A-major is general with occasional alterations
in some of the harmonies. Notice particularly the series of chords in
block formation with their surprise color elements. The section ends in
measure 38 in A-major with addition of the major 7th and 6th. This
figure continues in the piano part and is developed sequentially for
four measures becoming a coda. The chords used contain added color
tones, especially major 7ths. Foreign tones are at a minimum, since
primarily this music contains arpeggios and block chords.

    The following items are of particular interest:

1. Valid interpretation achieved by: setting the text of the poem to appropriate music, vocally and instrumentally; good voice leading
especially under circumstances of prevailing dissonance; piano accompaniment for harmonic support, for effecting rhythmic pulsations, for
supplying counterpoint, for enhancing the vocal message; commendable use of voices in four parts, unison, and duet

2. Standard rhyme
3. Unusual narrative form of themes arranged consecutively, A, B, C, D
4. Conventional phraseology with the exception of the 3-measure phrase in A
5. Evidence of unity, variety, and coherence
6. Obvious use of twentieth century influences: block chord structure with color tones added; altered chords; quartal element; polytonality; chromatics; expanded tonality
7. Absorption of obvious foreign tones within the harmonic structure
8. Conservative range of all parts
9. Melodic wave of each part
10. Changes in meter and tempo
11. Proper interpretation with observation of dynamics

Shout Unto the Lord – Psalm 98

Debby Rothstein

194

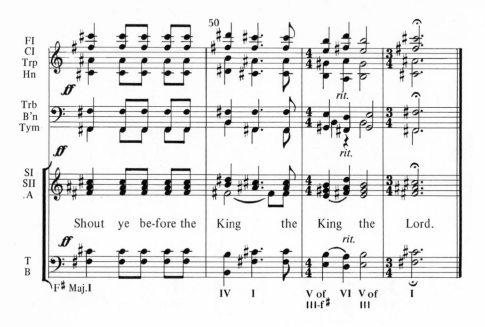

SHOUT UNTO THE LORD – PSALM 98   Debby Rothstein, Grade 10

Music played an important part in the religious worship of the ancient Israelites. Voices and instruments of various sorts were used in the Temple as an important adjunct to the service. Composer Debby, following the example of many of the great composers, past and present, who have reaped a harvest of inspiration for their choral music from the Bible, selected the second stanza of Psalm 98. She set this stirring text to appropriately stirring music, harmonized for mixed chorus of

1st and 2nd sopranos, altos, tenors, and basses, for wind ensemble consisting of flute, clarinet, bassoon, trumpet, horn, and trombone, and for harp and timpani.

Because of its dramatic quality, the piece could be used as an accompaniment to the action and dialogue of a biblical play, film, or theatrical production.

Debby has gone beyond the confines of the practices used in the music of the ancient Israelites. In those days harmony was unknown. Music was all monophonic. Female voices were not employed except in occasions other than religious ceremonies. Musical instruments were primitive compared to those used today. Debby's piece is primarily homophonic with a little polyphony. It requires female voices as well as the modern day instruments whose ancestral counterparts are mentioned in the Scriptures. For example, in Daniel III reference is made to the cornet, flute, harp, sackbut (ancestor of the modern trombone), psaltery, and dulcimer. In Psalm 8, mention is made of the sound of the timbrel (a small drum), of the sweet harp with the psaltery, of the blowing of the horn at the new moon. The importance of vocal and instrumental music in biblical times to glorify and magnify the Lord, His power and love is also found in: the singing of praises to the Lord with an instrument of ten strings and the psaltery, Psalm 92; the singing of praises to God with the harp, with trumpets and the sound of the horn, Psalm 98; praising the Lord in the dance, with the timbrel and the harp, Psalm 149; praising God with the psaltery, the harp, the timbrel, string instruments and the pipe, and with loud sounding and clanging cymbals, Psalm 150; and, finally, Samuel VI, 5 where it is stated that "David and all the house of Israel played before the Lord on all manner of instruments made of fir wood, even on harps, and on psalteries, and on timbrels, and on sistrums and on cymbals."

The text is narrative and without rhyme. Musically, the structure consists of 4-measure phrases. The entire piece is in unitary form and contains two fundamental motifs. The first is:

EXAMPLE VI-12

in measures 1 and 2 followed by the second:

EXAMPLE VI-13

in measures 3 and 4. Both of these are fully explored throughout the piece, each appearing either literally exact or with modification of pitch and harmony (adhering to the rhythmic patterns), or with variations of rhythm and pitch along with a constant metamorphosis of tonalities.

The first motif, as it appears in the first fore-phrase, is somewhat static melodically but redeems itself with its moving ♩♩. ♪ rhythm. As a contrast, the second motif, also somewhat static, has a smooth rhythmic flow of even quarter notes. In the after-phrase, motif 1 is presented in variation rhythmically for 2 measures, while no change appears in motif 2. The next 4-measure fore-phrase, 9 through 12, finds the motifs rhythmically as they were in the original. In the after-phrase, the second motif in measures 15 and 16 is varied with the pattern ♩ ♩ , but a high climactic point is reached on the cadence in measure 16. Motif 2 continues with the same variation pattern in the next phrase (measure 17) interrupted by a variation of motif 1 in measure 18 leading to cadence in measure 20. Returning to the original level in the next two 8-measure sentences (21 through 36), motif 2, employing the same rhythmic variation, is quite predominant and climbs slightly to a moderately high point. From measure 37 through 40, starting at a higher point, motif 1 persists in its original rhythmic form. At its cadence in measure 40, motif 2, slightly varied with the pattern in reverse ♩ ♩ , continues into the next phrase at a lower level, varied multiply and interrupted once by motif 1 in measure 43. Finally in measure 45, the first fore-phrase, consisting of the first two motifs in their original form, reappears. This is followed by a repetition, in the last 4-measure phrase, made rhythmically exciting by a slight variation of motif 1 in measure 49. The piece ends on the authentic cadence in measure 52.

Unity is achieved by the reiterations of these motifs; variety, by their diversifications and modifications.

The metamorphosis of tonalities creates an atmosphere of surprise, invigoration, and renewal. Sudden modulations shift to tonalities that appear remote, but are accepted as correct according to twentieth century procedures, which relax the restrictions of conventional tonal writing.

The keys at the beginning of each of the first five 4-measure phrases (1 through 20) differ from the keys at their cadences. The keys of the next two 8-measure sentences (21 through 36) begin and end the same, as does the next 4-measure phrase (37 through 40). In the next two 4-measure phrases, the keys at the beginning differ from those at their cadences. In the final 4-measure phrase, the key begins and ends the same.

Free of dissonance, the piece nevertheless has a contemporary feeling because of the unexpected harmonic progressions. For example, in the second and third measures, the roots of the major chords proceed in parallel motion and progress by major seconds. In measures 9 through 11, the roots of the major chords do likewise in thirds, first a major third, then a minor third. Between measures 13 and 14, a piquant cross relation, D-sharp and D-natural, adds a spicy and zestful flavor. In measure 19, the triad on "D," the lowered 7th degree of the key of E, minus its third, suggests the Mixolydian mode. In measure 34, the use of the dominant minor triad on "D" again suggests the Mixolydian mode.

The incorporation of secondary dominant chords and the interchange of parallel major and minor keys inject added color. For example, in measure 3, second beat, the chord is V of VI in the key of B minor, parallel to B-major. Other similar situations are indicated in the score.

This contemporary sound is made more colorful by the scoring of the wind band which plays in antiphonal treatment with the voices. (This is reminiscent of the sixteenth century Venetian school of music as instituted by Willaert and developed by Gabrieli; the chiaroscuro style of dark and light, paralleling the Titian school of painting, was incorporated into their music.) The harp continually supports the vocal forces wherever the harmonies change. In several places, the entire wind band is not used. In measures 21 through 26, bassoon with timpani punctuations reinforce the voices of the basses. From measure 29 through 36, the bassoon and timpani are joined by a moving counterpoint assigned to the flute. Again, from measure 41 through 44, the bassoon punctuates as before. Concerted harmonies in vertical arrangement predominate throughout.

These scoring changes are good for they offer a relief from what could become a tiring stereotyped format, and the tutti wind band which follows is enhanced after their silences.

The scoring for the winds and voices is consistently open in order to give breadth. The range of each vocal part is less than an octave except for the basses which cover an interval of a major 9th.

Foreign tones are necessarily absent because of the prevailing consonant harmony. Several passing and auxiliary tones occur in the flute counterpoint.

Because this piece combines both choral and instrumental forces, it offers unique procedures and avenues of approach:

1. Function of music to glorify and praise God
2. Use of unitary form in which the 4-measure phrase is basic

3. Repetition of motifs to achieve unity, and the diversification of motifs to obtain variety

4. Unexpected harmonic progressions and modulations, assimilating the 16th century Venetian school style with contemporary style

5. Antiphonal treatment between wind band and voices, both scored in open concerted vertical harmonies

6. Absence of foreign tones because of the consonant harmonic structure

7. General normality of the range of each voice contributing to facility in performance, except in flute counterpoint

8. Inspirational quality of the music and good choral and instrumental scoring in which dynamics and flexibility of tempos are at the discretion of the conductor—all conducive to proper and gratifying interpretation

Chorale with Theme and Variations

David Jodrey

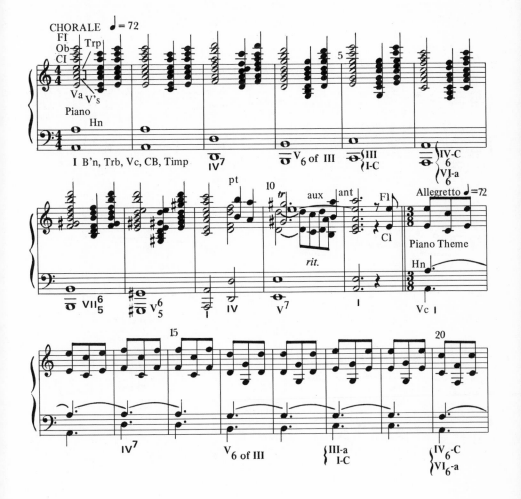

201

206

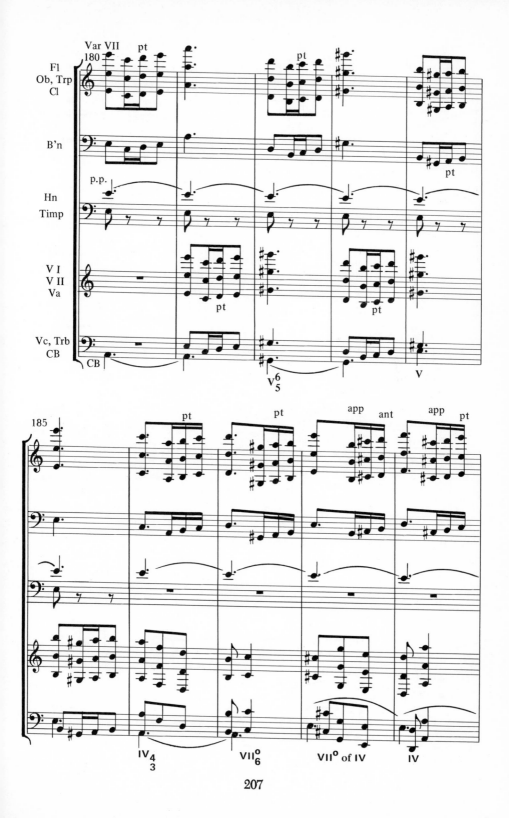

207

209

CHORALE WITH THEME AND VARIATIONS   David Jodrey, Grade 10

Robert Dumm of *The Christian Science Monitor* wrote as follows concerning David Jodrey's composition:

> Chorale with Theme and Variations in D minor (the Baroque reminder) managed rich color variety within a repeated harmonic frame.*

Stylistically, this piece, orchestrated for flute, oboe, clarinet, bassoon, horn, trumpet, trombone, piano, timpani, and strings is reminiscent of early 18th century music. It begins and ends with a chorale of impressive grandeur. The main body of the piece is a theme with variations.

In the chorale marked adagio in $\frac{4}{4}$, the motif:

EXAMPLE VI-14

is stated, repeated, and successively transposed until the authentic cadence is reached in measure 11. The melody range is limited, but this is compensated for by the flowing harmonic progressions. In measure 5, the relative major key is heard temporarily, after which the tonality of A-minor is definite, concluding the chorale in a dignified manner. Instrumentally, the tutti is most moving and majestic. Upper woodwinds and trumpet are treated in concerted harmony, giving brilliance and color. They are duplicated in the lower octave by the strings. The horn, bassoon, trombone, celli, basses, and timpani in unison produce notes basic to these harmonies as support.

Without any fanfare, the motif of the main theme in $\frac{3}{8}$ in measure 12:

EXAMPLE VI-15

appears pulsating without respite for sixteen measures through a series of transpositions. This motif is fundamentally related to and

---

* From a review by Robert Dumm in *The Christian Science Monitor*, June 2, 1961. Used by permission.

based upon the chorale theme harmonically and melodically. The fore-phrase of eight measures ends on an imperfect tonic cadence in C-major, while the after-phrase of eight measures ends on a perfect tonic cadence in A-minor. Beginning in measure 28, the motif develops in an ascending sequence for a 6-measure phrase extension. The next nine measures, beginning in measure 34, form a codetta divided into three groups of 3-measure phrases. The second group rises to climax in measure 38, descending into an authentic cadence in measures 41 and 42. The first note of each measure delineates the outline of the melodic line. Keeping this in mind will make the entire section more intelligible. Flute and clarinet in octaves bear the responsibility of the melody supported by horn and celli sustaining the harmony. All instruments are reinforced by the piano.

In the first variation, measure 43 with the following motif:

EXAMPLE VI-16

the phraseology is traditional with the 8-measure fore-phrase and the 8-measure after-phrase. The former begins in A-minor, modulates to the relative major in measure 46, but returns to A-minor with cadence in measure 50. The melodic line in the soprano voice corresponds to that of the original theme except that there are half as many measures. The after-phrase, beginning in measure 51, becomes more vigorous in both downward and upward squences based on the dominant harmony throughout. The melody takes many liberties.

In this variation, the upper woods and violins have the melody with bassoon and celli in unison on the triplet motif accompaniment with harmonic support in the basses. In measure 54, an exchange of material occurs when: the upper woodwinds are assigned the triplet motif; the violins take the melody; the basses sustain a pedal point; bassoon and celli add to the harmonic support.

The motif of the second variation:

EXAMPLE VI-17

is presented in measure 59. The treatment becomes more ambitious, involving chromatics, the use of a tonic and submediant chord in the

parallel major key in measures 65 and 66, a modulation to G-major in measure 70, a return to A-minor in measure 77.

The first phrase consists of twelve measures. The motif repeats itself, as it is gradually sequenced downward. With each transposition, the harmony changes. The next phrase of seven measures, beginning in measure 71, is characterized by continuous downward sequence generally without repeats. Notice the chromatic bass line, which creates an atmosphere of apprehensive endlessness dispelled finally by the re-establishment of the tonality of A-minor in measure 77. Now comes an 8-measure phrase characterized by an expansive treatment of diatonic motion upward and downward. This brings about a feeling of abandon and relief after the previously tension-packed passage. First, a 2-measure section ascends by scale. This is answered by a section of two more measures—the first down, the second up—which is freely sequenced downward for four more measures. The remaining six measures act as a codetta, concluding the variation on the authentic cadence in measure 91. Melodically, this variation would become more understandable if the first note of each measure were used in continuity. Strings perform in concerted harmony throughout the variation, supported by celli and basses.

In measure 92, the motif of the third variation:

EXAMPLE VI-18

appears. The structure involves four 6-measure phrases and a concluding 5-measure phrase. In the first 24 measures, the accompanying motif establishes a new pattern in which the eighth rest assumes rhythmic significance. Guided by the harmonic structure in the first 6-measure phrase, the melodic line of the motif progresses downward by sequence. The interval of a third plays an important part with each 2-measure section. In the next phrase beginning in measure 98, the sequential idea continues downward. The interval of an ascending second is important with each 2-measure section. The third phrase in measure 104 embraces a step-wise upward motion of the melody. It is followed by the next phrase in measure 110 which is a repetition melodically and harmonically of the first phrase. A 5-measure phrase leading to cadence in measure 120 completes the variation. The melodic line of the accompaniment motif in many places reinforces the principal melody of the variation. From the beginning of the variation, strings punctuate chords pizzicato providing a subtly-brittle background for the piano solo, while horn sustains basic harmony notes. In the last six measures, strings resume arco.

In measure 121, the fourth variation begins with the motif:

EXAMPLE VI-19

At first the motif appears to be phraseologically orthodox, but suddenly it changes its course. Two phrases of four measures each, one of three, one of eight, and finally one of two comprise the structure. The motif starts out boldly in the temporary key of G-minor which surrenders to D- and A-minors. The triplet motif keeps persisting. In the first 4-measure phrase, it is treated again in sequence with the interval of the third predominating as before. On the next phrase in measure 125, the expected procedure does not occur. Instead of continuing up by step to the note "C," the motif assumes a lower level on "E." For the next two phrases (4 + 3 measures), the motif frolics about sequentially. Throughout the following 8-measure phrase, the motif, which up until now has been generally step-wise with occasional skips, enters upon a leaping pattern, engaging very effective appoggiaturas in upward sequences. At the highest climactic point in measure 140, the motif descends on a 2-measure phrase to cadence in measure 142. To discern the melodic line, use the same procedure as used with the theme and with variations 2 and 3.

The motif throughout is given to flute and clarinet in unison with harmony supplied by bassoon, horn, and celli.

The cadence of variation 4 becomes the beginning of variation 5 in which there are two 4-measure phrases, one 7-measure phrase, and, finally, a 4-measure phrase.

The motif in the lower part:

EXAMPLE VI-20

announces itself in a 2-measure upward scale passage developing in sequence through measure 151. Then, the motif reverses by skips and diatonic progression for four measures. In the final five measures, it becomes stagnant in a sustaining capacity. Meanwhile, the soprano for the first four measures at the beginning of variation 5 engages in the upper motif:

EXAMPLE VI-21

which is a syncopated melodic variation freely related to the original. Its directional pattern is changed on the following 4-measure phrase. A mixture of the two treatments occupies the next seven measures. Cadence is approached within the last four measures. The soprano takes over the scale passage originally presented by the lower part. The variation ends in the unexpected key of D-minor. Instrumentally, the variation begins with oboe and violins, which join forces in octave unisons with flute and clarinet on the syncopated theme. The bassoon and celli produce the triplet accompaniment with harmonic support by the basses.

The sixth variation is structured into three phrases, eight measures in the first, three in the second, eight in the third. In measure 161, the variation begins in D-minor, but it would be more advisable to think of it as the sub-dominant chord in A-minor, since this tonality is now restored:

EXAMPLE VI-22

The relative major, which has been utilized in the fundamental harmonic structure established in the beginning, is also evident. It had been obviously absent in the previous two variations. The primary instrument in this variation is the piano, which functions again in the solo capacity. Accompanying it is a solo violin, which offers a sensitive counterpoint appropriate to the character of the solo material.

The final seventh variation in measure 180 has a bold, fearless, audacious motif:

EXAMPLE VI-23

which seems to predict the approaching finale. The rhythm is impelling. In the first 6-measure phrase, it is treated sequentially in imitation between woods and strings with trombone. From measures 186 through 200, the motif becomes more forceful by adopting a fresher and more animated rhythmic thrust. In measures 186 through 189, it is developed in sequence generally in an upward motion. The melodic pattern changes for the next ten measures, 190 through 199. During these measures, it continues its development in sequences, down for four measures, up for the next four. Then there is a leap upward followed by a downward sequence for three measures. Then one measure, diatonically going downward, leads to cadence. After the imitation in the first six measures, the strings and trombone take on the triplet rhythm of the original motif along with a syncopated figure in antithesis to the syncopated figure of the upper voice in variation 5. This is an excellent example of unity and variety. However, the triplet figure seems to dominate most of the section.

Consistent with the character of this final variation, an orchestra tutti in all its glory signifies the inevitable climax. The antiphonal treatment of woodwinds and trumpet as against strings and trombone for the first six measures is most effective and colorful, all in octave relationships. As the section progresses, the forces indicated above carry on their respective mission, the thematic motif given to woodwinds and trumpet, the accompaniment given to strings and trombone. Throughout, the horn sustains a pedal point, which the basses eventually double after having supplied harmonic support in the first eight measures.

Beginning in measure 203, the second chorale in $\frac{3}{4}$ completes the piece. Its fore-phrase consists of two motifs:

EXAMPLE VI-24

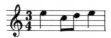

EXAMPLE VI-25

They appear successively in the first two measures. Notice the resemblance of motif 1 to the motif of variation 7. Both motifs are then transposed in the next two measures. The after-phrase is an outgrowth of the fore-phrase material leading to the final cadence.

A magnificent orchestral tutti again is displayed in this chorale. Concerted melodically and harmonically, it adds considerably to the angelic message.

The following observations about the piece are most pertinent:

1. Written in the baroque style
2. Theme and variations all in triple meter bounded by two chorales each in a different meter
3. Constructive principles achieved: unity by use of the triplet motif prevalent throughout the piece, developed through devices of transposition, sequence, imitation, and by relationship of motif to the first chorale, and relationship of variation 7 to the second chorale; variety by the seven variations of the theme, by the change of direction relative to the continuity of the motif, by the rhythmic variation and syncopation of the motifs; coherence by the common bond inherent in each variation as well as in the chorales
4. Unusual phraseology where the use of the 4-measure phrase is relaxed resulting in odd numbers of measures in the various sections
5. Harmony generally orthodox incorporating various secondary dominant chords, which increase color and interest and allow for temporary modulations; variety of foreign tones such as auxiliaries, passing tones, appoggiaturas, anticipations, a suspension, cambiatas and a free tone
7. Discreet choice of instruments for solo, ensemble, and tutti passages; concerted harmonic treatments and contrapuntal devices paralleling those of early 18th century
8. Opportunities for proper interpretation available even though dynamics not included to conform with baroque practices; nature of lines with their high and low points creating interesting melodic curves

Duet for Flutes

Christine Olton

219

DUET FOR FLUTES   Christine Olton, Grade II

The late Cyrus Durgin, Music critic of the *Boston Globe,* wrote rather
glowingly about the "Duet for Flutes" by Christine:

> For sheer ingenuity, this piece was remarkable because in writ-
> ing for just two instrumental voices with the comparatively
> limited technical resources and tone color of a pair of flutes,
> there is not too much one can do. But Christine figured how to
> produce variety and a degree of contrast.*

How true all this is. When composing and orchestrating for a
limited number of instruments, especially when the possibilities for
instrumental contrast in timbre are at a minimum, the composer must

* From a review by Cyrus Durgin in the *Boston Globe,* May 27, 1960. Used
by permission.

exercise his imagination and ingenuity all the more decisively. In this way, he can compensate for the lack of color contrasts to achieve his objective. Counterpoint plays an important and significant role especially in the case of two of the same instruments as we have here. With two separate melodic lines, each one equally important, the distinction between the instruments becomes that much more evident.

The style resembles that of the rococo period with its atmosphere of grace, courtliness, refinement, lucidity, elegance, and nobility. The piece's sensitivity, its moving melodic and contrapuntal lines, and the employment of trills so characteristic of the eighteenth century is reminiscent of François Couperin.

In form, it may be considered a free rondo, A,A′,B,B′, codetta (abridged A), C, interlude, A, codetta with variations and extensions.

From the outset, an andante 5-measure sentence is established with the fore-phrase of two measures in A-minor, harmonic form. It consists of a triplet motive and trill:

EXAMPLE VI-26

This is played by the first flute, while the second flute effects a simple quarter note counterpoint:

EXAMPLE VI-27

In the after-phrase of three measures, the natural and melodic ascending forms are used in antiphonal treatment between the two flutes with eighth notes predominating. Notice the feminine ending on the cadence.

In the next four measures, beginning in measure 6, both instruments reverse themselves, followed by an extension of four measures.

The B theme, beginning in measure 14 in E-minor, consists of an 8-measure sentence subdivided into 3 + 5 measures. The principal motif appears in the first three measures:

EXAMPLE VI-28

They are simply constructed rhythmically with a sustained note played by second flute. The next five measures take up the triplet motive of the A theme more ambitiously assigned to the two flutes in harmony. This is followed by the eighth note motif and the continued use of the harmonic form between the instruments.

At B' (measure 22), the triplets appear again with flutes reversed. A variation and extension follow using the material of the extension of A and the first motif of B inverted. This leads to a codetta in measure 30 of five measures using the original triplet motif, a reminiscence of A abridged.

At the allegro at C in measure 35, with a change of tempo, mood, and key (A parallel major), the motif:

EXAMPLE VI-29

is presented which grows into the subject of a fugue. It is presented by the first flute and answered by the second flute in an unorthodox way, since it remains in the tonic key. It enters on the third beat of measure 40 anticipating the expected entrance on the first beat of measure 41. In this way, shifted rhythm occurs creating excitement and interest, which is plainly evident as the first flute plays the countersubject:

EXAMPLE VI-30

Instead of the answer being six measures as was the original subject, it is extended to the 48th measure in the key of A parallel minor, followed immediately in measure 49 in the key of E-minor. The quarter notes used are related to the extensions of themes A and B'. Now the music becomes more exhilarated and more vibrant by using episodes in both flutes consisting of eighth notes in counterpoint. This culminates with sixteenth note runs leading to cadence in bar 58. At this point, material from the extension of B', which is derived from the extension of A, is played by the second flute and appears in the first flute through measure 63. Simultaneously, the second flute sustains a tonic pedal point. In measure 62, the harmony signifies I in E-major or V in A-major functioning as a pivot chord. C is then repeated in the key of A-major. The andante tempo returns as the cadence in measure 92 approaches. An interlude in measure 93 appears, made up of eleven measures of varied material. At first there is effective syncopation in the second flute, but only ephemerally. Then both flutes are involved in independent rhythmic lines introducing a little imitation leading to triplet material derived from A. Suddenly a new rhythmic motif enters in the form of quarter note triplets in measure 103, with both flutes concerted on the cadence in both parallel and contrary motion. Section A returns, measure 104, with the codetta in measure 117 slightly changed, possibly to effect a more determined conclusion.

The constructive principles are clearly delineated. Unity is apparent in the repetitions of themes. Especially obvious is the triplet motif of A, which appears in B and B′, in the codetta before C, in the following interlude, again in the recapitulation of A, and then in the final codetta. The quarter note motif of the extension of A appears in B and before the interlude. The contrasted nature of the various themes and the changes of keys effect ample variety. The manner in which the themes are developed and integrated makes for coherence.

Harmonically, the primary chords i, iv, and V and a minimum of the ii° chord are used exclusively. Modulations are clear and unobtrusive. The interest is increased by the use of foreign tones such as passing tones, suspensions, auxiliary tones, anticipations, appoggiaturas, echappées, as well as some quartal element in the codetta, pedal points, and changing tones.

All three motions, parallel, contrary, and oblique, are used discreetly, contributing to the melodic waves of the two voices.

In performance, interpretation involving contrast of dynamics between the two instruments is essential to do justice to the piece. At times, one instrument would have to be subdued to the other depending upon the importance of the material at that instant. At other times, both would have to play their roles equally.

The following are the important aspects of this piece:

1. Free rondo form
2. Perception necessary in writing effectively for a small group of instruments, especially for a duet of instruments in the same family, to achieve color contrast, contrapuntal and rhythmic interest
3. Technique of reversing instruments on repetition of material; use of antiphonal treatment, shifted rhythm and syncopation
4. Knowledge of a style, such as the rococo, and use of it consistently

requiring an understanding, objectivity, and appreciation, which can evolve only through education and experience

5. Unusual phraseology and extensions to help round out piece to avoid squareness and stereotyped treatment

6. Abundance of foreign tones to help spice up the conventional harmonies

7. Use of contrapuntal episodes in the C section to add to the interest and exuberance of the piece

Zwei Tänze

Donna Lawson

229

ZWEI TÄNZE   Donna Lawson, Grade 12

"Zwei Tänze" by Donna is succinctly described by Robert Dumm of
The Christian Science Monitor:

> They were there—Haydn's beat and Schubert's song—plus a
> linear sense which swept her past the usual four square phrases
> of that time.*

The piece is representative of the music of the late 18th and
early 19th centuries—the classical period with suggestions of the early
romantic period. The piece is in rondo form with the arrangement,
introduction, A, B, A, interlude, C with variations, A extended, coda.

The introduction, which was decided upon after the entire piece
was composed, is simplicity itself—a motif announced by clarinet,
which is then joined by the other woodwinds in octaves. A fermata,
then a luftpause, and the main theme of A, sprightly, animated, and
typically Haydnesque, are announced in measure 7.

The principal motif of the fore-phrase:

EXAMPLE VI-31

* From a review by Robert Dumm in *The Christian Science Monitor*, June
2, 1961. Used by permission.

constructed as an arpeggio, is followed by the secondary motif:

EXAMPLE VI-32

consisting of eighth notes diatonically.

Both are inverted in measures 9 and 10 respectively. In the after-phrase, an outgrowth of the secondary motif is treated in sequence for three measures. Observe a small but important detail in measure 13. Under the ordinary circumstances of sequence writing, it should have started with a "D." By starting with the "E," which leads to the "G," the climactic objective "A" in measure 14 is anticipated more successfully. In this measure, the phrase would have ordinarily ended, but the composer chose to extend the secondary motif four more measures leading to the tonic authentic cadence in measure 18. Examine measure 14, the second and third beats, through the first beat of 15. Compare this material with measure 16, which is a transposition lower. Notice how Donna skillfully treats the material not only in downward sequence, but also in shifted rhythm where the series of six eighth notes begins on the second beat of measure 14. In measure 15, they begin on the third beat. What rhythmic excitement this produces!

The entire A theme is played by first violins. Accompanying them are the other strings. Celli and basses in unison produce a percussive tonic pedal point on the first beat of each measure of the fore-phrase. Replying to them with double stops, outlining the harmonies on the second and third beats, are the second violins and violas. Three measures of sustained chords follow; then there is a return to the previous accompaniment for two measures. Finally, three measures of sustained chords end the sentence.

With the conclusion of the A section, which is repeated, new material, B, enters in measure 19. The first 4-measure fore-phrase consists of a syncopated motif:

EXAMPLE VI-33

followed by a transposition played by woodwinds in octaves, while the flute and horn sustain a dominant pedal point very effectively.

This is emphasized by off-beat punctuations in the lower strings and timpani. Through the use of the tie, the impression of $\frac{2}{4}$ and $\frac{4}{4}$ is created instead of $\frac{3}{4}$ throughout. What a glorious mixture of ingredients—the theme in syncopation, a pedal point sustained and simultaneously syncopated, with each ingredient effected by different choirs!

In the 4-measure after-phrase, celli pick up the melody, a variation of the motif, while the upper strings continue to punctuate syncopated chords concerted with basses and timpani on a tonic pedal point. At the same time, woodwinds and horn sustain the harmonies. Notice how the notes of the harmonies are distributed above and below the celli. B is then repeated followed by the return of A.

Starting in measure 39, a bridge of ten measures to the new C theme consists of a motif:

EXAMPLE VI-34

which is an outgrowth of the material of the last two measures of the B theme. It is played by flute, answered by clarinet using the material literally from the fifth and sixth measures of A in free inversion. The bassoon and celli in measures 43 and 44 then take up the motif of the bridge. They continue on for the next three measures with transpositions of the fifth and sixth measures of A, while the flute and clarinet in parallel tenths effect an interesting counterpoint. Involved before the cadence are a IV $^{6}_{3}$ $^{+}$ chord, a vii^{07} of V leading to the dominant half-cadence in measure 48. After a fermata, the new theme enters in measure 49 in the parallel minor key, slow, stately, dignified, almost in the manner of a pavane:

EXAMPLE VI-35

For 24 measures, the string orchestra, first violins on the melody, other strings on the harmony, exudes forth in an outburst of romantic utterance, espressivo and rubato, in contrast to the bright and gay sections which precede it. What a glorious change, these 24 measures! The motif is followed by an upward transposition, which in turn is transposed upward, but which results in an inversion leading to dominant half-cadence in measure 52. Its fore-phrase is balanced beautifully by its after-phrase, ending in authentic cadence in measure 56.

Now follows C', a development that is higher melodically, with harmony in open position mostly. In the fore-phrase are upward sequences, in the after-phrase are downward sequences. Notice how the theme soars, lifting to seemingly greater heights. The tension is relieved by the downward contrapuntal figure played by the second violins in measure 60. This is beautifully complemented in measure 64 on the V half-cadence by the violas answering the previous counterpoint of the second violins. The theme continues but descends into apparent resignation and submission, taking upon itself, in measure 69, the romantic utterance that resembles the very first two measures of C. Then it leads to tonic authentic cadence in measure 72. How well-integrated this whole section is—an 8-measure sentence followed by a 12-measure development, then a recapitulation of the very first statement modified. The melodic waves produced throughout can very well serve as an excellent example of good writing.

In measures 73–80, the oboe states a variation of the preceding theme, while the lower woods are in imitation and in harmony with one another. This imitation involves principally the eighth note motif of the variation, which is an outgrowth of the secondary motif of A. It is tossed around continuously among these lower woods. Throughout, the horn sustains an effective dominant pedal point.

Then in measure 81, the first violins take over the melodic responsibility of the variation, while the other strings toss the eighth note imitation around.

A most interesting phenomenon occurs in measure 87, where the beginning of the authentic cadence would be expected. Instead, the eighth note motif is developed through sequence for the next two measures, followed by a rhapsodic rhythmic treatment of the eighth notes. A high climactic point is reached, and then it descends to half-cadence in measure 94. This entire part may be divided into phrases of 6 + 8 measures—six being the theme, eight being the development. When the development begins, the woods gradually join the first violins on the melody, flute, clarinets, oboe, on harmony, while the bassoon, horn, and percussion join the lower strings in harmony. What a glittering and sparkling effect from the triangle supported by the vibrant timpani tremolo with a determined single crash of the cymbal at the climactic point in measure 91! To get the effect of a crescendo, adding instruments gradually is a standard technique.

The orchestration thins out as it approaches the dominant half-cadence in measure 94. This passage is a lesson in the coordination between orchestration and climactic development and its subsequent diminuendo.

In the next eight measures, the C theme is concluded by the oboe supported as before by its related instruments. Here again, the eighth note motif engages in frolicsome play, being tossed around antiphonally.

Throughout the C section, foreign tones of all varieties are used, as they are in previous sections. Especially effective as description are the suspensions that occur on the weak second beats of measures. Automatically, these beats become strong, because of the emphasis placed upon them by the suspensions. (Ordinarily suspensions should occur on the strong beats.) The dissonance is made more emphatic by the syncopation that results.

In measure 103, the A theme recurs, treated as before with strings. After measure 110, an extension begins, which reaches a climax in measure 113 in anticipation of the close of the piece. After the climax, a gradual descent leads to the tonic authentic cadence in measure 118.

In the coda in measure 119, material of the previous two measures is used and continues antiphonally between lower strings and flute. Then strings with a gradual addition of woods combine on the theme in unison with added counterpoint. Pizzicato chords and triangle conclude this piece in a very light and delicate manner similar to the daintiness associated with 18th century tradition.

The highlights of this composition are:

1. Combination of 18th century classical with 19th century romantic styles
2. Rondo form with introduction, development, and coda
3. Constructive principles achieved: unity by repetition of themes, by relationship of eighth note material of A to that used in the bridge, in the variation of C, and in the coda, and by the relationship of B material to material in bridge; variety by use of different themes, and by the variations in C; coherence by the common bonds in all the material
4. Phraseologically: prevalence of 4-measure phrases with extensions of phrases for more interest; incorporation of shifted rhythm
5. Harmonically: traditional, discreetly selected; use of parallel major and minor keys; prevalence of foreign tones such as passing tone, auxiliary, appoggiatura, cambiata, changing tone, anticipation, upward suspension, free tone, echappée, an abundance of standard

suspensions as well as pedal points, all creating dissonance; subtle counterpoint throughout

6. Development of motifs by inversion, transposition, and sequence

7. Select orchestration in all sections for transparency, dramatic purposes, antiphonal treatment, syncopated accompaniment

8. Interpretation easily achieved by adherence to tempo and dynamic requirements suggested by the material of the different sections and by the lyrical quality of the melodies

Episode No. I

Michael Bielski

238

239

241

EPISODE NO. I   Michael Bielski, Grade II

Michael orchestrated his Episode for one flute, oboe, clarinet, bassoon, horn, a pair of timpani, cymbals, and strings. Music critics McLaren Harris of the *Boston Herald* and Elliot Norton of the *Boston Record American* recorded the following remarks in their respective newspapers after a performance of Episode by the Boston Symphony Orchestra. Harris commented:

> Episode contained melodic charm and wit characteristic of Grieg, exhibited some understanding of some advanced theoretical practices.*

Norton wrote that the piece "is a commendably rich and mature work."

In this piece, a variety of moods and emotions is sensed. The themes are buoyant, frolicsome, melancholy and pulsating. In places there are tinges of oriental mystery as if Scheherazade were relating an adventure out of the Arabian Nights. The piece is in extended rondo form principally, with a bit of variation form. The plan is:

A, B, A, C, D, C, interlude

A, B', E, E', E, interlude, A, coda

The first violins, supported by the other strings with harmony generally in closed form, announce the buoyant material of A in F-major, with timpani support, which persists for eight measures. In measure 1 of the fore-phrase, the principal motif of the A theme:

EXAMPLE VI-36

is immediately followed by the secondary motif in measure 2:

EXAMPLE VI-37

---

* From a review by McLaren Harris in the *Boston Herald,* February 9, 1964. Used by permission.

Particularly interesting is the construction of these motifs rhythmically. In the fore-phrase, the dotted quarter and eighth rhythm of the first measure is reversed in the second measure as an eighth and a dotted quarter. The eighth notes of the second measure are heard in the third, but varied slightly. The dominant half-cadence occurs in measure 4. The after-phrase, which is a repetition of the fore-phrase, leads to the authentic cadence in measure 8.

The B theme appears in measure 9. It consists of a principal motif:

EXAMPLE VI-38

and a secondary motif:

EXAMPLE VI-39

For eight measures, also in F-major, the B theme is played by flute and bassoon in unison three octaves apart. A rather frolicsome atmosphere is created not only because of the nature of the theme, but also because of the extremity of the registers in which these colorful instruments are playing. In the odd measures, the notes have an element in common—exact repetition of both the rhythmic and melodic patterns. In the even measures, the rhythmic pattern is constant, made especially attractive by the sixteenth note flourishes, which, however, differ in motion. In measures 10 and 14, they ascend, while in 12 and 16 they descend by inversion, creating a rhythmic wave.

Accompanying the solo instruments are the strings playing harmonies in closed form; on the first and third beats are the lower strings; on the second and fourth beats are the upper strings. With all of them performing pizzicato, and with timpani support, a pixie-like atmosphere results, adding to the frolicsome feeling of the theme.

The B theme phraseologically contains a 4-measure fore-phrase closing on an imperfect tonic half-cadence in measure 12 with the third of the tonic chord in the soprano on the last two beats. At the end of the 4-measure after-phrase in measure 16 is an authentic feminine cadence with the dominant ninth on the first beat progressing to a tonic on the third beat.

The A section returns in measure 17 with the first violins and the other strings playing an octave higher, making this arrangement richer than the first appearance of A. Notice that the basses join by supplementing the celli an octave lower to provide an added foundation. An interesting dominant pedal point, assigned to the horn throughout these eight measures, tends to consolidate the strings. The voicing seems more open and so consistent with the brilliance desired by this repetition.

In complete contrast to the first two themes is the C theme in measure 25 in D-minor, relative to F-major, consisting of the principal motif:

EXAMPLE VI-40

and the secondary motif:

EXAMPLE VI-41

The C theme is ushered in by the celli, melancholy in character. The harmonies in the upper strings above the celli are voiced open, while the basses provide a solid foundation below. Phraseologically, the 4-measure fore-phrase is complemented by the 4-measure after-phrase, which ends with an authentic feminine cadence in measure 32. In the principal motif of the fore-phrase, note the dotted quarter and eighth rhythm. In measure 25, it occurs on the second and third beats, then in 26 on the third and fourth beats for contrast and rhythmic drive. The direction of the theme is generally downward, while, in the next two measures, the secondary motif soars upward in quarter notes. The same format is repeated in the after-phrase.

Customarily, one would expect a return to either A or B according to strict rondo form, but instead a brand new pulsating theme, D, arrives, with the principal motif in measure 33:

EXAMPLE VI-42

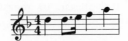

followed by the secondary motif:

EXAMPLE VI-43

   Continuing in the relative minor, the D theme is played by the
clarinet and bassoon two octaves apart, with timpani support, while
the strings accompany pizzicato just as they did in the B theme. Notice the sudden involvement of chromatics in motif 2, a refreshing
contrast to the thus far diatonic character of the three preceding
themes. At the same time, a glittering and sparkling effect is obtained
by flute trills. The distribution of the rhythmic components of this
entire 4-measure fore-phrase, the dotted eighths and sixteenths, and
the eighth notes, add an exciting impetus to the theme. The format
is carried through the after-phrase which ends in measure 40 on a
vii diminished seventh chord, the half-cadence resolving directly into
the C theme in measure 41. An interlude is then heard in measure 49
based upon the material of the last measure of the C theme. It is first
presented by the strings in closed voicing, and then is answered antiphonally by the woodwinds in both closed and open voicing. A scale-
like modulation to F-major brings back the A theme in measure 54 as it
was presented the second time. B follows in measure 62 instrumentally
the same as its first appearance, but this time functioning as a development for twelve measures, a deviation from the stereotyped
4 + 4 measure format. Modulation, sequence, and the use of a secondary dominant seventh eventually lead to a half-cadence in the
key of A-minor in measure 73.
   At this point, the new E theme enters in measure 74:

EXAMPLE VI-44

It is in the Phrygian mode with its final on "A" because of the presence
of the B-flat in the melody.
   This theme depicts the oriental atmosphere, a land of fantasy
and adventure. Appropriately it is assigned to the oboe supported by
woods, horn, and timpani with a pedal point played by bassoon. The
motif is repeated literally and then inverted. The 4-measure fore-

phrase ends on a half-cadence at this point, in A-minor. This key sup-
plants the Phrygian mode in the ensuing 4-measure after-phrase in
which the E theme continues with the same instrumentation. It also
ends on a half-cadence on the dominant in measure 81. Suddenly
there is a magic transformation in measure 82 to the relative major
key. In the next 4-measure fore-phrase, the persistent E theme in C-
major is taken by the flute supported by the woods, horn pedal point,
and tremolo violins ending on the dominant half-cadence in measure
85. The next 4-measure after-phrase, using the same material, returns
to A-minor when it reaches its dominant on its half-cadence in measure 89. Now there is a recapitulation of the theme in the Phrygian
mode for four measures, ending with an authentic feminine cadence,
V^7 to i, on the last beat in measure 93. One would now expect the
A theme to return. But no! An interlude occurs in measure 94. The
motif of the E theme is taken up by the clarinet with horn and string
support harmonically. It is continued for four measures. Then starting in measure 98, a little development occurs in which the new
motifs of this interlude:

EXAMPLE VI-45

EXAMPLE VI-46

are transposed down and up for eight measures. The principal motif
of the E theme returns. It leads by downward sequence for six
measures to the half-cadence, V^7 of IV in C-major (measure 111),
which as a pivot chord becomes V^7 in the key of F-major. The expected is about to happen.

In measure 112, A makes its final appearance exactly as it was
in the very beginning of the piece. After eight measures, the coda
commences in measure 120 with the principal motif of A slightly
shortened. Performed in unison by oboe, clarinet, first violins 8va with
harmonic support in the other strings, bassoon, and horn, it rises in
an upward sequence. Then it is followed by a return of the quarter
note motif of the B theme. Added instrumentation with a climactic
crescendo aided by the inclusion of timpani roll and cymbal crashes
brings the piece to a close on the final cadence.

There is a great deal of thematic material in this piece, all of which is of value to the student. The principal elements that should be emphasized are:

1. Written in a classically-romanticized style
2. Free rondo form with interludes and coda
3. Constructive principles achieved: unity by repetition of themes and motifs, as well as instrumentation; variety by contrasting themes, contrasting material within each theme, and devices of inversion, transposition, sequences applied to material development, and change of tonalities; coherence by consolidation of material throughout
4. Phraseology fundamentally square with the 4-measure phrase predominating; incorporation of the 12- and 6-measure phrase in the interlude
5. Harmonically transparent with conventional, properly voiced chords and progressions; modulations subtle and clear; use of foreign tones such as passing tones, changing tones, appoggiaturas, auxiliary tones, echappées, free tones, anticipations as well as pedal points to create interest and dissonance; use of Phrygian mode
6. Instrumentation economical showing understanding of timbre, color, mixture, function; percussive use of strings; use of percussion instruments confined to timpani and cymbals
7. Opportunities for good interpretation because of melodic simplicity, melodic waves, varied material, romantic style, tempo and dynamic contrasts

Fantasy Gavotte

John Harutunian

250

253

259

FANTASY GAVOTTE John Harutunian, Grade II

After a performance by the Boston Symphony Orchestra, Harold Rogers of *The Christian Science Monitor* wrote:

> Mr. Harutunian's "Fantasy Gavotte" was a good example of what a young composer can do while assimilating established forms and traditional methods of handling the orchestra. At this point of his development he could hardly be called a neo-classicist but simply a classical imitator. What he turned out, however, was highly engaging. The dancing melodies are passed back and forth from orchestra to piano which he himself played with some skill.*

* From a review by Harold Rogers in *The Christian Science Monitor*, April 4, 1966. Used by permission.

The style is definitely a mixture of classicism and Slavic romanticism. Orchestrated for strings, piccolo, two flutes, oboe, two clarinets, bassoon, horn, two trumpets, two trombones, timpani,

Composer John Harutunian taking a bow at Symphony Hall, Boston, after a performance of his piece by the Boston Symphony Orchestra.

triangle, cymbals, and piano, it is written in the concerto grosso style in which there is conversation between orchestra and piano.

The form is rondo with variations arranged as:

A, A', A", B, B', A''', A'''', A''', interlude, C, C'
A''''', A'''''', A''''', A'''''''', A, A", coda.

At the outset, the orchestral tutti announces a three-note motif:

EXAMPLE VI-47

which establishes itself confidently as though announcing the fact that it is to play a decisive part in the unfolding of the dramatic material, which it does, since it appears throughout the 8-measure sentence rather persistently.

In measure 2, it is followed by motif 2:

EXAMPLE VI-48

which is an outgrowth of motif 1.

After the half-cadence in measure 4 of the fore-phrase, the after-phrase begins in measure 5 in a way that reveals the composer's maturity. Here the average composer would be tempted to repeat measure 1 as is, possibly with a slight change of the melodic treatment to conform with the V $\frac{4}{2}$ of iv chord. Instead, John utilizes the material of measure 2, which is the second motif, in shifted rhythm, giving the music a drive and vitality it would have lost had the ordinary been used. He follows this measure with a transposition to a high point. Motif 1 returns followed by motif 2 inverted leading to authentic cadence in measure 8.

In simple concerto grosso style, the orchestral tutti is answered in contrast by the piano beginning on the anacrusis in measure 8, followed by a repetition of the first eight measures accompanied very subtly and unobtrusively by pizzicato strings. By this time, the tonality of D-minor has been securely established. Tonal contrast now must be introduced in the next 8-measure sentence. Beginning in measure 17, the material of A is presented in the key of F-major, the relative major of D-minor. In the fore-phrase, the rhythm is consistent with that of the fore-phrase of the original theme.

A modulation to D-minor occurs at the beginning of the after-phrase in measure 21. Compare this beginning rhythmically with that of A. In A, shifted rhythm of motif 2 is used instead of the expected balance to measure 1. In A'', the composer employs balance, but he uses the shifted rhythm of motif 2 in measure 22, thus avoiding the triteness that would have resulted. The cadence compares literally to that of A. In this section, the oboe solo is supported by harmony in the clarinets and bassoon, later joined by strings and by the horn sustaining the dominant pedal point. What a delightful contrast all this is to the orchestral treatment of the previous theme! D-minor is used only temporarily. Immediately, a new theme, B, in the key of B-flat major which is the submediant of D-minor, is introduced in bar 25 with the motif:

EXAMPLE VI-49

Notice, however, the similarity to motif 2 of A, definite evidence of unity in the piece. In the fore-phrase, the brass, with the sparkling tremolo triangle, announce the theme in an audacious masculine manner. They are imitated rather unobtrusively, but confidently, by the piano. On the after-phrase in measure 29, what seems to be the answer is expressed delicately in a feminine way by the woodwinds and strings modulating to "F," the dominant of B-flat. The entire format of B is repeated, but this time the cadence of the after-phrase remains in B-flat major.

A series of variations of A now begins in measure 41 for eight measures. The series consists of a predominance of eighth notes in arpeggio and scale-like formations. The first variation is presented by the piano in B-flat major with low strings accompanying pizzicato. Then follows the next variation in "F" in measure 49 played by the flute supported harmonically by woods and strings reinforced by brass in measure 53. The variation originally played by the solo piano returns in measure 57. For the next three measures, beginning in 64, the last eight notes of the piano variation are exploited in antiphonal treatment between flute and violins. This serves as an interlude modulating to the dominant of G-minor.

In measure 67, the C theme in G-minor is ushered in. This is a decided contrast to the previous material in meter, tempo, and mood. It is in $\frac{3}{4}$, andante, and is lushly romantic.

Consisting of two motifs (measures 67 to 70):

EXAMPLE VI-50

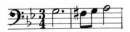

EXAMPLE VI-51

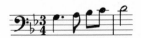

they are presented by the celli who sing out its rich, colorful, and vibrant theme majestically. The woods complement them with chordal punctuations, their positions ever-changing as if wishing to heighten the emotional intensity engendered by the celli. The horn and basses in unison sustain the tonic pedal point as a unifying element, which at the same time creates occasional dissonance and tension. Observe the line of the theme in both 8-measure sentences. Notice how it waves and how it progresses toward its half-cadence in measure 74 and its authentic cadence in measures 81–82 with an abundance of step-wise motion, skips being kept at a minimum. In the background, the triangle softly and effectively makes its glittering function crystal clear.

In measure 83, the C' theme occurs again in B-flat major with the first clarinet as the solo instrument. It is supported by upper strings in harmony and lower strings pizzicato. The tonic pedal point is continued on the first beat of each measure. To avoid monotony in the repetition of the C′ theme, which has returned to G-minor, slight variations are introduced. Compare measures 71 and 72 of the first 8-measure sentence of the C section with the corresponding measures, 87 and 88, of the first 8-measure sentence of C′. The direction of the former is generally downward, while the latter is up and down. Compare measures 76 and 77 of the second sentence of C with the corresponding measures, 92 and 93, of the second sentence of C′. The direction of the former is generally upward, while the latter is downward. How cleverly the composer has utilized inversion in the C′ section followed by variation in measures 95 and 96. Measures 97, 98 and 99 in G-minor are treated antiphonally in this cadence between the flute and bassoon.

After this quietude and serenity, there is a bursting forth in measure 100 of the variation of theme A, allegro in E-flat major, for eight measures presented for contrast by the violins, supported harmonically by upper strings and pizzicato by lower strings. A second sentence of eight measures begins on the IV_6 chord in measure 108 with solo piano and string harmony. This variation of the A theme leads through secondary dominant chords, V $^6_5$ of vi and V $^4_3$ of iii to a cadence on V^7 of vi. In measure 116, material that began in measure 100 returns exactly in E-flat major for eight measures with strings. As would be expected, the same format occurs in measure 124. The material that began in 108 returns with piano solo.

Secondary dominant chords, V^7 of vi and V^7 of ii, are used, insuring the cadence in E-flat major in measure 132. How resonantly vibrant and vigorous! A dominant 7th chord in D-minor announces the return to the A theme in measure 132.

The orchestral tutti blazes forth for eight measures magnificently, triumphantly, audaciously, and confidently. Here the piano does not answer as it did in the beginning. Instead, the theme in F-major is heard in measure 140, as before, played by the woods, but only for four measures when the piano appears in measure 144 where the coda begins. With string support in the harmony, the piano in the home key of D-minor develops the principal motifs through the use of secondary dominant chords, leading to a deceptive cadence on the submediant in measure 153. Here the second motif of A is tossed about from bassoon to flute to clarinet. Finally, the violins take over, after which the piano resumes in measure 158. The piano engages in ascending scale passages enhanced by punctuations of tonic and

dominant chords by the tutti. All are united on the final three chords.
Observe the following important aspects of the piece:

1. Classic-romantic in style
2. Rondo variation form with coda
3. Constructive principles well-observed: unity by repetition and development of material and relationship of the motif of theme B to
the second motif of theme A; variety by contrast of material, variations of theme A, variety of tonalities to prevent monotony such as:
F-major relative major of D-minor, B-flat major related to D-minor
as its submediant, relative minor of B-flat major (G-minor, which is
the subdominant of D-minor), E-flat major remote from D-minor
but related closely to B-flat major as its subdominant, use of inversion
and shifted rhythm
4. Orthodox structure of phrases in measures of four graduating to
8-measure sentences
5. Harmonic structure based consistently on: use of primary chords,
tonic, dominant, subdominant; use of secondary dominants for variety
and for purposes of modulation; foreign tones confined to auxiliary
tones, passing tones, echappées, occasional appoggiaturas, and pedal
points
6. Contrapuntal lines used judiciously in support of and in logical
relation to material
7. Appropriate use of orchestral forces in conformity with the style
and idiom; instruments individually and collectively selected dis-
cretely; composer's understanding of the orchestral forces obvious;
percussion sparingly but suitably used
8. Proper interpretation by contrasts of themes, tempos, dynamics, instrumentation, rise and fall of melodic lines, qualities of freshness,
exuberance, youth, and sentiment

Capriccio

Ross Capon

269

271

274

277

CAPRICCIO   Ross Capon, Grade II

Elliot Norton of the *Boston Record American* wrote of Ross' "Capriccio" after a Boston Symphony Orchestra performance of the work:

> "Capriccio," an imposing work, is a simple, modest, melodious piece of music which utilizes most of the instruments of the full orchestra in interesting harmony.*

Subsequently, at "Newton High School Night at the Boston Pops," the piece was repeated. It is orchestrated for two flutes, two oboes, two clarinets, one bassoon, two horns, two trumpets, one trombone, one tuba, timpani, triangle, snare drum, cymbals, and the usual strings.

This two-movement piece was one of the most ambitious and resourceful compositions produced at Newton High School. It is definitely in the romantic style showing influences of Beethoven, Berlioz, and Mahler, with a chromatic element predominating.

In form, the first movement is based fundamentally on one main theme with the use of a subordinate motif briefly and a variation of the main motif. Actually, it is in free rhapsodic form.

The second movement is composed of the exposition containing a main scherzo-like theme that is very predominant, a development section in which new motifs are introduced, and an abridged recapitulation of the scherzo theme followed by a coda containing themes from both movements. The second movement may be considered to be in free sonata form.

At the very beginning of the first movement in moderate tempo, the first violins announce the first theme audaciously with aplomb and definiteness of purpose. The theme contains two motifs which are similar in that they both descend. The principal motif is:

EXAMPLE VI-52

and the secondary motif is:

* From a review by Elliot Norton in the *Boston Record American*, March 8, 1965. Used by permission.

EXAMPLE VI-53

Immediately, in the 4-measure fore-phrase, chromatics are introduced by the second violins, while the violas support the violins with a dominant pedal point which creates dissonance. Suggestions of the Mixolydian mode are apparent. It is carried into the 4-measure after-phrase and mixed with the D-major tonality. The material used is derived from the secondary motif of the fore-phrase. The violas are reinforced by the celli and basses on the dominant pedal point, which pinpoints the half-cadence at the end of the phrase. Beginning in measure 9, the material is repeated for the next eight measures but with fuller orchestration. The lower strings provide a pizzicato accompaniment on the tonic pedal, emphasized by timpani; the violas and horn play a dominant pedal point; the lows and highs of the orchestra imitate one another; and finally a concerted tutti is reached. On the cadence in measure 16, a bit of polytonality occurs with the V chord over the tonic pedal. In measure 17, the secondary motif of the theme begins a development by transposition and upward sequence in the upper strings and woodwinds. In contrary motion, the lower strings tremolo on a descending diatonic scale. This all occurs for five measures over timpani pedal. A 2-measure plagal cadence of progression V to IV over V over I leads to a return of the fore-phrase of the theme in measure 24. For the next six measures, the upper woods canonically imitate the strings and trumpet, while the lower woods and brass reinforce the lower strings in an upward chromatic scale. A magical effect is dramatically created by string tremolos.

Excitement increases when the upper parts of the orchestra are assigned the secondary motif of the theme in diminution, while the lower parts of the orchestra in contrary motion ascend chromatically, also in diminution. This is repeated several times. Finally in measure 32, the climax is reached with the reannouncement of the first motif of the theme. Calm immediately follows. For five measures, a new whimsical and capricious motif beginning in measure 33 with suggestion of the Dorian mode:

EXAMPLE VI-54

is ushered in by unison bassoon and basses, imitated by flute, then by clarinets with support by woodwind chords. The motif is restated by unison bassoons, celli, and basses. Notice effective use of triangle.

In measure 38, the clarinets for four measures take over the motif, which is transformed, in the key of D-harmonic minor, while the lower strings continue the tremolo characteristic already established. In this way, the dramatic element is consistently maintained. A sudden change to the tonality of E-minor occurs in measure 42. The upper woods help to establish this new color. The lower strings continue to tremolo. After four measures of this activity, an extension of two measures follows consisting of eighth notes related to the diminution of the second motif of the theme. From bar 48 through 51, the tonalities change successively beginning with A-flat major and going through D-flat, "G," and back to A-flat major. The material consists of scale passages in eighth notes treated antiphonally. Upper woods and upper strings in an ascending A-flat major scale are answered by woods and lower strings and trombone in a descending D-flat major scale. In the next bar, upper woods and upper strings are joined by trumpets in an ascending G-major scale only to be answered by lower strings, woods, and trombone in a descending A-flat major scale. In the next two and one-half measures, in complete contrast to the enterprising busy instrumentation thus far, strings function alone with horn pedal, followed immediately by the principal motif transformed with upper woods on the third beat of measure 54. Eventually two measures later, the motif falls on the first beat because of the subtle interpolation in measure 55 of $\frac{2}{4}$ rhythm. A tutti dwells on the motif sufficiently, leading to a concluding authentic and added plagal cadence in measure 59 with timpani on the tonic.

The second movement is indeed a most imaginative one. A change of mood and temperament takes place. The 3-measure grave introduction in $\frac{3}{4}$ time in D-minor:

EXAMPLE VI-55

is appropriately scored so the low instruments of the orchestra can contribute toward the solemnity and seriousness of the music. How cleverly the composer transforms this. With a sudden change to allegro, a 5-measure phrase begins in measure 4, with a decisive tutti chord promptly followed by a vibrant scherzo-like motif related to the introduction:

EXAMPLE VI-56

This motif is played in harmony by the upper woods and strings. In the next measure, another tutti chord is heard after which the motif reaches a higher point followed by still another tutti chord. This leads to a downward sequence of the motif to measure 7 where contrary motion with each part harmonized adds to the excitement. Here, the normal 4-measure phrase ends, but a measure follows serving as an extension. With the change of the rhythm signature to $\frac{4}{4}$ in measure 9, the violins carry on the triplet pulse of the scherzo, utilizing the motif of the grave introduction in diminution. The violins are supported harmonically by the celli. The skill of the composer is evident by the way he carefully and clearly relates the triplet pulsation to the material of the introduction, contributing to unity.

In the 3-measure phrase, the melody of the third measure is an exact transposition by a perfect fourth of the second measure, while its accompaniment is a perfect fifth lower. The next two and one-half measures beginning in measure 12, consist of a sequence accompanied by a descending chromatic scale. For the next six and one-half measures, beginning in the last half of measure 14, an extension appears, in which the motif in the upper parts rises chromatically in contrary motion to the lower parts, which descend chromatically. Flute and violins play antiphonally. Throughout, the music becomes more colorful as more instruments are added in both lines leading to the climax of repeated tutti dominant chords through measure 20, which is in $\frac{2}{4}$ time. They resolve to the tonic in measure 21 when the main theme returns, still in D-minor, treated in concerted tutti harmony for three measures. In the next four measures, the introductory motif appears tutti with harmony concerted transposed as the rhythm signatures change to $\frac{2}{4}$, $\frac{3}{4}$, $\frac{2}{4}$ while modulation proceeds simultaneously to A-minor in measure 27. Then, the concerted strings and woods develop the main theme for six measures. Antiphonal treatment occurs among the woods and between the woods and strings. The ascending chromatic element returns in the low instruments. All converge to cadence in A-minor tutti in measure 34. For three measures, syncopation in the upper voices of the orchestra adds to the sparkle of the descending chromatics in the low voices of the orchestra.

In measure 37, the exposition ends; the development begins. For the first 15 measures, the composer engages in a rhapsodic excursion with solo instruments carrying the responsibilities of theme development. Celli and basses announce the first motif in A-minor for two measures:

EXAMPLE VI-57

Here the triplet motif of the scherzo theme is predominant, thereby achieving unity. The tempo changes to andante in measure 40. The mood is subdued. The core of this material is repeated by solo cello with bassoon in unison all supported by celli and basses. The key has changed to the parallel key of A-major which is a good contrast. This persists for four measures, in which the triplet motif is varied by inversion and imitated by celli and basses. Elaboration of eighth notes is perceptible. In measure 46, a 2-measure extension leads to motif 2:

EXAMPLE VI-58

Melodically, the tonality is A-natural minor in contrast to the accompaniment in which A-major occurs intermittently. A conversation between solo cello and solo violin is carried on for six measures ending on a tonic half-cadence in measure 51. An extended cadenza follows. The cello announces motif 1:

EXAMPLE VI-59

while the violin executes counterpoint for four measures starting in A-major and modulating to F-sharp major in measure 55. The violin then carries on the theme with cello counterpoint for twelve measures principally in F-sharp major, though there are suggestions in F-sharp minor. The cello also includes a portion of an Alberti bass, a reminiscence of a technique used during the classical period. The section ends on cadence in F-sharp major, which becomes, as a pivot chord, V in B-minor. This is the tonality of the next section beginning in measure 68. Here at the allegro, a new motif 2:

EXAMPLE VI-60

capers along for eight measures with the responsibility divided between the violin and cello in imitation. The section ends on cadence
in B major, which acts as a pivot chord, V of V in A-major in measure 75.

In the next four measures, counterpoint between the two instruments continues from A-major through A-minor. Especially important
are the upward suspension and the A tempo that occur within this
portion. Officially, the cadenza ends in measure 79, since the solo
string instruments are henceforth joined by others. The motif that was
first announced by the solo cello returns in measure 80. The violin and
flute present it in both A-minor and A-major for two measures. Below
in A-minor, creating a bit of polytonality, the cello contrapuntally
reintroduces very deftly and unobtrusively the scherzo-like triplet
motif from the main theme of movement two. Notice the two against
three metric rhythms reminiscent of Brahms. In the next three
measures, 82–84, instruments are gradually added toward a tutti in
which the scherzo motif is developed in sequence. At the authentic
tonic cadence in measure 85, a basso ostinato in A-minor persists
for eight measures. At the same time, the upper instruments, after an
A-major 2-measure interlude, present motif 1 of the cadenza for four
measures rising up with vigor and purpose. At the authentic cadence
in measure 91, a 2-measure extension begins over the continuation of
the basso ostinato. A return to the $\frac{3}{4}$ rhythm signature occurs in measure 93. The main motif of the scherzo appears and is used in upward
sequence extensively. It is assigned to woods, then to strings, then to
both, while the motif of the grave intro is taken over in the lower
parts. Curious but interesting changes in tonality keep one wondering
where the final objective is to be. In measure 100, an authentic
cadence in D-minor is reached. For the next three measures, the
lower instruments carry on the scherzo motif in sequence and then
in upward chromatics, while the upper parts continue on the grave
intro theme. For four measures, beginning in measure 104, the upper
instruments carry on the motif in a series of major and minor triads
most likely selected and accepted justifiably by experimentation at
the keyboard. The lower instruments, at the same time, continue with
the intro motif until the authentic cadence in D-minor is reached in
measure 108. With the development concluded, the recapitulation

begins in D-minor. It is abridged, enduring for only five measures, repeating the same material that appeared at the beginning of the second movement. The time changes to $\frac{4}{4}$. The theme continues for two measures literally in the woods, with brass and lower strings sustaining harmonies. This is followed in measure 115 by a chromatic sequence of the motif upward against a chromatic descending quarter note bass line for two measures. A change to $\frac{3}{4}$, involving a sixteenth note figure and an extension of one measure, culminates in a cadence in D-major in measure 119. Here the coda begins. In $\frac{4}{4}$ the main theme of movement one returns in unison celli and bassoon followed by two tutti dramatic chords in D-minor. The scherzo motif in $\frac{3}{4}$ reappears in the woods and strings, but only ephemerally. From here on in, $\frac{4}{4}$ persists. The main theme of movement one is interrupted by the scherzo motif of movement two. For two more measures, both motifs alternate. Then they join contrapuntally in measure 126—the scherzo motif in the upper instruments against the first movement motif in the lower instruments in a glorious tutti. A dramatic D-minor chord is sustained, while the timpani majestically beat out a tonic, dominant series of notes. Again, the scherzo motif appears, but only once in a subdued manner preparing for a D-minor triad in the low register orchestrated conservatively. A gradual crescendo begins, directed toward a final utterance of the D-minor triad fully orchestrated.

The student will derive a great deal from the analysis of this piece, because of its musical content and the manner in which it is treated and developed:

1. Stylistically written in the romantic tradition
2. Structurally: first movement, free rhapsodic form; second movement, free sonata form
3. Constructive principles achieved: unity by repetition and graphic relationship of themes and subsequent use of fundamental material throughout; variety by use of different themes, changes of key, meter, tempo, mood, dynamics, and especially the rhapsodic treatment of the development in the second movement; coherence by the consolidation of the material throughout
4. Phraseologically: predominance of 4-measure phrases and a mixture of odd numbered phrases such as 2, 2½, 3, 4, 5, 6, and 6½, adding considerable variety
5. Harmonically: generally traditional with occasional elusiveness into chromatic passages, suddenness of tonality changes, presence of polytonal sounds resulting from key mixtures, use of secondary dominant chords leading to modulations; mixture of the modes with major scale;

abundance of foreign tones such as passing, auxiliary, changing, appoggiaturas, echappées, cambiatas; evidence of independence of all parts; absence of stagnation; accompaniment always vital
6. Well-balanced and well-developed presentation of themes by imitation, transposition, sequence, modulation, antiphonal treatment, and extensions
7. Superb orchestration showing an understanding of all instruments and their uses; percussion used discreetly in appropriate places
8. Opportunities for interpretation great because of clarity of directions in tempos and dynamics and because of quality of the melodies, which are beautifully curved

Shades of Thought

Dale Shuman

288

SHADES OF THOUGHT   Dale Shuman, Grade 12

"Shades of Thought" is written in the atonal idiom employing the twelve-tone serial technique. The tone row appears initially in its original form. There are times when it crosses from one instrument to another without an interruption of its continuity. Fragments of notes of the original are heard. Pedal points appear, in which one note of the series is constantly being repeated over a period of time by one instrument, while another voice functions serially. The retrograde of the original, fragments of the retrograde, the inversion of the original, fragments of the inversion, the synthesis of the notes into chordal structures, and the retrograde inversion are all utilized throughout the piece.

The arrangement of the tones of the original is compatible with the principles of atonality, because of the type of intervals used consecutively as the row or its fragments unfold. Generally, every time the row appears, it assumes a new rhythmic pattern, thereby maintaining a liveliness throughout, which is vitally important for a piece in this idiom. The phraseology differs in length necessarily because of the rhythmic mutations with each presentation.

The score is analyzed minutely. Each note is numbered according to its appearance in the tone row. The following abbreviations will be helpful:

$$O = \text{original}$$
$$R = \text{retrograde}$$
$$I = \text{inversion}$$
$$RI = \text{retrograde inversion}$$

The piece is orchestrated for flute, oboe, clarinet, bassoon, horns I and II, trumpet, trombone, timpani and percussion, consisting of triangle, snare drum, and cymbal.

The tone row consists of a mixture of quarters and eighths:

EXAMPLE VI-61

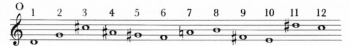

This serves as a basis for the entire piece, since all subsequent material is derived from and related to it. It is first announced by the
clarinet in a 4¾-measure phraseology. Immediately in measure 2, the
bassoon enters on the last half of the first beat, establishing a feeling
of syncopation, which is carried through a 5½-measure phrase, in
which the eighths are predominant. In measure 7, the phrase ends on
the twelfth note of the series surprisingly played by the clarinet.
Thus, the series has crossed over from the bassoon to the clarinet.
In the interim, the clarinet, after completion of the initial row in
measure 5, begins a new rhythmic pattern of the original, presenting
only its first three tones. The bassoon takes over in measure 7 and
completes the row in measure 10, making a 5¼-measure phrase. On the
last quarter of measure 7, the clarinet once more attempts the original row, but is interrupted by the flute. The flute borrows the third
note of the row from the clarinet and, beginning in measure 9 over a
triangle roll, effects the third note as a pedal point staccato which
persists for fourteen measures through measure 22. During this
phrase, the clarinet, after a 2½-measure rest, restores itself in measure
11 by continuing the row in the form of a triplet motif. After a
measure rest, the eighth note motif returns briefly. Then more rests
are followed by a restatement of the triplet in measure 14 into the
beginning of 15, completing what amounts to a 7½-measure phrase.
In measure 15, antiphonal treatment occurs between the clarinet and
the bassoon on the eighth note motif consisting of the retrograde of
the original, which assumes the following series:

EXAMPLE VI-62

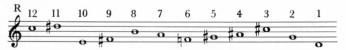

This lasts for three measures. Strangely enough in the following
measure, 18, the bassoon begins a statement of the original. The first
four tones imitate the last four tones of the previous measure played
by the clarinet. Then in measure 19, the clarinet, in mild syncopation
for two measures, continues the row, which is taken over by the
bassoon for the next two measures, 21 and 22, in rhythmic imitation,
completing the row of a 5-measure phrase. During these interruptions,

the bassoon, in measures 19 and 20, begins a rather free retrograde involving notes 7, 8, 6, and 5 of the original in a rhythmic pattern. This pattern is imitated by the clarinet in the next two measures, 21 and 22, involving notes 12, 11, 10, and 9 of the retrograde of the series.

In measure 23, an elaboration of the pedal point over a snare drum roll, which appears intermittently through measure 48, is presented by the flute and oboe in unison using notes 12 and 10 of the series in retrograde for four measures. This gradually is developed by repetitions of groups of notes arranged numerically from the original as: 9, 10 in measure 27; retrograde as 9, 8 in measure 28; then 8, 9 and 9, 10 in measure 29, representing the original; an arbitrary retrograde jump as 12, 9 in measure 30; again 12, 10 in measures 31 and 32; 4, 3 of retrograde inversion in measure 33; original 10, 11 in measure 34; 3, 4 of the inversion in measure 35; retrograde as 11, 10 and original as 10, 11 in measure 36 where the trumpet solos; then 10, 11 as original and 11, 10 as retrograde in measure 37 presented by the clarinet, followed by groups of consecutive notes in retrograde in measures 38 and 39. In measure 40, the clarinet is doubled in octave unison by the bassoon arriving in measure 44 at the final 1. The parallel octaves in measures 40 and 41 between melody and bass are unavoidable because of the nature of the basso ostinato and the adherence to the rhythmic line of the original. Altering either one would be more objectionable than using parallel octaves, the lesser of two evils. During this persistent ostinato support, the clarinet and bassoon present the series in inversion as:

EXAMPLE VI-63

It is a five-measure phrase from 25 through 29. Rhythmically, it is similar to the original. For the next six measures, through measure 35, these instruments continue in a new rhythmic pattern utilizing only the first four notes of the inversion. Measures 36 through 39 already have been analyzed.

In measure 40, flute and oboe in octave unison present the original tone row series in a 5-measure phrase paralleling exactly the rhythm that is used in the inversion in measures 25 through 29. From 45 through 48, flute and oboe begin anew the original, but, in a 4-measure phrase, do not go beyond number 3 of the series, which is exploited in repetitions. At the same time, the clarinet and bassoon in octave unison continue an ostinato using notes 12, 11, 10, 9 of the retrograde whose eight remaining notes in the series are contained in a tutti concerted chord in measure 49. At the same time, these notes can be considered the first eight tones of the original. In this forte climactic 8-measure phrase, the sharpness of the dissonance together with the accelerated rhythmic motion produced by the repetitious chords with emphasis on the triplet motif create a feeling of increased tension, excitement, and agitation. Cymbal crashes passionately add to the drama. In measure 52, notes 9 and 10 are introduced. Finally in measure 57, after the excitement has abated, notes 11 and 12 of the series are heard purely and simply in the oboe followed by a retrograde treatment of notes 11, 10, 9. These very same notes then appear in the original. Throughout these two measures, in which a delicate triangle roll is employed, the triplet motif is emphasized. Measures 59 and 60 contain notes 8 through 1 of the retrograde. At the same time, the bassoon states the first four notes of the inversion of the series. This leads to the tutti forte chord in measure 61 enhanced by a cymbal crash, seemingly to disturb the tranquillity of the previous 4-measure phrase. The use of cymbals could very well be reminiscent of the earlier boldness of measures 49 through 56. The bassoon is left to carry the first five notes of the original in rhythmic simplicity for 2½-measures. The clarinet takes over for the next four measures dwelling upon the last four notes of the series, measure 64 in retrograde, then 65 in the original. In measure 66, the clarinet carries on, beginning with note 8 and continuing through note 1 in retrograde. Throughout this 4-measure phrase over a triangle roll, the triplet motif is prominent. In the last two measures of the phrase, the flute in measure 66 and the oboe in 67 imitate what the bassoon did in measures 59 and 60, using the first four notes of the inversion of the series. Again the tutti chord with cymbals is heard in measure 68, an exact repetition of the one in measure 61, with the bassoon carrying on exactly as before for five measures. This time the bassoon completes the entire series, in which the triplet motif continues to appear. In measures 73 and 74, flute and trombone respectively imitate antiphonally the last four notes of the series. For the ensuing 4-measure phrase, the original is heard again in rhythmic variation with the responsibility mostly on the bassoon; the flute contributes only the third note of the series; the trumpet consummates the series with the last three notes. With the trumpet, a bass drum punctuation is established, persisting for three more measures. The trumpet continues with the retrograde inversion utilizing the triplet motif:

EXAMPLE VI-64

(R of I)

Throughout these three, a frolicking Alberti type of basso ostinato in sixteenth notes is assigned most appropriately to the bassoon using notes 6, 7, 8, 9 of the original.

In measure 82, numbers 1 through 6 of the inversion are synthesized into a chord produced by all instruments except the oboe and clarinet. While the snare drum rolls, the bassoon carries on the inversion of the series aided by the trombone, which establishes another eighth note basso ostinato using number 5 of the series repeatedly. The clarinet enters in measure 85 after an effective quarter rest with the triplet motif consisting of notes 6, 7, 8 of the inversion. Another quarter rest, two more consecutive repetitions of the triplet, a return to the eighth note motif, another quarter rest, and finally another triplet, syncopated by virtue of the tie, close this phrase of 6⅔ measures. During this time, the triangle asserts itself in a continuous penetrating roll. In measure 89, the clarinet presents a rhythmic variation of the original series through measure 93, while the bassoon, presenting the inversion of the series in imitation through measure 94, adheres to the rhythmic pattern it had established in the phrase beginning in measure 25. In measure 94, as the bassoon finishes the series, the clarinet, as if in retrospect, proclaims the first two notes of the original, followed, as in imitation, by the bassoon playing the first two notes of the inversion over a snare drum roll. In the final measure, a triangle roll prepares a conclusive announcement by the clarinet, which unobtrusively ejects numbers 3 and 4 of the inversion. Notice how the piece decreases in intensity by slowing down in motion and by using milder dissonances.

Writing a piece in the twelve-tone technique is indeed a challenge for the neophyte composer. Interesting aspects are:

1. Compatibility of the tone row with atonal principles involved in the relationship of the intervals
2. Constructive principles achieved: unity by the repeated use of the triplet motif, the eighth note motif, repetitions of characteristic chords, and pedal points; variety by the use of different rhythmic patterns of the rows as they continually appear in the original, inversion, retrograde, and retrograde inversion; coherence by the assurance of the homogeneity of the piece through the permeation of the whole struc-

ture by the tone row and its motif relationships, which represent the unifying idea as conceived originally by Schoenberg

3. Unsymmetrical phraseology consistent with the atonal style and contrapuntal character of the music

4. Mild and sharp dissonances producing harmonies characteristic of the idiom

5. Contrapuntal style obtained by an abundance of contrary as well as parallel and oblique motion

6. Rhythmic interest resulting from the sharp dissonances, the accelerated motion, and increased tension leading to culmination points

7. Good understanding of instrumentation in the production of melodic, harmonic, and contrapuntal ideas

8. Proper interpretation dependent on dynamics and tempos consistent with the piece

Conflict in Solitude

Tina Currens

296

298

299

CONFLICT IN SOLITUDE Tina Currens, Grade 12

After hearing Tina Currens' "Conflict in Solitude," Harold Rogers, in *The Christian Science Monitor,* commented:

> It shows teen-agers' uncertainties in an atomic world. It expresses qualities of cynicism, uncertainty and doubt in effective tonal combinations and careful choice of instrumentation.*

The composer indeed has achieved these philosophical objectives by combining her musical ideas with contemporary methods of expression.

Tina orchestrated the piece for two flutes, oboe, two clarinets, bassoon, horn, three trumpets, trombone, triangle, cymbals, wood block, timpani, and strings. It is in three-part form with A highly developed, B repeated, and the return of A abridged, with the plan, A, B, B, A abridged.

* From a review by Harold Rogers in *The Christian Science Monitor,* June 1, 1962. Used by permission.

From the very beginning of the andante, the first motif:

EXAMPLE VI-65

stated by unison oboe and clarinet, consists of downward chromatics signifying uncertainty, followed by the second motif:

EXAMPLE VI-66

which proceeds upward also in chromatic movement. The tonality of A is established by the accompanying bassoon and celli progressing in contrary motion, also chromatically.

In the next two measures, the motifs are repeated, but the bass line is subtly reversed not only to obtain variety and to avoid a stereotyped treatment, but also to help emphasize the tonality of A on the cadence.

The absence of the color tones, the thirds, in the accompanying chords creates a feeling of incompleteness and insufficiency consistent with the cynicism of the piece. In measure 5, the after-phrase begins on more secure ground, A-flat major, made more colorful with the addition of the flute.

In the after-phrase, unison bassoon and celli introduce a moving eighth note motif:

EXAMPLE VI-67

which, as the piece progresses, will play an important role. Following immediately is a derivative from the first motif inverted in an upward ascent involving the tonality of E-major. On the cadence at measure eight, a clashing impact is caused by the double inflection of E-minor over E-major—G-natural over G-sharp.

The first 8-measure sentence is repeated with a modification of motif 1 in measure 15 slightly retrograded leading to a tonality change to G-sharp in measure 16. After a repetition of 15 and 16 (the cadence), a whole series of eighth notes derived from motif 3 is treated in free expanded tonality embracing the twelve tones of the chromatic scale punctuated in each measure by chords progressively changing. These eighths are treated in sequences with imitations between instruments in antiphonal treatment, building up to a climax in measure 25 as instruments are added for crescendo and tone color.

A sudden drop in register in measure 27 sets the stage for another ascent toward more dramatic climax in measure 32. The following not only create dissonance, but also bear out the philosophical uncertainties and skepticism in the piece: double inflections as in measure 20, "G" over G-sharp; polytonality as in measures 21 and 23; altered notes as the G-sharp in measure 28; and additions of color tones to fundamental chords such as 6ths, 7ths, 9ths, as well as chromatics in multiple places. This section, measures 19 through 31, consists of the rather unusual phraseology of 13 measures subdivided into two 4-measure phrases and one 5-measure phrase. Penetrating this entire action is the sparkling triangle, which adds a piquant flavor to the ingredients of cynicism and skepticism.

Motif 1 is the basis of the material in the next eight measures, 32–39, a series of downward major triads followed by a bass treatment, reminiscent of Moussorgsky, played by unison trombone, bassoon, and lower strings. The importance of the motif is emphasized by the several repetitions of this material, contributing to the dynamic climax assisted by timpani and tremolo cymbals. Tension is relieved by a simple A 7th chord in measure 40, while the accompaniment suggests the rhythm of the motif. Relief from dissonance is only temporary. A minor 9th is created by the injection of repeated B-flats by horn and violas in unison. While the bass line persists with the rhythm of the motif, the upper strings reintroduce the first two original motifs from measures 44 through 47. Motif 1 keeps being repeated for four more measures by strings and oboe, while the lower strings (celli), doubled by clarinet and bassoon, ascend, pulsating the motif rhythmically. By interval, they proceed for four measures from an augmented fourth to a perfect fifth and then to two diminished fifths, making the tonality vague. In measure 52, the tonality of E-major is established, while a type of Alberti bass played by celli suddenly makes its appearance in true classical style. This is ephemeral, for in the next measure, poly-tonality reappears only to be followed by a return of the Alberti bass in measure 54 to complement its earlier appearance. Beginning in measure 56, the strings function alone. For nine measures, the upper strings take on the Alberti bass in an upward sequence, at times con-sonant, then dissonant, with the celli who continue to expand on motif 1. At the cadential point in measure 65, the tonality of "E" is re-established followed by the clarinets playing the rhythm of the motif above the lower strings. Both clarinets end with an augmentation of motif 2.

With a tempo change to allegro and a meter change to $\frac{2}{4}$ in measure 69, at B, a frolicsome basso ostinato on a "G" pedal point pre-cipitously announces itself for four measures:

EXAMPLE VI-68

It continues through measure 85, supporting a theme based on the motif:

EXAMPLE VI-69

It is a theme of vitality and power made so by its rhythmic pulsations and its expanded free chromatic tonality creating excitement and tenseness. The music moves with abandon and force. Clarinet, then flute, persist for 13 measures consisting of two 4-measure phrases and one 5-measure phrase. At measure 86, the pedal point changes to "F"

enduring for eight measures, the last four supporting the clarinet on the theme. At measure 94, unison bassoon, celli, and basses carry the thematic responsibility for 17 measures consisting of three 4-measure phrases and one 5-measure phrase. The upper strings take over the frolicsome basso ostinato pedal point changing from B-flat to B-natural to "C," ending with a single C-sharp. French horn effectively reinforces the strings by sustaining the notes above. As this section progresses, the woodwinds, and eventually the brass, enter at suitable points with harmonic support, helping to build up the anticipated climax. The roll of the timpani and the trenchant persistence of the wood block beating out the rhythmic frolicsome accompaniment contribute abundantly to the desired effect. In measure 111, bassoon and lower strings (celli) are suddenly left by themselves to continue the persistent ♩. ♫♩. ♪ rhythm for 9 measures descending gradually to a point where the original basso ostinato begins again in measure 120. The whole section is repeated through measure 164. From 165 through 170 unison bassoon and lower strings continue with the ♩. ♫♩. ♪ rhythm as before. In anticipation of a change of pace, the ♪. ♪ notes become uniform eighths for two measures dissolving into quarter notes from measure 173 through 179 in gradual descending chromatics. It is as if the preparation is set for the return to the original theme. How subtle the quarter note triplet is in measure 180 preparing for the change to the ¾ meter of the first theme, A, which is now recapitulated exactly for eight measures. This is followed by a repetition of the last two measures leading to a series of three consonant chords with an optimistic undertone played by woodwinds and lower strings (celli). The chromaticism of motif 2 is the last to be heard, as if to substantiate the truism that problems will always exist; the warmth of the clarinets alone seems to reassure that all will not be lost.

This piece is a musical essay on the philosophical concept that although life has its trials, tribulations, and frustrations, it is rewarded with compensations. The piece contains these items of interest:

1. Contemporary style with its dissonant flavor, appropriately expressing the philosophies inherent in the piece
2. Three-part form, A, B, B, A abridged
3. Constructive principles achieved: unity by the predominance and repetition of the motifs; variety by the contrasts of material; coherence by the tightly-knit fabric
4. Phraseologically: 4-measure structure generally, with occasional 5-measure phrases

5. Harmonically: predominance of dissonance in the abundant use of chromaticism, free tonality, polytonality, double inflections, alterations and addition of notes in chords, incorporation of pedal points, as against occasional reversion to consonant classicism and use of Alberti bass; foreign tones easily detectable if analyzed as relative to the harmonic structure

6. Contrapuntal techniques apparent throughout A section, inversions, imitations, antiphonal treatment instrumentally, uses of retrograde motion

7. Evidence of rhythmical power especially in the basso ostinato of the B theme and in the character of the B theme itself; subtle transformation of rhythm at end of B in anticipation of the return of A in $\frac{3}{4}$ meter

8. Careful choice of instrumentation producing proper effects for color; appropriate use of percussion in places demanding them; discreet addition of instruments for climaxes, as well as switching of melodic and accompanying motifs for contrast

9. Opportunities for interpretation of dynamics and tempos at the discretion of the performer or conductor; within A, importance of flexibility of tempo rubatos, accelerandos, and upward suspensions; within B, importance of tempo constancy

Les Emotions Changeantes

Liz Little

Movement I - Moderato

308

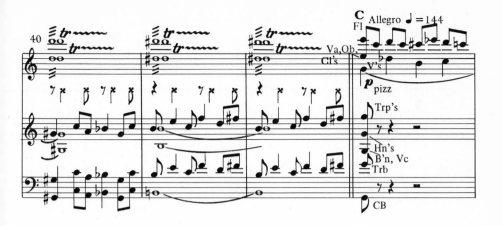

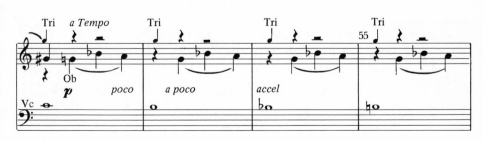

Movement II - Andante

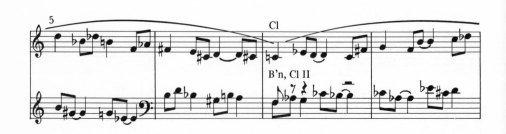

311

Movement III - Presto

312

313

LES EMOTIONS CHANGEANTES   Liz Little, Grade 12

Following a performance at Newton High School, Robert Dumm, in *The Christian Science Monitor,* wrote:

> "Les Emotions Changeantes" by Liz Little (as if only the French could vacillate) was the most technically accomplished of all

pieces leading its atonal lines surely between solo and duetting instruments and never missing a churning climax.*

At a concert presented by the Greater Boston Youth Symphony Orchestra, Marvin Rabin conductor, "Les Emotions Changeantes" was given another performance.

The conditions under which this piece was composed warrant an explanation, since any composer at some time in his career finds himself in this situation. Liz, who had never composed before, had tried for some time to conceive an idea that she could accept as a basis for a composition, but to no avail. She felt she was completely bereft of inspiration, or, possibly because she was her own severest critic, she was not completely satisfied with any of her initial attempts. One day before the theory class had begun, she started to improvise at the piano with a minimum amount of technique, since cello was her instrument. Suddenly the motif:

EXAMPLE VI-70

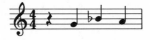

* From a review by Robert Dumm in *The Christian Science Monitor,* June 2, 1961. Used by permission.

which was to become the introduction of her piece, came forth. Recognizing its value as a potential starting point for her piece, I urged
her to consider this as its germ.

She scored the piece for two flutes, oboe, two clarinets, bass
clarinet, bassoon, two horns, two trumpets, trombone, triangle, wood
block, snare drum, cymbals, and strings. The piece is in three movements, Moderato, Andante, Presto. It is written in a contemporary style,
reminiscent of Bartók.

First Movement   This movement is in a free unitary form. In the 4-
measure introduction, the three note motif is assigned to the oboe. As
it repeats itself persistently and quietly, it is accompanied by a chromatically moving bass, which is in keeping with the somewhat chromatic nature of the motif. This counterpoint is played by celli enhanced
by triangle punctuations.

At the end of the introduction, the 4-measure fore-phrase enters
with a rather wandering chromatic-type theme, played by flute, based
upon the motif:

EXAMPLE vi-71

The introduction continues in the background creating a polytonal effect with the theme. The celli meanwhile maintain a stagnant
"C" pedal point giving the feeling of the tonality of "C" rather than
continuing its chromatic movement, which would have been too much
activity at this time.

This material is followed by a 2-measure extension in the form of
a cadence, consisting of a single sustained note, the climactic part of
the theme. The accompaniment still continues. On the after-phrase in
measure 11, the flute repeats the first three measures of the theme, eli-
minating the fourth measure, while the accompaniment continues as
before. A change occurs in the next two measures. It is another extension in the form of a cadence balancing measures 9 and 10, but this
time it is a half-step lower as is the accompaniment by the oboe and
celli. The tonality of B is now established for the next five measures,
beginning in measure 16. The flute continues to play, developing its
theme and transposing it a half-step lower than the original for four
measures with a 1-measure extension. The oboe and celli function as
before.

An outgrowth of the theme follows incorporating shifted rhythm and syncopation presented first in measure 21 by clarinet and answered in measure 23 by flute and bass clarinet. Here the shifted rhythm and the syncopated motif are combined. Two measures of limited activity and a 1-measure extension with syncopation over the piognant taps of the wood block complete this portion. Throughout these six measures, the celli take on a completely new type of activity, more or less consistent in its chromaticism.

A seemingly new thematic presentation in measures 27, 28, and 29 by the bassoon is reminiscent of material in 20, 21, and 22. A gradual rise rhythmically suggests an approaching climax. In measure 30, double stops in the upper strings reinforced by pizzicato basses and wood block begin pulsating a sequence of major chords supporting a theme of ever-increasing intensity played by the celli. This lasts for six measures. Eventually, the celli are joined by bass clarinet and bassoon. Meanwhile, the changing harmonies are sustained by horns. At this point in measure 36, the busy theme is taken over by upper strings doubled by upper woods for three measures as the bassoon and lower strings supply a chromatic bass line with limited activity. The brass in octaves of minor seconds punctuate off-beat dissonances reinforced by snare drum. The brass rise with the theme creating tension and excitement until a climax is reached in measure 39. With trills in the upper woodwinds and tremolos in the upper strings, the theme is carried by low strings, trumpets, and bassoon, while horns and trombone sustain octave unisons. This 2-measure climax is repeated reaching a higher point in measure 43 when, suddenly, the tutti evaporates and the tempo becomes allegro. The flute continues alone quietly and ethereally on the thematic material for five bars progressing in a free downward sequence. Meanwhile, the violins unobtrusively supply an accompaniment, which resembles that played by the celli in measure 21. After the previous climactic tension, this indeed is a refreshing relief. A 4-measure codetta, measures 48–51, in which the theme is continued in a subdued fashion a cappella by clarinet, brings the A tempo restatement of the original motif from the introduction by the oboe for four bars, beginning in measure 52. This restatement is accompanied by the chromatically moving counterpoint associated with the celli and by the penetrating triangle in the introduction. Quietude and repose have been reestablished. Suddenly they are interrupted abruptly in measure 56 by an impetuous and agitated tutti presentation of the theme in unison by flutes, clarinets, bassoon, celli and upper strings, while the other instruments sustain a pedal point in octaves, securing the fundamental tonality of "C." A series of cymbal crashes helps to bring the movement to a frenetic finish.

Second Movement   The material in this andante movement, which is in three-part form, complies in style with that of the first movement. Chromaticism and free tonality continue throughout, creating tension, vitality, and power even in the transparently thin passages, which are economically orchestrated.

The first theme with its motif:

EXAMPLE VI-72

is presented by the first violins. In the 6-measure fore-phrase, the melody gradually soars upward reaching a high point in measure 4, after which it gradually descends, its activity ceasing in the beginning of the next phrase. Observe how this theme expands. Melodically, it consists of a series of arches curving upward and downward, downward and upward. They either alternate or follow consecutively. In this way, a beautiful melodic curve is achieved. The rhythm is animated sufficiently by syncopation. Accompanying the first violins are the second violins and violas in unison counterpoint, involving material resembling the principal melody melodically and rhythmically. The counterpoint seems to gain equal importance for itself.

The 6-measure after-phrase imitates the fore-phrase in exact fugal imitation. The first clarinet assumes the melodic responsibility, while the second clarinet and bassoon function in unison on the counterpoint. Both lines have been transposed a fifth below the original, a curious aberration from the usual fifth above. This procedure is justified doubly—first, because of the natural freedom of the piece itself, and second, because it is transposed consistently throughout.

A 1-measure extension in $\frac{6}{4}$ meter adds intensity in anticipation of theme II, B, beginning in measure 14, which resumes the $\frac{4}{4}$ meter. Its motif:

EXAMPLE VI-73

is developed in the 4-measure fore-phrase by imitation between first violins and celli. Sequence and inversion are applied most freely, consistent with the general character of the piece. In the 6-measure after-phrase, beginning in measure 18, the imitation of the motif ceases, its treatment now becoming a function of sequential continuity by the violins, subsequently joined in unison by the flute and first clarinet.

At the same time, the counterpoint is assigned to violas and celli, subsequently joined by second clarinet and bass clarinet in unison. In measure 21, a tutti is proclaimed, in which the acompanying quarter note motif:

EXAMPLE VI-74

is given to the flute, oboe, first clarinet, trumpet, trombone and violins in unison, intensified by wood block. The eighth note motif, derived from the principal motif of theme II:

EXAMPLE VI-75

is assigned to second clarinet, bass clarinet, violas, and celli in unison.

In the background are the French horn, bassoon, and basses on a sustained pedal point. All this material, the quarter note motif, the eighth note motif, and the pedal point, is developed for three measures sequentially to an almost tempestuous climax in measure 24 at which point a 4-measure extension begins. Here group one, flute, oboe, first clarinet, and violins, in octave unison declare a ♪♩ ♪♩ ♩ rhythm complemented by a reversal of this rhythm ♩ ♩ ♪♩ ♪ proclaimed by group two, second clarinet, bass clarinet, violas and celli, also in unison. Sustaining an octave unison pedal point are the trumpet, trombone, horn, bassoon, and basses. In the next three measures, instruments of groups one and two continue, proceeding in concerted and alternating rhythm above, with the continuation of the above sustained pedal point. A codetta of two measures, combining the eighth note and syncopated motifs in the upper strings in unison against a unison counterpoint by the second clarinet and violas, re-introduces theme II in measure 30. The melody originally played by first violins in measure 14 is now played by first clarinet; the imitation originally played by celli, also in measure 14, is now played by second clarinet and bassoon in unison. This persists for four measures. After a 1-measure extension, theme I returns in measure 35 as it was initially presented at the beginning of the movement by strings proceeding to cadence in measure 40, ending rather quizzically with an upward suspension in B-major tonality.

Third Movement In this movement in ¾ meter, the tonality continues to be vague and free adhering to the style established in the previous two movements. It is in rondo form, in which themes I and II alternate, with the latter subject to variations. Its plan is A, B, A′, B′, B′′, A′′, codetta (A).

Theme I, which is revealed by the first clarinet, contains two significant motifs. The first motif is:

EXAMPLE VI-76

The second motif is:

EXAMPLE VI-77

In both the fore- and after-phrases, the motifs are developed by inversion and by freedom of interval relationship.

Accompanying the first clarinet are the bassoon and celli in unison on a diatonic counterpoint which could be related to the original counterpoint of movement one:

EXAMPLE VI-78

Theme II enters in measure 9 with its two motifs:

EXAMPLE VI-79

EXAMPLE VI-80

the latter related to motif 2 of theme I. The upper strings and clarinet
in unison present the theme with its two motifs, while the lower strings
and bassoon in unison imitate the former by reversing the two motifs.
Each group develops its material by sequence throughout the fore- and
after-phrases. Notice that in the former, the interval relationship again
is free. Major and minor thirds are used arbitrarily rather than literally, and inversion is included to some extent. However, the counterpoint climbs to its high point by chromatic regularity in measure 15,
and then descends slightly to cadence in measure 16. Themes I and
II are then repeated.

Unison flute and first clarinet in measure 17 present theme I as
A′ in the 4-measure fore-phrase in a freely-conceived treatment inter-
vally and directionally, but with the rhythm remaining constant. Accompanying is the contrapuntal diatonic line as first presented, which
now appears in diminution in unison bass clarinet, bassoon, and lower
strings, but with a chromaticism introduced in measure 20. On the
after-phrase, the rhythm of motif 1 is treated by the upper instruments
in sequence, involving chromaticisms and sequence, while the accompanying instruments execute a syncopated rhythm against it. After
this portion is repeated, a new variation of theme II, B′, in measure 25
appears in the upper strings, while the lower strings continue the syncopated figure established previously. The first clarinet joins the upper
strings in measure 29 on the after-phrase. Bass clarinet and bassoon
join the lower strings on the syncopation. Notice that the material of
the first three measures of this after-phrase is a minor third transposition upward of the fore-phrase. Contrary motion chromatically in the
fourth measure, 32, leads to a new phrase for eight measures in which
the rhythm of the first motif of theme I is taken repeatedly, by inversion and repetition, and by unison lower strings, bass clarinet, and
bassoon. At the same time, the counterpoint, related to that which
appeared in measure 17, is played and also successively repeated by
unison oboe, first clarinet, and upper strings chromatically. Its last
two measures, 39 and 40, are transposed upward by a half step, while
the motif by the melody instruments remains the same.

A melodic and rhythmic variation of the first motif of Theme II
returns in measure 41, as B″, played by the unison lower strings, bass
clarinet, and bassoon, while the counterpoint continues in the other in-

struments. A repetition of the first two measures invites a transposition of all material in the next four measures. Gradually, instruments are added on each part, until a tutti climax is reached in measure 49 (A″), where motifs 1 and 2 of theme I and the counterpoint related to them return for two measures only to be repeated literally. In the next 4-measure phrase, 53 through 56, everything is transposed upward freely. The final codetta, beginning at measure 57, comprises the re-iteration of the first motif of A, a syncopation in measure 59, and a unison "D" octave throughout the entire orchestra, accentuated by a cymbal crash, boldly signalling the final conclusion. Throughout this tutti portion, a continuous snare drum roll, ever-increasing in intensity, adds to the excitement.

This music is broad in aspect and scope and teaches many things:

1. Consistency of style throughout the three movements with Bartókian flavor

2. Different form for each movement: unitary form in movement one; three-part form in movement two involving fugal treatment; and rondo form with variations in movement three

3. Constructive principles achieved: unity by repetition of material within each movement, resemblance of both melodic and contrapuntal material throughout all the movements, relationship of counterpoint of third to first movement, and relationship of motif 2, theme II, third movement to motif 2, theme I, third movement; variety by a multiplicity of themes throughout three movements; coherence by the consolidation of all material which, in many respects, may differ but which, in many respects, is the same

4. Phraseologically: predominance of 4-measure and some 6-measure structures, extensions of 1- and 2-measure structures

5. Harmonically: existence of free tonality and chromaticisms throughout all movements as well as polytonality, resulting in dissonance; obvious understanding of the contemporary idiom by exposure to music of the period and by experimentation at the piano with the intention of imitating and incorporating these concepts; use of foreign tones relative to harmonic analyses

6. Contrapuntally: evidence of imitations of material; antiphonal treatment between voices; development of motifs by freedom of interval relationship

7. Abundance of shifted rhythm and syncopation creating drive, vitality, a feeling of ever-present refreshment

8. Orchestration beautifully conceived in solos, duets, and tuttis; economy of instruments evident especially in the tuttis where only two lines

may exist; percussion relegated to triangle, wood block, snare drum, and cymbals, indicating transparency and clarity of material not requiring instruments of a ponderous quality such as timpani and bass drum

9. Interpretation achieved by natural observation of the development of the music dynamically and instrumentally with flexibility of tempos and rubatos wherever logical

Huapangos

Geoffrey Hale

325

326

327

328

329

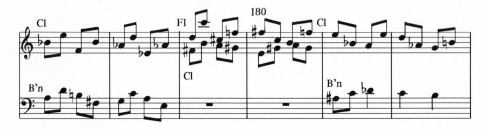

HUAPANGOS   Geoffrey Hale, Grade 12

Elliot Norton, upon hearing this piece performed by the Boston Symphony Orchestra, wrote in the *Boston Record American:*

> "Huapangos" by Geoffrey Hale is bright in color and tone, a gently jocular piece in a Spanish style.*

Geoffrey orchestrated this for flute, oboe, two clarinets, bassoon, horn, two trumpets, trombone, timpani, cymbals and strings. It is a piece which fundamentally is in three-part form, A, B, A, codetta. The

---

* From a review by Elliot Norton in the *Boston Record American,* March 8, 1965. Used by permission.

second part is a fugue followed by new material developed also as a fugue in ever-quickening strettos.

A 4-measure introduction in $\frac{4}{4}$ consists of a motif:

EXAMPLE VI-81

presented by flute very humorously. Tonally, it appears to be in G-minor but in relation to the main theme, it is in D-minor. This motif, which becomes the material of the main theme, is answered in the next measure by a rather grotesque motif:

EXAMPLE VI-82

played by bassoon. In the following two measures, these two motifs are heard again, the first by trumpet an octave lower, the second continued by the bassoon in a transposition a minor third higher.

In measure 5 in $\frac{2}{4}$ the main theme, A, is presented with its two motifs:

EXAMPLE VI-83

EXAMPLE VI-84

The motif in the bass clef is reminiscent of motif 2, measure 2, of the introduction. The theme is presented in 4-measure phraseology by the violins and clarinets. Simultaneously the violas, celli, and bassoon, and later the basses, take up the bassoon accompaniment motif of the introduction with bravado and conviction. They begin exactly with the notes of the transposition of the motif in the introduction and flow directly into the notes of the original.

The main theme is obviously in D-minor, while its accompaniment creates a polytonal effect at first, only to resolve itself into tonal D-minor on the cadential motif:

EXAMPLE VI-85

In measure 13, added to the violins and clarinets are the oboe and flute which create more color. The accompanying orchestral forces assume a downward chromaticism for four measures followed by a reversal upward, also chromatically. In spite of this chromatic treatment, the tonality of D-minor still persists. Suddenly, what appears to be a new theme is heard. Actually it is the main theme inverted and varied rhythmically. The trumpet presents it rather ironically, while the strings merrily hold forth in a pizzicato accompaniment. The theme consists of major and minor triads, mostly major, progressing by root in intervals of minor thirds principally. In customary fashion, the celli and basses provide the roots on the beats. The second violins and violas supply the thirds and fifths on the off-beats. All chords are voiced open in relation to the roots. With this distribution, the dimension becomes more expansive. The lines of the eighth notes played by each instrument are related to the second motif of the main theme rhythmically and by interval, even though the direction is not completely consistent.

In this way, polytonality is created, made more apparent by the many double inflections between notes of the accompaniment and notes of the melody indicated by a bracket in the score. The 3-measure phrase is followed by a 2-measure phrase, during which a very impulsive flourish of triplets by flute and violins adds zest to the grotesqueness already established.

In measure 26, the trumpet continues on the theme transposed three half steps higher and still inverted. The reversal of the accompaniment pattern injects a slight rhythmical surprise, which adds more spice to the music. After this 3-measure phrase, a well-planned interlude for five measures, beginning in measure 29, appears, brilliantly orchestrated with antiphonal treatment involving strings, then woods, then brass. What excitement! By resorting to the progression of chords arranged in the cycle of the fifth, a tonal concept is maintained. A suspended D-flat octave in the lowest strings in measure 33 creates a feeling of anticipation, almost apprehension. It is followed at A' by a prolonged pedal point for 9 measures, which secures the tonality of "D." The flute takes up the theme, transposed and still inverted. In counterpoint to it, the clarinet brings back the original theme with note changes for polytonal effect. After three measures of this, the flourish by first violins returns exactly as before, not a transposition as would be expected in light of the previous treatment of the theme.

During this flourish, the clarinet continues with the theme's second motif of eighth notes inverted in sequence while trumpet executes a pedal point. In the next three measures, the flute and clarinet repeat the material of measures 34, 35, and 36 and lead to cadence (measure 42), which is related to the original cadence of the main theme. Here the soprano is a free inversion of the bass of the original theme. The slurred motif from the previous interlude now appears, played by the brass. It is answered in the next measure by the cadential motif played by woods, treated similarly to measure 42. The slurred motif by brass and the cadential motif by woods are transposed in the next two measures.

The development of the cadential motif begins in measure 47, involving sequences chromatically and antiphonal treatment between brass and woods.

In measure 50, the development continues. Transpositions, antiphonal treatment between woodwinds engaged in duet formation, and double inflections creating more dissonance are readily evident. Structurally, this developmental section consists of phrases of 3, 4, and 6 measures. Suddenly, in measure 60, a new dramatic element enters. The vibrant timpani is the center of attraction, followed by an extremely intense dissonance resulting from the combination of the A-flat major seventh chord over the "B" octave. This combination, played tutti with cymbals, becomes more prominent as the piece progresses. It is as if it were functioning in defiance of the cynicism expounded in the music to this point. Several tutti chords are transposed higher as they appear. They are interrupted by the cadential motif, which is treated contrapuntally as a duet and also transposed as it appears successively.

In the beginning of the middle portion of the piece, B, measure 67, the bassoon announces a new 4-bar theme with the motif:

EXAMPLE VI-86

Moving and pulsating, it becomes the subject of a fugue. The violins tremolo a high pedal point, which, in combination with the bassoon subject, creates an atmosphere of mystery and apprehension. With the violins rising a half step, the answer, a perfect fifth above in measure 71, is taken over by second clarinet. Simultaneously, the bassoon continues on the counter-subject, which is related to the bass of the original cadential motif. The subject returns in measure 75 played by the first clarinet. The second clarinet performs a free treatment of the counter-subject, while a free part in the bassoon is treated in a sequential syncopation, in which the accent keeps shifting. All the while, the violins function on a pedal point still a half step higher.

In measure 79, the answer is taken over by the flute; the counter-subject is assigned to the first clarinet; the second clarinet plays the previous free part almost note for note. At the same time, the bassoon pours out the original main theme motif as a counterpoint in chromatics, sequentially and rhythmically free. During this quartet activity, the violins tremolo again on a pedal point a half step higher than before.

This whole portion, an excellent example of unity, contributes so much to a vibrant tension apropos of the musical message.

In measure 83, the subject of fugue II enters with the motifs:

EXAMPLE VI-87

EXAMPLE VI-88

played by the flute and oboe in octaves. Tonality of C-minor is suggested, while the counter-subject in the bassoon, an outgrowth of the free part of the first fugue, continues the chromatic personality of the work. In measure 88, the answer, a perfect fifth higher, enters in the strings on the first beat rather than on the second as originally conceived while the celli have the counter-subject. This time the counter-subject starts on the second beat of the previous measure rather than on the first beat as originally conceived. Now in measure 92, treatment of the material adds immeasurably to the excitement, energy and vibrancy of the piece. The subject, back to its original second beat entrance, is announced by the horn, which is imitated canonically on the corresponding beat of the following measure by the trumpet, creating a stretto. Throughout this treatment, the trombone takes over the counter-subject beginning on the original first beat. The same format appears in the next phrase. On the second beat in measure 96, woodwinds on the answer are imitated in canonic stretto in the next measure by trumpet, while bassoon takes over the counter-subject, this time starting on the second beat.

A free outgrowth of the eighth note motif, which completes the contrapuntal line, now appears starting in measure 101 with antiphonal imitations between woods and brass. In measure 106, the closer proximity of the strettos of the subject by the strings, a welcome contrast orchestrally, becomes more apparent, creating more rhythmic excitement and mobility. The celli and basses hold forth on the chromatic counterpoint related to the second motif of the subject. Attention must be called to the treatment of this stretto section. Notice how the imitation of the theme in succeeding instruments appears one beat later than the previous appearance—a most subtle device for the purpose and objective in mind.

Suddenly, in measure 111, the flute and first violins announce the theme in inversion above the continued counterpoint in the lower strings and bassoon. The culmination point occurs in measure 114 when the horn and trombone present in octaves the original subject on the second beat. They are imitated by the trumpet in the inversion on the second beat. This creates more complexity made more predominant by a repeated pedal point on the timpani. This is then cleverly followed in measure 118 by a transposition in the form of an answer to all this material. It is as though the fugal treatment already established were continuing with the horn and trombone on the subject, the trumpet on the inversion, and the timpani on the pedal point. As if to allay the height of emotional pitch, four measures of the material of the interlude that appeared in measures 30–33 make their second appearance, measures 123–126, treated in a similar manner orchestrally, only in reverse order, woods, brass and strings. Indeed this is a welcome respite from the intensity that has been building up so continuously. But alas! This is not to last, because in measure 127 the bassoon, in a very stealthlike and furtive manner, commands attention by its announcement of the motif of the second fugal subject modified in diminution. Pauses and repetitions of the theme greatly increase the dramatic element, when suddenly emotional intensity returns. From measure 131 through 140, the subject is taken in syncopation and treated in canonic imitation between clarinet and flute one beat later and then two beats later. During this time, the bassoon grotesquely spurts forth the theme in diminution. Beginning in measure 136, a transposition a fifth higher brings back the tutti dissonant chord of A-flat major 7th over "B" octave in measure 141. This is followed by a reminiscence of the flourish that first appeared in measures 24 and 25. This time it is played as 16th notes by celli supported by a magical tremolo on the timpani. Again the chord is heard in syncopation several times, immediately followed by the flourish played by violins over continued timpani tremolo in measures 145 and 146. This same format is repeated with more syncopations of the chord transposed higher as an A-major 7th over a "C" octave in measures 147 and 148. Another flourish on the violins over timpani tremolo occurs, followed by more syncopations of the chord, which has again been transposed higher as a B-flat major 7th over a C-sharp in measures 151–153.

With the climax consummated in measure 153, celli, basses and a bass drum roll occupy the attention on the next measure as if in relief of the extreme intensity. This is the invitation for the return of the simple and pure introduction followed by the recapitulation of material as before at A' in measure 159.

Finally in measure 184, the point of dramatic conclusion arrives. The timpani powerfully announces the return of the ever-important and characteristic dissonant chord, this time a B-major 7th over a "D" octave in measure 185. At first repeated in syncopated beats, it is transposed twice, first as a C-major 7th over a D-sharp octave, then a C-sharp major 7th over an "E" octave, each time reaching a higher climactic point.

In the final measure, 190, as if in defiance of everything that is cynical, with aplomb and confidence, two more punctuations, the first, an A-flat major 7th over a "B" octave, the second and final, a pure C-minor chord, rhythmically use the eighth note motif of the original main theme. Energetically, with vigor and strength of conviction, they both bring the piece to its conclusion.

Creative imagination, understanding of technical treatment and development of material are all embodied in the piece:

1. In many respects, style is 20th century atonal with several evidences of secure tonality
2. Fundamentally in three-part form, with introduction and coda, and second part consisting of two consecutive fugues
3. Constructive principles evident everywhere: unity achieved by motif and theme relationships such as the introduction to the main theme, the use of the original as a counterpoint to the inversion, the

development and use of the cadential motif in many places, such as the counter-subject of fugue I, the use of the main theme motif as a counterpoint in the first fugue, the use of the free part of fugue I as a counterpoint to the subject of fugue II, repetition of themes in the fugues by imitation and strettos, simultaneous use of subject of fugue II in original and inversion and the reminiscence of the flourish idea; variety achieved by many different themes such as the main theme, the interlude, the fugal subjects, rhythmic interest and vitality created by the entrance of themes on different beats, variations of themes; coherence obtained by the tight-fit relationship of material

4. Phraseologically: mostly 4-measure construction with occasional 3 + 2, 4 + 3, and 5-measure phrases

5. Harmonically: combination of tonal, atonal, and polytonal elements, contributing to dissonance; analyses of harmonies and foreign tones relative because of linear structure; twentieth century character secured by sequence of chords based on roots progressing in minor thirds, double inflections, chords with color tones added

6. Contrapuntally: subtle throughout utilizing related material in its linear structure

7. Orchestrally: understanding of the colors of instruments, their appropriate use in solo and accompaniments, and their characteristics to help increase the emotional aspect

8. Interpretation secured by the orchestration, which is sensitive to the style, idiom, and character of the piece; dynamics result naturally without being imposed artificially

Study for Orchestra

Walter Wagenknecht

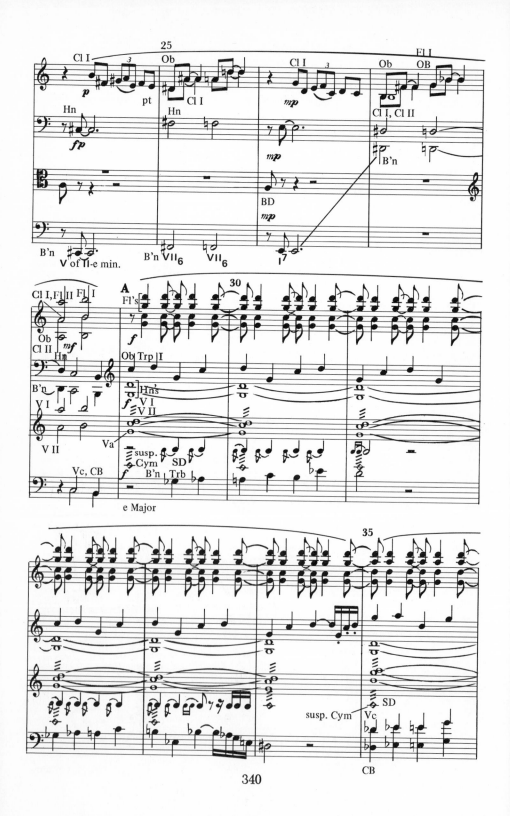

340

343

III

345

347

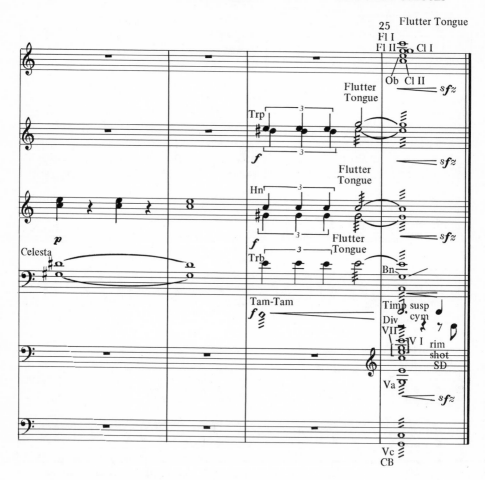

STUDY FOR ORCHESTRA   Walter Wagenknecht, Grade II

Following the performance of Walter Wagenknecht's "Study for Orchestra" by the Boston Symphony Orchestra, Harold Rogers, in *The Christian Science Monitor*, wrote:

> Mr. Wagenknecht captured something of a Renaissance mood in his Study for Orchestra, especially in the modal Andante. He can spin out a melody with considerable skill; he handles his orchestral colors with imagination. Though his final Allegro seemed too short (as if he had run out of time rather than ideas) the three movements together gave evidence of a fine talent. *

* From a review by Harold Rogers in *The Christian Science Monitor*, April 4, 1966. Used by permission.

This piece, after its two performances at the Boston Symphony Orchestra Youth Concerts, was presented at "Newton High School Night at the Boston Pops," Arthur Fiedler, conductor. At the request of the president of the National Education Association, who was in the audience, it was performed by the Symphony of Greater Miami at the convention of the Association in Miami.

The instrumentation for this piece includes two flutes, oboe, two clarinets, bassoon, two horns, two trumpets, trombone, timpani, bass drum, snare drum, triangle, tam-tam, suspended cymbal, crash cymbals, xylophone, celesta, and strings. The style is contemporary involving polytonality and atonality, as well as modal influences. In the allegro first movement, the form is fundamentally three-part with coda based on theme II.

The principal material of the A theme, a 10-measure sentence divided into two equal 5-measure phrases, is based upon the harmonies assigned to the upper strings tremolo. Both the fore-phrase and after-phrase are constructed in groups of 3 and 2 measures with harmonies changing in the initial measure of each group. The motif presented by oboe and trumpet in unison:

EXAMPLE VI-89

is derived from the notes of the first chord played by the upper strings. The ensuing harmonic changes, performed dauntlessly and boldly by tremolo strings, provide notes that the solo instruments incorporate into their melodic development. Notes of the after-phrase are an exact transposition of the fore-phrase, a perfect fifth higher. The combined notes of the entire sentence, with the exception of the chromatic changes that have been inserted parenthetically for color changes on the last two beats of measures 5 and 10, spell out the Dorian mode.

Throughout this exciting and vibrant A theme, syncopations are effected by flutes and clarinets in harmony on the off-beats as accompaniment, outlining the harmonies of the string tremolos and solo instruments. Meanwhile, the bassoon, trombone, and lower strings in unison create a feeling of atonality with their accompanying descending chromatic octaves in the fore-phrase, which are also transposed proportionately in the after-phrase. Here the basses continue on an "E" pedal point which defines the tonality around which the movement revolves.

A tremolo suspended cymbal enhances the tremolo strings, while snare drum punctuates the rhythm of the solo instruments. Through all of this activity—solo theme, syncopated woodwinds, chromatic bass notes creating the atonal atmosphere, and tremolos on the upper strings and cymbal—the horns sustain pedal points in fifths and fourths conforming to the harmonies based on the Dorian tonality. Before this section finally ends, a 2-measure extension beginning in measure 11 finds the flutes, oboe, and trumpets in unison on a series of eighth note triplets against ascending chromatic eighths in twos, played in unison by bassoon, trombone, and lower strings. In measure 12, the former group on eighths against the latter group on quarters leads to the second theme.

A complete contrast is felt with the motif of the second theme in measure 13:

EXAMPLE VI-90

The fore-phrase has a 3-measure structure. The theme is assigned to clarinet in E-minor tonality. The tonic, dominant, sub-dominant, and mediant minor predominate. Syncopations occur in both the theme and the accompaniment assigned to lower woods, horn, and strings. In the 3-measure after-phrase, the theme is suddenly transformed into A-flat minor, during which the oboe takes over the melody accompanied by lower woods and horn. On the tail-end of the theme in measure 18, descending chromatics are incorporated in the lower woods and strings, which continue through the next 1-measure extension.

In measure 20, a 4-measure phrase begins in D-minor. The theme is antiphonally treated in the upper woods accompanied by bassoon and horn in continuous syncopation. In measure 23, a cadence of melody and accompaniment in concerted harmony falls into the unexpected key of E-flat minor.

In the next 5-measure phrase, the clarinet continues the theme in E-minor. It presents the original material of the second theme, B, transposed for two measures, doubled in measure 25 by oboe. The next three measures, 26–28, are essentially the same as before except for fuller orchestration. Percussion throughout this B section consisting of cymbal, snare and bass drums, and timpani is economically but subtly used.

Theme A returns, this time in C-major in diminution. It is a tutti with: the strings and suspended cymbal tremolos, and snare drum punctuations of the rhythm of the solo instruments; syncopations by the flutes and clarinets in harmony on off-beats; solo by unison oboe and trumpet; and accompaniment assigned to bassoon, trombone, and lower strings. At this time, the accompaniment is not chromatic. It is a rather free abandoned type line, in which the tonality is vague, while horns sustain pedal points in perfect fifths throughout. This is all presented for six measures. Then everything is transposed up a perfect fifth for another six measures, with rhythmic elaborations toward the end of the phrase.

Notice that the accompaniment, which in measure 29 began on the third beat, now begins on the first beat of measure 35, an example of shifted rhythm. Finally, the second theme returns in a 5-measure phrase as a coda occurs with shifted rhythm in measure 41. It begins on the first beat in the key of E-major presented by flute. Eventually, the original first three measures of the theme are played by the clarinet. Low strings descend almost chromatically in octave accompaniment. A sub-dominant tutti chord is dramatically contrasted by flutes and triangle alone, answered by bass drum and low strings on the final dominant, which ushers in the second movement.

An idyllic pastoral picture is painted in the second movement, andante, which is in three-part song form, A, A′, B, A′, codetta. Appropriately, it is in the Aeolian mode interchangeable at times with the harmonic minor scale whenever the D-sharps appear. The woodwinds and strings carry the responsibility of theme presentation and development. A very nostalgic theme with two motifs:

EXAMPLE VI-91

EXAMPLE VI-92

sings out in the clarinet with bassoon counterpoint for three measures in the fore-phrase. The 4-measure after-phrase is presented by flute and clarinet accompanied by bassoon. They effect contrapuntally mobile material derived from and related to the material of the fore-phrase, especially measure 3, which is an outgrowth of the motifs. A sixteenth note running passage by woods, after an E-minor cadence in measure 7, reintroduces the first theme as A', which appears in variation with the first violins on the melody and the celli on the counterpoint for a 3-measure phrase. An extension for six measures follows, containing a repetitious motif, which is an outgrowth of motif 2, played by bassoon. A lower contrapuntal line, chromatic and diatonic, is played by basses embellished by timpani tremolos on a dominant pedal point.

In measure 17, new material of B theme enters with the motif:

EXAMPLE VI-93

in the strings with violins on the melody supported by harmony in the lower strings. The clarinet, in reminiscence of the run in measure 7, completes the 4-measure phrase. In measure 21, the celesta and oboe follow with an extension of the material for six measures accompanied by celli. The first theme returns in measure 27 for seven measures, as at first. Then A' in measure 34 appears as before, only this time enhanced by the addition of the celesta. A short codetta of three measures by the woods with a brass chord subdued brings the movement to a close, again on the dominant.

The third movement, allegro, in three-part form, is brief but pulsating throughout. It consists of a main theme, A, with the motif:

EXAMPLE VI-94

The oboe immediately sets forth a nervous utterance, canonically imitated by the clarinet, but with rhythmic change and direction, creating contrary motion. Throughout, the tonality is obscure, suggesting V⁷ chords with lowered fifths and quartal chords. After the first three measures, the fore-phrase, the ♩. ♩ 's and ♪♩. are exchanged for the next four measures, which together with the ♩♫ rhythm developed by sequence in the next two measures, make the after-phrase. All the while, the woods and strings with snare drum and timpani roll are the principal instruments. A tutti, involving the ♪♫ motif in contrary motion in measure 9 with cymbal crash and triangle, ends the theme.

Low strings present a throbbing pulsating and vibrating motif of the second theme, B, in measure 10:

EXAMPLE VI-95

An interesting suggestion of the motif of the A theme of the first movement is announced by trombone in diminution very briefly in measure 12, an evidence of cyclical unity.

Beginning in measure 13, a rhapsodic outpouring of sixteenth notes in arpeggios and in contrary and parallel motions occurs, involving a conversation between strings and woodwinds. Their harmonic structures, when combined, produce unquestioned polytonality. They are brilliantly enhanced by the xylophone, doubling the violins and then functioning independently.

The motif of the A theme is heard in the woods beginning in bar 15. The ♪♫ motif from the last of A returns immediately; it is repeated several times, and then leads to the tutti in measure 18 as presented before in measure 9. In the coda beginning in measure 19, this motif is repeated tutti for dramatic effect over and over, continuing in contrary motion between the upper instruments in unison against the lower instruments in unison. Especially effective are the trombone glissandos, as well as the percussion effects by cymbals, triangle, and timpani. Except for the celesta uttering an unobtrusive dissonance of a G-sharp eleventh in measures 22 and 23, there is abrupt silence. Precipitously the brass in concerted harmony punctuate a quarter note triplet audaciously, as if announcing that the end is about to be. With a crescendo tam-tam roll, a tutti on a pure C-major triad brings the piece to a close.

Unusual maturity and imaginative ideas are reflected in this opus. The salient features are:

1. Contemporary in style harmonically, melodically, and rhythmically
2. Three-part form prevalent in each movement
3. Constructive principles achieved: unity by repetition of themes within each movement literally or in variation, with slight suggestion

of theme I of first movement briefly in the last movement; variety by use of new material in each movement and by variation of themes; coherence by consolidation of material

4. Structurally: predominance of 3-measure phrases with extensions of 1- and 2-measures

5. Harmonically: presence of tonality, atonality, polytonality, and modal influences; abundance of chromaticisms; altered chords, quartal chords, chords with the addition of the 11th and 13th recognizable; subtle diffusion of harmonic structure into melodic and rhythmic treatment simultaneously as in movement 1; presence of foreign tones relative to harmonic analysis; existence of foreign tones more evident when harmony is vertically recognizable; passing tones, appoggiaturas, echappées, auxiliaries, a cambiata and free tone detectable

6. Contrapuntal treatment ever active and contributive to the character of the piece

7. Rhythmically exciting due to syncopations, shifted rhythm and rhythmic transformation

8. Orchestrally: instruments used appropriately and with discretion in solos and accompaniments and in antiphonal treatment; percussion economically applied

9. Dynamics, instrumentation, changes of tempos contribute to proper interpretation

Toccata

Claire Rubin

356

357

358

359

362

TOCCATA   Claire Rubin, Grade 12

After a performance by the Boston Symphony Orchestra, McLaren
Harris of the *Boston Herald* commented:

> Claire Rubin's Toccata, an orchestral essay with robust sonorities
> reminiscent of Prokofiev, exhibited strong understanding of some
> advanced theoretical practices.[*]

The piece is orchestrated for two flutes, oboe, two clarinets,
bassoon, two horns, three trumpets, two trombones, timpani, cymbals,
triangle, and strings. The form is free rondo, A, B, C, C', C", interlude, A, B, C, Coda. Its style and medium is contemporary.

From the very beginning, the entire orchestra plunges into the
first theme. The motif is:

EXAMPLE VI-96

Here the tonality is vague, though the key of F-minor seems to be
the tonal center. In the first three measures of the fore-phrase, a triplet
rhythm is played by high woodwinds and brass, reinforced by double
stops in the upper strings which punctuate the beginning of each triplet. Supporting this material, the low instruments of the orchestra
play single bass notes, which are generally foreign to the triplets
above. The monotony that could have resulted from repetition of the
same material within this short phrase has been avoided by the transposition down a half step of the last triplet. This ushers in a 1-meas-
ure conclusion of the fore-phrase consisting of a series of eighth-note
chords. Syncopation results from the subtle placement of accents
emphasized by bass notes, which occur at the same accented spot. In
the after-phrase beginning in measure 5, the triplet motif again continues for three measures, repeating earlier material with a slight
change in motion and harmony. In measure 8, 1-measure conclusion
of the after-phrase follows, using the eighth note motif with accented
syncopations. This measure parallels the same one in the fore-phrase.
In measure 9, the triplet motif is continued with new harmonies, but,

[*] From a review by McLaren Harris in the *Boston Herald*, February 9,
1964. Used by permission.

interestingly, the triplet is divided between upper and lower parts of the orchestra, thereby creating more syncopation. This pattern comprises a 4-measure phrase, with chord changes on the end of the fourth measure. A 3-measure phrase follows beginning in measure 13. In this phrase, a series of the eighth note motif is repeated and occasionally varied with contrary motion between upper and lower lines.

After the basic melody line had been composed, it was suggested that, to avoid triteness, each note of the line be supported with a chord that would sound unusually exciting and interesting. This required a great deal of experimenting at the keyboard, an exercise highly recommended for the neophyte whose ear must absorb the complexities of twentieth century sonorities. Only by digging in at the piano can he select the sounds which to him will be appropriate for his purpose. He must also open his ears and mind to avenues hitherto unexplored and begin to realize the existence of sounds that at first may seem strange or even sound "wrong." As the neophyte becomes more mature and open-minded, he will reject the trite and commonplace and will begin to use techniques and sound combinations, which will add immeasurably to the value of his work.

Using this kind of preliminary experimentation, Claire chose, for her first section, chords of various denominations, all of them consistent with contemporary usage. These include: augmented and diminished, major triads, quartal chords, dominant 7th chords, minor triads with the added major 6th and major 7th, and dominant 7th chords using the raised 5th. As mentioned before, these chords in most cases are foreign to the bass notes heard with them. If each note of the bass line is considered a fundamental chord root, it becomes apparent that these root positions occur in thirds and seconds, a common twentieth century technique.

To continue with the melodic material, in measure 16 a faster second theme B appears whose motif is:

EXAMPLE VI-97

in which the triplet motif of the first theme is only rhythmically applied. The melody, played by flute and clarinet in octaves, begins in the key of A-flat. It capers and leaps in a frolicking way, using free chromatic progressions, which create a feeling of atonality. Sequences help to develop the motif, while pizzicato upper strings punctuate the beginning of each triplet. Triangle is used sparingly but effectively. Against these two 4-measure phrases, which are repeated, runs a pizzicato bass line played by lower strings and bassoon; this creates a rather eerie and mysterious atmosphere, at times offering dissonance with the melody through the use of double inflection. As the theme nears its end, a bold tutti makes a sudden appearance. Here, chords fundamentally derived from the dominant, with double inflections with the bass line, interrupt the triplet motif several times. Within a 5-measure phrase beginning in measure 24, both motifs are repeated with shifted rhythm. This increases the excitement, only to culminate in an unresolved dominant 9th chord with double inflection.

In measure 29, the third theme, C, with the motif:

EXAMPLE VI-98

appears in a much slower tempo. Tonality is vague, though suggestive of F-major. The music seems to question, rather cynically and ironically, the existence of things. The theme is characteristically made up of minor seconds and is divided into a 5-measure fore-phrase, followed by a 4-measure after-phrase. Both are repeated, after which another 4-measure phrase completes the section. Horns and woodwinds bear the responsibilities here. Portions of the motif, as well as the entire motif and all its transpositions, inversions and sequences, are passed around antiphonally between both choirs. In spite of the bar line, it is interesting to see how rhythmically the horn material gives the feeling of $\frac{3}{4}$ in the first measure. Although the woodwinds answer on the fourth beat, this may be considered as though it were the first beat of the measure; eradicate the bar line, and $\frac{4}{4}$ rhythm is felt. The horns return on the original fourth beat (to be considered now as the first beat of the measure), and with the eradication of the bar line the woodwind material on the first two beats of the original measure becomes the second and third beats. With the horns on the simulated first beat, a feeling of $\frac{3}{4}$ rhythm again results. From here on, the duple rhythm becomes orthodox. Altogether, this section represents a classic example of an asymmetric division.

The material gains momentum in speed and dynamics, and in measure 42 the theme is varied, C'. The motif in the low instruments is imitated for six measures either literally or by inversion in contrary motion, and at times freely, by the high instruments. In the next 4-measure phrase beginning in measure 48 the pattern is reversed, with the highs being imitated by the lows, not literally but sometimes in parallel motion, then contrary motion, then freely. In measure 52, a 6-measure phrase begins, and harmony again appears in the highs and is imitated in the lows, this time literally and freely and also in contrary motion. In measure 58, a new variation of the third theme appears again in F tonality, C''. Here, in another 6-measure phrase, the lows are imitated by the highs literally, with two eighth notes occurring on the second beat of each measure in the highs. In the next 5-measure phrase, the two eighth notes played by the lows appear on the third beat for variety. All is concerted in the final 8-measure phrase beginning in measure 69, and both quarter and eighth notes are used consecutively. (Observe the eighth notes as they keep appearing on different beats in consecutive measures, creating a rhythmic vitality which culminates in a series of eighth notes for measures 74 and 75, in syncopation. A sustained "E" octave, the leading tone of "F," diminuendos and gives a feeling of suspension and anticipation.

From C' through C'', tutti has been used. In measure 77, the interlude, a contrast in tempo and dynamics, with an economy of instrumentation, occurs. The low strings play a downward diatonic and then chromatic line which is made mysterious by constant repetition of a vii^{o7} of the dominant triad over the dominant note played by trombone. Below, the horns bring back an abridgement of the third theme in a 5-measure phrase, when suddenly the triplet motif of the second theme in measure 82 returns chromatically for four measures in the upper woodwinds, imitated by the low instruments chromatically in contrary motion. This prepares the way for a recapitulation of the first, second and third (abridged) themes, to coda in measure 86, ending in a sustained F-major triad in measure 93. Finally, a tutti appears in measure 94, with the motif of theme 1 slightly elaborated, ending with three bold and dynamic chords, F-major, VI in F-minor with added G-flat, and F-major, the fundamental tonality of the piece.

A most powerful and creative piece not only in material, but also as a lesson in orchestration, this piece is of great value:

1. Twentieth century style with "robust sonorities reminiscent of Prokofiev"
2. Free rondo form because of the unorthodox sequence of themes
3. Constructive principles achieved: unity by the repetition of themes, rhythmic use of the triplet motif of the first theme within the second

theme, and use of the motif of the first theme in the coda; variety by the many themes used, the changes in mood and tempo, and the variations of theme 3; coherence by the skillful use of unity and variety

4. Phraseologically: work rich in the combination of: 3 + 1 measures: 4+3, 5, 5+4, 6+4, 6, and 6+5

5. Harmonically: chords treated in a variety of ways: fundamental notes altered; quartal chords apparent; color tones added to produce double inflections with the accompaniment; polytonality and atonality suggested; root positions of chords in thirds and seconds evident; foreign tones to be considered in a relative manner because of atonality and polytonality

6. Material repeated literally up to a point, then varied melodically and rhythmically, especially at the ends of phrases to avoid monotony; pattern of theme occasionally reversed; motifs transposed, inverted and sequenced; contrary motion between the parts employed liberally; rhythmically, syncopation obtained by the use of accents at appropriate places, by the alternation of fragments of a line between parts, and by shifted rhythm; interest and intensity increased by use of asymmetric meter

7. Orchestrally, understanding of the instruments and economy of percussion shown by their appropriate uses throughout: in the tuttis, in the antiphonal treatment, and sometimes for purposes of economy, especially in theme 3 where an enigmatic quality requires the use of instruments suitable for dynamic effects

8. A philosophy readily perceived in: the powerful first theme made massive by its orchestral forces; the frivolity of the second theme as defined by capering woodwinds and a percussive string pizzicato; and the enigmatic third theme with its variations and their characteristic minor seconds; quality of themes conducive to proper interpretation emotionally and dynamically with adherence to correct tempos

CONCLUSION TO CHAPTERS 5 AND 6

I would like to point out that all these young composers, though exposed primarily to a free creative experience, knew that they had to practice certain musical disciplines in order to hear their music properly performed. Among the most important of these are the mechanics of notating manuscripts clearly, legibly and intelligibly. They were taught to set up a vocal line with lyrics and piano accompaniment, to write harmonized voices to a solo part, and to arrange and organize geometrically an instrumental score, whether for small chamber group or a larger orchestral ensemble. All these techniques are necessary for a good, professional-appearing product. Extracting parts from an instrumental score correctly was an experience that added to the importance of their work and to their personal feelings of accomplishment.

It is my theory that if a child is made to feel important, as if he were a professional, his product will have the earmarks of a professional piece. He never should be made to feel like an amateur, a word that is better not used if the teacher wishes to inspire the student toward future accomplishment. Weaknesses should not be condoned because the composer is "an amateur." It is far better to emphasize that errors are a product of inexperience and that even a professional makes mistakes. The objective is to instill in the youthful composer a sense of pride, something he cannot realize if his mistakes go unobserved. With only a little more concentration and dedication, the young composer will be able to reach the point where inconsistencies become the exception rather than the rule.

Conclusion

Music as a language is a psychological and cultural mainstay of our civilization; it is also a vital force in the health of our society. Today, too many educators and administrators feel that the primary objective of music is entertainment, and, therefore, consider it a peripheral subject. Perhaps they would do well to recall the words of Shakespeare: "The man who hath no music in himself, nor is not moved with concord of sweet sounds, is fit for treasons, stratagems, and spoils. Let no such man be trusted." Or remember Plato's thesis that "musical training is a more potent instrument than any other because rhythm and harmony find their way into the inner places of the soul." It was Plato's philosophy that made the study of music by all young men in Greece mandatory, with the realization that this would contribute importantly to their understanding of harmony in government. To quote once more, Robert Browning observed that "There is no truer truth obtainable by man than comes of music."

How salutary it would be if administrators today could respond to the central, life-giving quality of this heritage! Perhaps music educators might then gain the support and equipment they need to give children the same opportunities they now receive in more recognized fields. Music, like philosophy and literature, enriches; its entertainment value is secondary. To establish music as a vital force in our society, teachers must equip themselves accordingly. The children they teach do not have to become professional musicians. How many students in a creative writing class become practicing authors or poets? How many students who have taken courses in chemistry or physics become professional scientists? The parallel holds true for other educational areas—the importance of learning the fundamentals of different disciplines, as part of the over-all educational process, is widely accepted. The same holds true for music. It should, like other subjects, be taught in depth, not by superficial shortcuts. Students have a right to learn this language and to learn it well. Thus may they come to understand intelligently a symphony concert, a Broadway show, or even a simple folk song—and appreciate them all the more—just as the creative writing student, who has since become a physician or businessman, appreciates the theater or a good book.

To develop musicianship, a child must discipline himself to practice daily in order to establish a feeling of being at home, of confidence, when he picks up a piece of music and wishes to "hear" it in his mind. In the long run, he will be gratified by knowing he has acquired a reading skill, which strengthens him mentally, emotionally, and culturally. This skill will become more evident when he has developed, without reservation or hesitancy, an understanding of and feeling for music. At first, his creative efforts will be spontaneous or emotional, but as he gains more experience and becomes more mature, he will realize the importance of developing a technical facility. Better compositions will result, giving him more intellectual satisfaction. His appreciation and understanding of harmony and counterpoint will make his creations that much more exciting.

What better foundation is there for the belief that creativity is innate in every human being, especially evident in those from ages 5 through 17, than that shown by the many examples appearing in this book? From all that has been said in this book, it is evident that to compose music a person does not have to be inducted into an occult society living in an ivory tower. Everyone has latent creative ability of varied dimensions. It is my sincere hope that all music educators will take it upon themselves to carry on as missionaries, spreading the important gospel that age is no factor in creativity. Talent is too often inhibited; young people must have encouragement, guidance and understanding, and it is incumbent upon their music teachers to provide these. Without such dedicated leadership, much will be lost, not only in productivity, but also in the personality development of our children. Simply watching the reaction of these young composers to a performance of their own work is reward enough. As one student put it, "My three years in Newton High School were years of common everyday occurrences, and not until I began writing my piece, and especially after hearing it, did I consider anything important or significant. This experience was the only real thing that happened to me in high school."

Primarily, we must be concerned with the emotional future of these youngsters. What better way is there to help them enjoy emotional stability than to help them express inner feelings through their own artistic creations? To be sure, inevitably there will be some frustrations, especially in the case of insecure children who, because of previous traumatic events or rejection, find it difficult to express themselves at first. These children need special help. Given patience, understanding and proper direction, they too may eventually emerge from their shells and learn the excitement of creative achievement. Is this not the ultimate goal of *all* teaching?

Above all, it must be clearly pointed out and understood by everyone concerned that the creative student must develop an attitude of tolerance for the works of others. He must avoid impetuosity or impulsiveness in making decisions and in accepting and rejecting material created. He must develop an attitude of temperance and objectivity. For the composer, it is difficult to be free of subjectivity toward his own work. He can become so identified with his opus that very often he may not see the forest for the trees. He should invite the opinions of others, teachers and colleagues. As he gains more experience, he will mature and become more objective and secure. The ultimate will be achieved when a composer can be his own severest critic.

Creative expression in the lives of young people will develop creative power individually and collectively, not only in music, but also in any field of endeavor, which may eventually be of interest. It will establish a healthy and balanced attitude toward life and may even rescue and rehabilitate those whom society may have rejected.

As far as this book is concerned, I have already stated that my aim is not to make all our students professional composers. It is rather to encourage creativity for its own sake and for what it can do to stimulate the imagination of children generally. In the area of music, the approaches and programs outlined here clearly demonstrate the enormous potential that already exists. Carried out with skill, knowledge and wisdom, perhaps these approaches and programs *can* provide a bridge for the younger generation to join the ranks of the Bachs, Beethovens, and Bartóks of the future.

Appendix

Listed below are books on harmony, melody, counterpoint, orchestration, ear training, musical notation, form, avant-garde and electronic music, and jazz which will be helpful.

HARMONY AND MELODY

1. Alchin, Carolyn A., *Applied Harmony*. Hollywood, Calif.: Highland Music Co., 1959.
2. Harder, Paul O., *Harmonic Materials in Tonal Music*, Parts I and II. Boston: Allyn and Bacon, Inc., 1968.
3. Marquis, G. Welton, *Twentieth Century Music Idioms*. Englewood Cliffs, N.J.: Prentice-Hall, Inc., 1964.
4. Piston, Walter, *Harmony*, third edition. New York: W. W. Norton & Company, Inc., 1967.
5. Rauscher, E. J., *Chromatic Harmony*. New York: Free Press of Glencoe, Inc., 1965.
6. Robinson, Raymond C., *Progressive Harmony*, revised edition. Boston: Bruce Humphries, Inc., 1962.
7. Schönberg, Arnold, *Structural Functions of Harmony*, revised. New York: W. W. Norton & Company, Inc., 1969.
8. Siegmeister, Elie, *Harmony and Melody*, Vols. I and II. Belmont, Calif.: Wadsworth Publishing Co., Inc., 1965, 1967.

9. Tapper, Thomas, *First Year Harmony,* revised edition. Evanston, Ill.: Summy-Birchard Publishing Co., 1969.
10. Tischler, Hans, *Practical Harmony.* Boston: Allyn and Bacon, Inc., 1964.
11. Ulehla, L., *Contemporary Harmony.* New York: Free Press of Glencoe, Inc., 1966.

COUNTERPOINT

1. Krenek, Ernst, *Studies in Counterpoint.* New York: G. Schirmer, Inc., 1940.
2. Merritt, A. Tillman, *Sixteenth Century Polyphony.* Cambridge: Harvard University Press, 1949.
3. Piston, Walter, *Counterpoint.* New York: W. W. Norton & Company, Inc., 1947.

ORCHESTRATION

1. Berlioz-Strauss, *Treatise on Instrumentation.* New York: Kalmus, 1948.
2. Forsyth, Cecil, *Orchestration,* second edition. New York: The Macmillan Co., 1937.
3. Kennan, Kent, *Technique of Orchestration,* second edition. Englewood Cliffs, N.J.: Prentice-Hall, Inc., 1952.
4. McKay, George F., *Creative Orchestration,* second edition. Boston: Allyn and Bacon, Inc., 1969.
5. Piston, Walter, *Orchestration.* New York: W. W. Norton & Company, Inc., 1955.
6. Rimsky-Korsakoff, *Principles of Orchestration with Musical Examples.* New York: Dover Publications, 1964.
7. Wagner, Joseph, *Orchestration.* New York: McGraw-Hill, Inc., 1959.

EAR TRAINING

1. McGaughey, Janet McLoud, *Practical Ear Training,* second edition. Boston: Allyn and Bacon, Inc., 1966.
2. McHose, Allen I., *Teachers Dictation Manual.* New York: F. S. Crofts & Co., 1948.
3. Thomson, William E., and DeLone, Richard P., *Introduction to Ear Training.* Belmont, Calif.: Wadsworth Publishing Co., Inc., 1967.

MUSICAL NOTATION

1. Donato, Anthony, *Preparing Music Manuscript*. Englewood Cliffs, N.J.: Prentice-Hall, Inc., 1963.
2. Read, Gardner, *Music Notation—A Manual of Modern Practice*, second edition. Boston: Allyn and Bacon, Inc., 1968.

FORM

1. Berry, Wallace, *Form in Music*. Englewood Cliffs, N.J.: Prentice-Hall, Inc., 1965.
2. Leichtentritt, Hugo, *Musical Form*. Cambridge: Harvard University Press, 1965.
3. Tyndall, Robert, *Musical Form*. Boston: Allyn and Bacon, Inc., 1964.

AVANT-GARDE AND ELECTRONIC MUSIC

1. Cage, John, *Silence: Lectures and Writings*. Middletown, Conn.: Wesleyan University Press, 1961.
2. Cage, John, *Year From Monday: New Lectures and Writings*. Middletown, Conn.: Wesleyan University Press, 1969.
3. Cross, Lowell M., *Bibliography of Electronic Music*. Toronto: University of Toronto Press, 1967.
4. Judd, Frederick C., *Electronic Music and Musique Concrète*. London: M. Spearman, 1961.

JAZZ

1. Dankworth, Avril, *Jazz: An Intro to Its Musical Basis*. London: Oxford University Press, 1968.
2. Markewich, Reefe, *Inside Outside: Substitute Harmony in Modern Jazz and Popular Music*. Riverdale, N.Y.: Markewich, 1967.
3. Schuller, Gunther, *Early Jazz: Its Roots and Musical Development*. London: Oxford University Press, 1968.
4. Wilson, Jan S., *Jazz: The Transition Years 1940–1960*. New York: Appleton-Century-Crofts, Inc., 1966.

Index

Aase's Death (Grieg), 32
Abbey Singers, 38
Abbreviations, list of, 59
A capella choir, 57
A capella melody, 87, 92
Accented syllables, 11, 18
Accompaniment:
    piano as, 148–50, 189, 367
    selection of, 44
Activity and stagnation, theory of, 40
Adagio for Strings (Barber), 46
Advanced music theory class, 5, 50, 55, 172
Aeolian mode, 114–15, 182, 184, 351
After-phrase, 32, 97, 115, 122, 124, 131, 135, 149, 167–68, 245, 318, 320, 351
    analysis of, 17
    concept of, 5
    defined, 15
Age of Anxiety (Bernstein), 46
Alberti bass, 36, 44, 130, 293, 304
Alchin, Carolyn A., 55
Aleatory music, 45
Alexander, Judy, 88–93
Alto harmony, 99
A-major key, 282–83
"Amateur," connotation of, 368
Amicangioli, Jonna, 94–100
A-minor key, 136
Anacrusis, 11, 18, 62, 70
Anderson, Marian, 38
Animals' Discussion, The (Tufts), 60–65
Annie Laurie (Douglass-Scott), 32
Antecedent, defined, 15
Anticipation, 143

Anti-climax, 36
Antiphonal treatment, 44–45, 115, 223–25, 281, 322, 333
Appalachian Spring (Copland), 46
Appassionata Sonata (*Sonata No. 23, Op. 57*) (Beethoven), 35
Applied Harmony (Alchin), 55
Appoggiatura, 63–64, 83, 115, 131, 137, 143, 186, 191, 247, 266, 285
Arpeggios, 75–76, 86, 97, 113–14, 131, 160, 232
    as accompaniment, 44
    in singing, 26
Atomistic philosophy, 2
Atonality, 42, 287, 337, 349, 354, 364
Augmentation, 43–44
    motif and, 32
Authentic cadence, 15–16, 21, 24–25, 52, 63, 71, 99, 124, 142, 148–49, 244
Auxiliaries, 143

Bach, Carl Philipp Emanuel, 37
Bach, Johann Sebastian, 32, 36–37, 43
Banks, Betsy, 73–77
Barber, Samuel, 37, 46
Bar lines:
    area between, 12
    indication of, 18
Baroque style, 36–37, 46
Barricades Mystérieuses, Les (Couperin), 35
Bartók, Béla, 36–37, 46, 143, 316

Bass, chromaticisms in, 108
  (*see also* Accompaniment)
Bass drum, 349
Basso ostinato, 160, 162
Bassoon, 210, 243, 245, 280, 289,
    301, 316, 330, 349, 363
  imitation by, 319
  solo, 290, 305, 317, 331, 333–34
Beats, continuity of, 39
Beethoven, Ludwig van, 30–37, 44,
    278
Berg, Alban, 36–37, 45–46
Berio, Luciano, 37
Berlioz, Hector, 36–37, 278
Bernstein, Leonard, 26, 46
Bible, inspiration from, 196
Bielski, Michael, 237–47
Bjoerling, Jussi, 38
Block chord structure, 192
Books (Kaplan), 66–72
Boston Globe, 221
Boston Herald, 242, 363
Boston Record American, 242, 278,
    330
Boston Symphony Orchestra, 242,
    261, 330, 348, 363
  Youth Concerts of, 349
Boulez, Pierre, 37
Brahms, Johannes, 32–33, 35–37
Brandenburg Concertos (Bach), 36
Britten, Benjamin, 35
Browning, Robert, 369
Bruckner, Anton, 37
Bull, John, 35
Byrd, William, 35

Cadence:
  authentic (*see* Authentic ca-
    dence)
  defined, 15
  half (*see* Half-cadence)
  rising, 15
  tonic, 106
Cage, John, 37, 46
Cambiatas, 285
Canonic imitation, 21
Canons, in electronic sound, 47
Capon, Ross, 267–85
Capriccio (Capon), 267–85

Carnival of the Animals (Saint-
    Saëns), 33
Case, Dottie, 186–92
Celesta, 349, 352
Cello:
  as counterpoint, 316, 319, 334
  motif by, 264
  solo, 144
  in string quartet, 119
Chamber music, 37
Child (*see also* Student):
  composing by, 1
  confidence of, 4
  creativity in, 2–3
  embarrassment of, 3, 368
  freedom of, 2
  innate creativity of, 370
  as musical automaton, 3
  pitch discrepancies in, 3
  uninhibited reaction of, 2
Child's Garden of Verses, A (Steven-
    son), 188
Chopin, Frédéric François, 33–34, 44
Chorale with Theme and Variations
    (Jodrey), 201–16
Chord(s):
  function of, 159
  intervals and, 26–27
Chord progression, 27
Chord vocabulary, 52
Christian Science Monitor, The, 180,
    210, 231, 261, 301, 314
Chromatic melodies, 36
Chromaticism, 318, 321
  in bass, 108
  in counterpoint, 124
  dissonance and, 306
Clarinet:
  B-flat, 130
  imitation by, 319
  solo, 131–32, 148–50, 161, 169,
    231, 233, 290–91, 304, 317,
    319–20, 333–34, 351–52
Clarinet and flute ensembles, 122–
    25, 128, 135, 166, 197, 234,
    242, 278, 289, 301, 316, 321,
    330, 349, 351, 363
Classical style, 37, 47, 266
Climax, 36
C-major chord, 63

C-major key, 136
  melodic motif in, 28
C-major scale, 13–14
  four-measure phrase in, 20
  tone row series in, 19
C-major triad, 13–14, 21
C-minor key, 136–37
Coda, 33, 231, 247, 266, 349, 353
Codetta, 142, 144, 159, 212, 317, 319, 322, 330, 351
Coleman, Ornette, 46
Color-basic principle, 52
Commonplace, rejection of, 364
Composer:
  child as, 1–2
  creation of motif by, 156–57
  imagination and ingenuity of, 222
  musical disciplines required in, 367–68
  as neophyte in creativity, 171
  as professional, 368
Composition (see also Creativity):
  fundamental principles of, 5, 31–48
  guidelines for, 1
  harmony and counterpoint in, 40
  melodic synthesis in, 40–41
  model in, 7
  mysteries of, 4–5
  singing as approach to, 8–10
  student self-criticism in, 53
  techniques in, 39–45
  Theory I course in, 52–53
  Theory II course in, 5, 50, 55, 172
  trial and error in, 40
  vocal treatment in, 37–38
Concerto, 35
Concerto for Orchestra (Bartók), 36–37, 46
Concerto for Piano More or Less (Singer), 151–62
Concerto Grosso (Handel), 36
Concerto grosso style, 263
Concerto for Violin and Orchestra (Berg), 36
Conflict in Solitude (Currens), 295–306
Conjunct interval, 19

Consecutive fifths, error of, 52
Consequent, defined, 15
Constructive criticism, need for, 54
Contact microphones, 47
Contemporary music, stylistic elements in, 36
Contrapuntal devices, 115
Contrary motion, 109
Cooke, Michèle, 121–25
Copland, Aaron, 37, 46
Counterpoint:
  in beginning composition, 40–41
  chromaticism in, 124
  harmony and, 40–42
  study of, 52–53
Couperin, François, 34–35, 37, 222
Cowell, Henry, 46
Creative Arts Center, Newton, Mass., 49
Creative Arts Program, 4, 50
Creative climate, establishing of, 49–57
Creative power, development of, 371
Creative teaching, essence of, 7
Creativity:
  channeling of, 1
  fear and, 171
  gradual approach to, 9
  harmonic approach to, 26
  high school composers as neophytes in, 171
  innateness of, 370
  jingle approach to, 10–19, 26
  latent, 370
  meaning and purpose of, 1–7
  melodic approach to, 25–26
  music composition as, 1–2
  rhythm approach to, 21–25
  singing approach to, 8–10
  teaching approaches in, 8–30
  tone row approach to, 19–21
  vocal, 38
Criticism, constructive, 54
Cross parts, 52
Currens, Tina, 295–306
Cymbal, suspended, 350
Cymbals, crash, 292, 301, 303, 316–17, 349–50, 363
Cynicism, in music, 333

Daniel (prophet), 197
David, King, 197
Debussy, Claude Achille, 37, 44–46
Déserts (Varèse), 46
Diminution, 43, 279
  motif and, 32
Disjunct intervals, 19
Dissonance, 63, 162, 184, 303, 333
  chromaticism and, 305–6
  complex harmonies and, 43
  harmonic scheme and, 108
  as melodic interest, 29
  romantic style, 42
  teaching of, 52
  tonal freedom and, 157
  in twelve-tone system, 294
  voice leading and, 191
D-minor key, 214, 280–81, 284, 331–32, 350
"Do," in scale, 21
Dominant chord, 17
Don Quixote (Strauss), 35
Dorian mode, 80–82, 113, 279, 349–50
  triads in, 82, 115
Dotted half-notes, 20
Doubling, harmonic balance and, 42
Drink to Me Only with Thine Eyes (Jonson), 34
Duet for Flutes (Olton), 217–25
Dulfano, Guila, 78–84
Dumm, Robert, 180, 210, 231, 314
Duple time, simulation of, 110
Durchkomponiert, 187
Durgin, Cyrus, 221

Ear training, 21, 55
Echappée, 64, 83, 143, 235, 247, 266, 285, 354
Education, traditional, 2
E-flat key, 136
Eighteenth-century style, 231–35
Electronic music, 45–47
Elijah (Mendelssohn), 33, 43
Embarrassment, of student, 3, 368
Emotions Changeantes, Les (Little), 307–23
Encyclopaedia Britannica, 38

Episode No. 1 (Bielski), 237–47
Eroica Symphony (*Symphony No. 3, Op. 55*) (Beethoven), 32, 36
Extended rondo form, 242

Fantastic Symphony (Berlioz), 36
Fantasy Gavotte (Harutunian), 248–66
Fauré, Gabriel, 43
Fear, creativity and, 171–73
Feedback, in tape recording, 48
Fermata, 231
Fiedler, Arthur, 349
Fifths, perfect, 36
Figured bass, 52
Final note, 81
Fine, Irving, 37, 46
First Chair Instruments of the Orchestra (Philadelphia Orch.), 38
Fisher, Linda, 174–85
Five Pieces for Orchestra (Schoenberg), 37, 46
Flute:
  antiphonal treatment of, 223–25
  as counterpoint, 199
  duet for, 217–25
  imitation by, 280
  oboe and, 291–92
  solo, 132, 233, 246, 290, 304–5, 316–17, 331, 334, 351
Flute-clarinet ensembles, 112–16, 128, 135, 142–45, 166, 197, 210, 234, 242, 278, 289, 301, 316, 321, 330, 349, 351, 363
Folk songs, 34
Foreign tones, 42, 64, 88, 109, 115, 143, 285
  defined, 159
  teaching of, 55
Fore-phrase, 61–62, 70, 75, 79, 86, 97, 122, 124, 142, 167–69, 182, 189, 231, 243, 263, 318, 320, 351, 363, 365
  concept of, 5
  defined, 15, 32
  essence of, 16
  four-measure, 21

Forms, types of, 32–35
Foss, Lukas, 46
Four-four rhythm, 20
Four-measure phrase, 16, 21
Franck, César Auguste, 35
Free Jazz (Coleman), 46
Free rondo form, 105, 170, 224, 247, 363, 366
Free tones, 143, 247, 318, 320, 322
French horn, 319
French Suites (Bach), 33
Frolic for Clarinet and Piano (Phillips), 146–50
Fugue, 35, 331, 334

Gabrieli, Andrea, 199
Gershwin, George, 42
Gerson, Beverly, 117–20
Gesang der Jünglinge (Stockhausen), 46
Glazer, Stuart, 85–87
G-major scale, 280
G-minor key, 264–65
"Good Morning" experiment, 11–13, 15–16, 20
Greater Boston Youth Symphony Orchestra, 315
Grieg, Edvard Hagerup, 32, 242

Hale, Geoffrey, 324–37
Half-cadence, 15, 17, 25, 32, 52, 63, 71, 99, 136, 142, 148, 233–34, 245–46, 263, 279
Half-notes, 20
Handel, George Frederick, 33, 35–37, 43
Harmonic balance, voicing and doubling in, 42
Harmonic dictation, 52
Harmonic progression, melodies and, 27–28
Harmonic rhythm, 52
Harmonic structure, 64–65, 118–19
Harmonies, secondary, 28–29
Harmonious Blacksmith, The (Handel), 35
Harmonization, in theory class, 52–55

Harmony:
in basic composition, 40–41
four-part, 27
intervals and, 27
Harmony (Piston), 55
Harris, McLaren, 242, 363
Harutunian, John, 248–66
Haydn, Franz Joseph, 32–33, 35, 37, 44, 231
Haydnesque style, 128, 231
Hearing, mental, 3, 52
High school music courses, 5, 49–50, 172, 370
Hindemith, Paul, 36–37, 46
Home key, 33
Home on the Range, 34
Homophonic music, 197
Horn, 289, 301, 316, 330, 349, 363
HPSCHD (Cage and Hiller), 46
Huapangos (Hale), 324–37

Imagination, 336
as gift, 1
need for, 222
Imitation, 32, 43
learning by, 56
Impressionistic style, 37
Individuality, stylistic, 48
Ingenuity, need for, 222
Insecurity, creativity and, 171–73
Instinct, in students' work, 54
Instrumental contrast, 45
Instrumental treatment, 37–38
Instruments:
antiphonal treatment of, 44, 115
compositions for, 112–70
in middle and junior high schools, 59
range and register of, 6
Instruments of the Orchestra (National Symphony Orch. of Washington), 38
Interval:
analysis of, 52
conjunct and disjunct, 19
as "heart and soul" of music, 26–27
understanding of, 27–28

Inversions, 32, 43, 108
  use of, 52
Irony and satire, in motif, 158
Israelites, music of, 196–97
Ives, Charles Edward, 46

Jingle, accented syllables in, 11
Jingle approach, to creativity, 10–19, 26
Jodrey, David, 201–16
Junior high school program, 55, 58–170

Kaiser Quartet in C-major (Haydn), 35
Kaplan, Marjorie, 66–72
Kontakte (Stockhausen), 46

Land of Counterpane, The (Case), 186–92
Late romantic style, 37
Lawson, Donna, 226–36
Leonore Overture No. 3 (Beethoven), 37
Liszt, Franz, 37
Little, Liz, 307–23
London Symphony Orchestra, 38
Love, eternity of, 181
Luftpause, 231
Lullaby (Brahms), 33

Madrigal, romantic, 180
Madrigal group, 57
Mahler, Gustav, 37, 278
Major scale:
  construction of, 5
  singing of, 26
Mathis der Maler (Hindemith), 46
Mazurka, Op. 33, No. 3 in C (Chopin), 33–34
Mechanistic philosophy, 2
Mellon, Jason C., 89
Melodic line, 17–18, 64
  contour of, 36, 55, 99
  unaccompanied, 87
  "waving" of, 84, 87, 92, 116

Melodic motif, as approach to creativity, 25–26
Melodic style, teaching of, 42
Melodic synthesis, 40–41
Melodic treatment, 35–36
Melodic unity, diagram of, 17–18
Melody:
  climax and anti-climax in, 36
  harmonic progression and, 27–28
  non-vocal, 36
  wave-like structure of, 35–36, 84, 88, 92, 116
Mendelssohn, Felix, 33–34, 37, 43
"Mental hearing," 3, 52
Mer, La (Debussy), 46
Merrill, Robert, 38
Messiah (Handel), 43–44
Meter:
  academic approach to, 10
  defining of, 18
  rhythm and, 12–13
Meyers, Donna, 126–33
Middle and junior high schools:
  creative work in, 58–170
  instruments used in, 59
Milhaud, Darius, 37, 46
Minor scales, harmonic progressions in, 27
Minuet form, 69
Minuet rhythm, 22
Mitchell, Howard, 38
Mixolydian mode, 80, 143, 197
  triads in, 81
Modes, *vs.* scales, 81–83
Modulation, 43
  motif and, 32
Moissoneurs, Les (Couperin), 34
Monophonic style, 87
Moog Synthesizer, 48
Moonlight Sonata (Op. 27, No. 2) (Beethoven), 33
Mormon Tabernacle Choir, 38
Motif, 97–98
  C-major melody and, 28
  concept of, 5
  creation of, 156–57
  development of, 16–17
  eighth-note, 99
  importance of, 16
  improvising of, 315
  in madrigal, 181

Motif (*cont.*)
  as musical basis, 31
  repetition and, 31, 200
  rhythmic, 23–25
  secondary, 99–100
  syncopated, 182
  unity and, 29
  variations of, 32
Motion, function of, 43
Moussorgsky, Modest Petrovich, 303
Mozart, Wolfgang Amadeus, 31–35, 37, 43–44
Musette en Rondeau (Rameau), 34
Music:
  creative teaching of, 7
  cynicism in, 333
  disciplines required in, 367–68
  instrumental and vocal treatment in, 37–38
  as language, 369
  listening to, 52–53
  measurement of, 10
  motion in, 43
  religious worship and, 196
  rhythm in, 10, 22 (*see also* Rhythm)
  setting of to poetry, 19
  twentieth-century idioms in, 45–48
  as vital force in society, 369
Music Club, Newton High School, 56
Music composition (*see* Composition)
Music courses, high school, 5, 50–52
Music theory, 5, 50–52, 55, 172
Musical ideas, expression of, 6
Musical notation, 3, 39
Musical piece, basis of, 31 (*see also* Composition)
Musical sentence:
  concept of, 5
  construction of, 16
  forms in, 32–35
  structure of, 32
Musicianship, development of, 370
Musique concrète, 47

National Education Association, 349
National Symphony Orchestra, 38

Ne'er to Part (Fisher), 174–85
Neophyte Rondo (Smoller), 163–70
Newton, Mass., Creative Arts Program, 4
Newton High School, 49–50, 172, 370
  Music Club of, 56
  "Night at the Boston Pops," 278, 349
New York Philharmonic Orchestra, 26
Nineteenth-century style, 231–35
Nocturne, Op. 37, No. 1 in g (Chopin), 33
Norton, Elliot, 242, 278, 330
Notation, 3
  rhythmic, 39
Notes:
  function of, 159
  mental response to, 15

Objectivity, need for, 371
Oboe, 210, 289, 301, 363
  flute and, 291, 334
  "oriental" atmosphere of, 245
  solo, 263, 352
Octaves, consecutive, 52
Olton, Christine, 217–25
Opera, improvised, 9
Orchestrating, as new experience, 6
Organismic theory, in education, 2
Ostinato rhythmic patterns, on tape machines, 47

Passacaglia and Fugue in C-minor (Bach), 4
Passing tones, 143, 183, 191, 247, 285
Pathétique Sonata (Sonata No. 8, Op. 13) (Beethoven), 34–35
Pavane, 233
Pedal point, 43, 63–65, 98, 144, 159, 232, 244–45, 279, 289, 291, 293, 304, 317, 319, 335, 349
Percussive rhythms, on tape machines, 47–48
Perfect pitch, 3
Personal philosophy, in music, 184

Philadelphia Orchestra, 38
Phillips, Rosalie, 146–50
Phrase:
    division of, 16
    musical, 32
Phrygian mode, 245–46
Piano:
    as accompaniment, 148–50, 189, 367
    in chorale, 210
    concerto for, 151–62
    concerto grosso style, 261–65
    experimenting at, 364
    pitch and, 15
    as reinforcement to orchestra, 210–11
    singing and, 9
    solo, 213
Pick-up beat, 18
Piece for Flute (Sapers), 112–16
Piece for Instrumental Ensemble (Meyers), 126–33
Pierce, Jan, 38
Piston, Walter, 7, 37, 40, 55
Pitch:
    in electronic sound, 47
    perfect, 3
    relative, 3, 9
    sensitivity to, 9
Pitch discrimination, introduction to, 21
Pivot chord, 63, 282
Pizzicato passages, 45, 130–141, 213, 235, 243, 264, 332, 365
Plato, 369
Playful Pup, The (Cooke), 121–25
Poem, setting music to, 19
Polonaise in A (Chopin), 34
Polytonality, 162, 349, 354
Popular song writing, 104–5
Preadolescence, self-consciousness in, 3
Prelude No. 1 in C (Chopin), 33
Prelude No. 7 in A (Chopin), 33
Prelude No. 20 in c (Chopin), 33
Price, Leontyne, 38
Progressive education, 2
Prokofieff, Sergei, 37, 46, 366
Psalm 8, 197
Psalm 92, 197
Psalm 98, 193–200

Psaltery, 197
Puccini, Giacomo, 37

Quartal tones, 36
Quarter notes:
    syllables and, 12–13
    value of, 20
Question-and-answer principle, 15, 131
Quintet for Strings and Flute (Starr), 139–45

Rabin, Marvin, 315
Rameau, Jean Philippe, 34–35, 37
Range, number of notes in, 17
Ravel, Maurice, 37
Recapitulation, 106
Recitative, 9, 44
Recorded musical examples, use of, 16
Relative major, 136, 214, 263
Relative minor, 136, 245
Relative pitch, 3, 9
Repetition, 31, 43
Requiem (Fauré), 43
Requiem, K.626 (Mozart), 43
Reverberation, in stereo machines, 47
Rhapsodic form, 278
Rhyming words, 61, 64, 68–69, 72, 189
Rhythm:
    changes or shifts in, 36, 44, 62, 110, 354
    harmonic, 52
    instinctive feeling of, 10
    mutations of in twelve-tone system, 289
    notations for, 22, 49
    sing-song, 105
    sophisticated, 104, 109
    wave motion of, 64
Rhythm signature, 13
Rhythmic styles, as idioms, 36–37
Rite of Spring (Stravinsky), 36, 46
Robert Shaw Chorale, 38
Rococo style, 37, 222
Rodgers, Richard, 42

Rogers, Harold, 261, 301, 348
Romantic style, 37, 46
Rondo a Capriccio in G-major, Op. 129 (Beethoven), 32, 34
Rondo Capriccioso (Mendelssohn), 34
Rondo form, 5, 34, 128, 235
    extended, 242
Rondo in C-major, Op. 51 (Beethoven), 34
Rondo-sonata form, 34–35
Rondo variation form, 266
Root positions, use of, 52
Rothstein, Debby, 193–200
Rubin, Claire, 355–67

Sadness, in madrigal, 180–81, 184
Saint-Saëns, Camille, 33
Samuel (Hebrew judge), 197
Sandler, Barbara, 134–38
Sapers, Joanne, 112–16
Sargent, Sir Malcolm, 38
SATB (soprano-alto-tenor-bass), 180–86
Satire, in motif, 158
Scales, *vs.* modes, 81–83
Scherzo motif, 283
Schoenberg, Arnold, 36–37, 42, 46, 294
School orchestra, access to, 6
Schubert, Franz Peter, 33, 37, 52, 231
Schuller, Gunther, 46
Schumann, Robert, 31, 34–37, 44
Scoring, mechanics of, 56
Self-discipline, need for, 370
Self-expression, creativity and, 1
Senior high school, creative output of, 171–368
Sentence, musical (*see* Musical sentence)
Sequence, 43
    motif and, 32
Seven Studies on Themes of Paul Klee (Schuller), 46
Shades of Thought (Shuman), 286–94
Shafran, Audrey, 101–11
Shakespeare, William, 369
Shaw, Alexander, 37

Shaw, Robert, 38
Shostakovich, Dmitri, 37, 46
Shout Unto the Lord—Psalm 98 (Rothstein), 193–200
Shuman, Dale, 286–94
Sibelius, Jean, 37
Signature, 13
Singer, Joey, 151–62
Singing:
    narrative or recitative manner in, 9
    pitch and, 9
Singing approach, to creativity, 8–10
Sing-song rhythm, 105
Six Pieces for Orchestra (Webern), 46
Slavic romanticism, 262
Smoke Gets in Your Eyes (Kern-Harbach), 34
Smoller, Ronnie, 163–70
Snare drum, 291, 316, 349–50, 352
Sonata No. 8, Op. 13 ("Pathétique") (Beethoven), 34–35
Sonata No. 14, Op. 27, No. 2 ("Moonlight") (Beethoven), 33
Sonata No. 16, Op. 31, No. 2 (Beethoven), 44
Sonata No. 23, Op. 57 ("Appassionata") (Beethoven), 35
Sonata in A-major, K.331 (Mozart), 35
Sonata in C, K.545 (Mozart), 32, 34
Sonata form, 35
Song, narrative, 9, 189
    (*see also* Singing; Vocal music; Voicing)
Song cycle, 188–89
Soprano:
    contrary motion with bass, 109
    harmonization of, 52–55
Soprano-alto-tenor-bass form, 180–86
Sound-on-sound recordings, 47
Stagnation-and-activity principle, 52, 115
Starr, Daniel, 139–45
Stevenson, Robert Louis, 73–74, 79, 83, 188
Stockhausen, Karlheinz, 37, 46
Story, student's writing of, 9–10

384INDEX

Strauss, Richard, 34–35, 37
Stravinsky, Igor, 36–37, 46
Stretto, 44
String Quartet (Gerson), 117–21
Student(s): (*see also* Child)
creative instinct in, 54
self-criticism by, 53
self-discipline in, 370
singing approach by, 8–10
Study for Orchestra (Wagenknecht), 338–54
Study in Jazz (Sandler), 134–38
Stylistic individuality, development of, 48
Suite Française (Milhaud), 46
Summertime (Glazer), 85–87
Swarowsky, Hans, 38
"Swing," 135
Swing, The (Banks), 71–77
Syllables:
accented, 11, 18
pick-up or anacrusis in, 11
quarter-notes and, 12–13
Symphonic Etudes, Op. 13 (Schumann), 35
Symphonic Variations (Franck), 35
Symphony No. 3 in E-flat ("Eroica") (Beethoven), 32, 36
Symphony No. 5 in C-minor, Op. 67 (Beethoven), 30–32, 35
Symphony No. 9 in D-minor, Op. 125 (Beethoven), 36
Symphony No. 1 in c, Op. 68 (Brahms), 32
Symphony No. 3 in F, Op. 90 (Brahms), 33, 36–37, 44
Symphony 1962 (Fine), 46
Symphony No. 94 in G-major ("Surprise") (Haydn), 32, 35
Symphony No. 104 in D-major ("London") (Haydn), 33, 44
Symphony No. 40 in G-minor, K.550 (Mozart), 31, 33, 44
Symphony No. 5, Op. 100 (Prokofieff), 46
Symphony No. 1 in B-flat, Op. 38 ("Spring") (Schumann), 31, 34, 36–37, 44
Symphony No. 2 in C, Op. 61 (Schumann), 36

Symphony No. 7, Op. 60 (Shostakovich), 46
Symphony No. 4 in F-minor, Op. 36 (Tschaikowsky), 36, 44
Symphony (Orchestra) of Greater Miami, 349
Symphony orchestra, growth of, 37
Syncopation, 36–37, 105, 109, 144, 290, 321, 335–36, 354, 363
in madrigal, 182
as "swing," 135
Syn-Ket, electronic synthesizer, 48

Talent, lack of emphasis on, 2
Tam-tam, 349, 353
Tape loop, 47
Tape recorder, for electronic music, 47
Teacher:
patience and understanding in, 54
techniques of, 6–7
Temperance, need for, 371
Tempo, in beginning composition, 40–41
Theme, concept of, 5
Theory I and Theory II classes, 5, 50–52, 55, 172
Thoughts of Spring (Amicangioli), 94–100
Three-four rhythm, 12–13, 20
Three-part forms, 5, 33
Three-Part Inventions (Bach), 32–33, 43
Three-part song form, 34, 69, 79, 83, 97
expanded, 33
Three-quarter rhythm, 12–13, 20
Till Eulenspiegel (Strauss), 34, 36
Timbrel, 197
Time Cycle (Foss), 46
Timpani, 301, 330, 349, 353, 363
Toccata (Rubin), 355–67
Tolerance, for work of others, 371
Tonal contrast, 263
Tonality:
free or expanded, 36, 157
shifts in, 198
Tone row, 289
atonal principles and, 293
vocal or instrumental, 21

Tone row approach, to creativity, 19–21
Tonic, as last note, 17
Tonic cadence, 106
Tonic chord, 17
Topic sentence, 16
Transposition, 32, 43
Travel (Dulfano), 78–84
Treasure Chest of Humor for Boys and Girls, A (Mellon), 89
Treble clef, 13
Triad:
    in Dorian mode, 82
    formation of, 26
    in Mixolydian mode, 81
    primary, 5
Trial and Error No. $\frac{3}{4}$ (Shafran), 101–11
Triangle, 278, 280, 289, 301, 316, 349, 363
Triple meter, 12, 22, 110
Tritones, 52, 143
Trombone, 210, 289, 301, 316, 349, 363
    antiphony with flute, 292
Trumpet, 210, 289, 301, 316, 330, 349, 363
Tschaikowsky, Peter Ilich, 36, 44
Tufts, Linda, 60–65
Tutorial sessions, 56
Twelve-tone technique, 36, 42, 289
Twentieth-century idioms, 45–48
Two-four rhythm, 20
Two-part forms, 5, 32–33
Two-Part Inventions (Bach), 32–33, 43

Varèse, Edgard, 46
Variations, 32, 35, 43, 213–15, 264
Variations on a Theme by Diabelli, Op. 120 (Beethoven), 35
Variations on a Theme by Haydn (Brahms), 35
Venetian school, 199
Verdi, Giuseppe, 37
V harmony, 21
Vienna Symphony Orchestra, 38
Viola:
    as counterpoint, 319
    solo, 144
    in string quartet, 119
Violin(s):
    antiphonal treatment of, 281
    solo, 144
    in string quartet, 119
Vocal creativity, 38
Vocal music, coordination of with texts, 110
Vocal treatment, in composition, 38–39
Voice leading, 52, 191
Voice records, listening to, 38
Voices, antiphonal treatment of, 44
Voicing, harmonic balance in, 42

Wagenknecht, Walter, 338–54
Wagner, Richard, 37
Waltz, Op. 64, No. 1 in D-flat (Chopin), 33
Waltz, Op. 64, No. 2 in C-sharp (Chopin), 34
Waltz in A-flat (Schubert), 33
Water Music (Handel), 33
Webern, Anton von, 37, 46
Well-Tempered Clavier (Bach), 32, 35, 43–44
White noise, on tape machines, 48
Whole notes, 20
Whole-tone formation, 44
Willaert, Adrian, 199
Wood block, 301, 316, 319
Woodwinds:
    antiphonal treatment of, 215, 333
    harmony of, 232–33, 263
    imitation in, 234
    as support, 245, 280
    tutti of, 210
World War II, 47
Wozzeck (Berg), 46

Xylophone, 349

You Can Always Tell the English (Alexander), 88–93
Young Person's Guide to the Orchestra (Britten), 35, 37–38

Zwei Tänze (Lawson), 226–36